The

Criminal Justice System

AN INTRODUCTION

THIRD EDITION

Bryan Gibson and Paul Cavadino

With the assistance of **David Faulkner**

❈ WATERSIDE PRESS

About the authors

Bryan Gibson is a barrister, former co-editor of *Justice of the Peace* and a regular contributor to legal journals and other media. He founded Waterside Press in 1989 and has since written, edited and published a wide range of books on aspects of crime and punishment whilst also compiling an *A-Z of Criminal Justice* (forthcoming).

Paul Cavadino is chief executive of Nacro, the crime reduction charity, which he has worked for since 1972. From 1979 until 2000 he was chair of the Penal Affairs Consortium, an alliance of 50 organizations concerned with the penal system. He has written and broadcast widely on issues related to crime reduction, criminal justice and the treatment of offenders.

David Faulkner CB was deputy under secretary of state at the Home Office where he worked with seven Home Secretaries, gaining unique insights into and experience of the workings of central government. He is a senior research fellow at the Centre for Criminal Justice Research at Oxford University and a prominent and respected commentator on criminal justice and constitutional matters. His writings include *Crime, State and Citizen: A Field Full of Folk* (Second edition, Waterside Press, 2006).

The **Criminal Justice System**
AN INTRODUCTION

CONTENTS

Foreword

Changes have been needed to every chapter of this handbook since the first edition appeared in 1995 under the title *Introduction to the Criminal Justice Process*. Indeed, the reforms of the last decade have been quite substantial, altering the overall landscape, creating new landmarks, points of reference and in certain cases introducing entirely new concepts or ways of proceeding. Within the confines of a basic introduction, we have sought to take account of all these dynamics, but nonetheless to capture and retain enduring values, standards, principles and doctrine.

The Criminal Justice System (CJS)
Previous editions of the handbook noted that the arrangements for crime and punishment that existed in England and Wales were more in the nature of a *process* than a *system*. To an extent this is still the case: various separate and independent functions and tasks bear upon a chain of events the outcome of which is the critical decision by a jury or magistrates as to whether or not someone is guilty of a criminal offence. Judges or magistrates then decide upon the appropriate sentences. Before and after these events, various people—'key actors'—perform other essential but often less visible roles. Each operates independently, but usually within a working partnership with (or constrained by) other parts of the criminal process: police officers, Crown prosecutors, probation officers, prison governors, members of the Parole Board and many others whose contribution may be less well-known. This relationship has been described as one of 'interdependence': a way of doing things that exists at all levels, national, regional and local. We say more about these developments in *Chapter 1*. They have occurred, in the main, over the past 25 years, leading to considerable progress in the way that criminal justice is administered. They now take place, since 2007, in the context of a Ministry of Justice (MOJ) and related developments. Hence, the title of this third edition. It is intended to convey that there is now what can be described as a Criminal Justice System.

A tried and trusted approach
This edition follows the tried and trusted approach of earlier versions. The contents are affected by a large number of changes, not least those concerning many aspects of criminal justice due to the creation of the MOJ. This new backdrop is outlined in *Chapter 1*, which also notes associated developments in relation to the Home Office and other government departments.

The handbook remains primarily about the day-to-day workings of the system, the ways in which it impacts on everyday life and at what is often termed 'grass roots' level, rather than at the level of strategy or policy-making.

Some of the latter is unavoidable, not least when describing the interaction of sentencing legislation and judicial independence, or the replacement of criminal sanctions by those built around civil behaviour orders and their separate code of procedures. For readers wanting a 'top down' perspective, much valuable information can be found in two companion handbooks to this work: *The New Ministry of Justice* and *The New Home Office*.[1]

The format of the handbook remains as before. *Part I* describes the structure of the courts—the hub around which the CJS revolves. Amongst the many updates here, we have included a note on the new Supreme Court that in 2009 will replace the longstanding arrangements for appeals at the highest level within the UK. In *Part II* all the main stages of a case are described: from the detection of crime, police dealings with suspects, the charging, cautioning and prosecution of offenders to bail, remand, trial, sentence and beyond. *Part III* describes the actors themselves, their work, daily routines and preoccupations. Finally, *Part IV* looks at *Aspects of Criminal Justice*, a selection of items which are intended to add flavour to the more descriptive parts of the handbook. One innovation is the *Glossary* that has been added at the end.

Throughout, we have tried to describe matters in a way that will leave the reader with a clear picture. A primary aim has been to avoid undue complexity, whilst nonetheless providing a sound description. The focus is on key features rather than minutiae. We hope that this approach will be of use not only to the beginner—whether as a student or an inquisitive member of the public—but also to the seasoned practitioner who wants to strengthen his or her understanding of the broader context for his or her day-to-day work.

Acknowledgements

Many people have contributed to this handbook. We would particularly like to thank the authors of those other Waterside Press publications mentioned at various points in the text or footnotes whose work has assisted our understanding of matters. Our thanks also go to David Faulkner of the Oxford Centre for Criminological Research for casting his expert eye over the final draft. Any remaining errors are, of course, our own entirely.

Bryan Gibson and **Paul Cavadino**

April 2008

---

[1] See the full references to these companion works in the text.

CHAPTER 1

Criminal Justice: An Overview

The notion of justice has traditionally had two components: first, a fair outcome to a process of negotiation, or the fair resolution of conflict; and, second, the exercise of authority through procedures which are recognised and legitimate (sometimes described as 'due process'). Hence, e.g. 'social justice' is about the fair distribution of power and wealth among a nation's citizens. All kinds of justice stand above the immediate interests of any one individual, section of society or community, and above those of government or other forms of power and influence. Either aspect of justice noted above may be stressed at different times according to shifts in priorities or concerns, but both must be present in any situation where it is claimed that 'justice is being, or has been, done'.

Criminal justice: a brief survey of context and meaning
The term 'criminal justice' is used in several contexts, but chiefly to encompass the chain of events, activities, tasks or functions that constitute the official response to perceived problems of law and order, including, such as

- crime prevention and crime reduction;
- the arrest and prosecution of suspects;
- the hearing of criminal cases by the courts;
- sentencing and the administration and enforcement of court orders;
- parole and other forms of licence for prisoners; and
- work with offenders or ex-offenders in prison or in the community.

Other common shades of meaning are those pointing to:

- a dedicated form of justice that applies in relation to criminal cases as opposed to civil, family or administrative matters—and that has its own laws, principles, rules, procedures, codes, practices and thinking; or
- any of a range of outcomes flowing from decisions at given stages of the criminal justice process, e.g. whether to interview or arrest someone, charge them with an offence, grant them bail, find them guilty, fine people, pass a community sentence or send them to prison, or—at the end of that process—whether to release them back into the community.

This handbook looks at each of these strands. It does so by focusing on day-to-day events from the point in time when an offence is discovered until the case has run its course. It describes the components of the official framework for criminal justice and the roles of the various 'key actors'. It deals with the effects of Criminal Justice Acts (and similar legislation) and notes the guiding principles, strategies and thinking that lie behind the modern-day arrangements for a Criminal Justice System (CJS) in England and Wales, including those involving the private, voluntary, charitable or non-statutory sectors.

KEEPING THE PEACE

As a rudimentary statement, criminal justice is about keeping the peace, or what is sometimes described as 'The Queen's Peace', given that the theory is that all criminal offences (*Chapter 2*) are offences against or 'remissible only by' the state as represented by the sovereign. A day-to-day reminder of this is the fact that prosecutions are brought or sentences administered in the name of the reigning monarch, as symbolised in *Regina v. Smith* or designations such as Crown Prosecution Service, Her Majesty's Court Service or Her Majesty's Prison Service. The need to keep the peace by using sanctions of one kind or another against people who do not obey the criminal law is confirmed by societal needs ancient and modern and few communities have existed without resort to such mechanisms.[1] The hue and cry of Anglo-Saxon times, the pillory, stocks and public executions of old are all part of the same continuum of controls that nowadays find expression in forms of imprisonment, fines and the generic community sentence. What is also different in the present day is, e.g. the speed of events, the vast range of crimes that exist, the opportunities and methods of committing many kinds of offence and the ease with which there may arise a concerted public (or media) outcry for something to be done. But the underlying—and ultimately political—question remains: what should be done about lawbreakers. Not everyone agrees that punishment is the answer. Whilst noting the existence of such views (see, e.g. the reference to restorative justice in *Chapter 13*), this handbook describes the practical arrangements for criminal justice as they exist today, whatever their imperfections.

THE CRIMINAL JUSTICE SYSTEM (CJS)

Certain parts of the criminal justice process are of quite ancient origin, such as the magistrates' courts, High Court and appellate jurisdiction of the House of Lords (pending a new Supreme Court: see *Chapter 4*), whilst others developed in the Victorian era, such as the first regular police forces. Some are of more recent origin such as the Crown Court (which was created by the Courts Act 1971),

---

[1] There are said to be a small number of remote and isolated communities untouched by crime as we know it that have largely attracted the attention of anthropologists rather than criminologists.

Crown Prosecution Service (CPS) (Prosecution of Offences Act 1985), the Youth Court (1991), Youth Justice Board (1998), National Probation Service (NPS) (under administrative changes in 2001),[2] Criminal Defence Service (CDS) (also 2001) and Serious Organized Crime Agency (SOCA) (2005).

An era of change

The past 20 years have seen an unprecedented acceleration in the pace of change alongside a greater concentration on crime prevention, crime reduction and the use of enhanced forms of surveillance, technology, databases and recording systems as aids to policing or evidence gathering. The many significant landmarks include:

- the Human Rights Act 1998: see, in particular, *Chapters 2* and *5*;
- a sequence of Criminal Justice Acts: *Chapter 2*;
- a revised sentencing framework (with new kinds of sentence and criteria for decision-making) as provided for in the Criminal Justice Act 2003 (*Chapter 9*) that also contains other landmark reforms;
- the creation of a Sentencing Guidelines Council (SGC) (again under the 2003 Act): *Chapter 9*;
- a Police Reform Act 2002, fresh methods of policing, police units and a National Policing Improvement Agency (NPIA): *Chapter 11*;
- the reorganization of many other criminal justice services, including the court, prison and probation services as noted at appropriate points in the chapters which follow;
- the creation of 3,000 extra criminal offences: *Chapter 2*;
- a joint Criminal Procedure Rule Committee (CPRC): *Chapter 2*;
- innovations such as the anti-social behaviour order (ASBO) (*Chapter 2*) and other secondary ways of tackling crime as used, e.g. by local authorities, government departments and the private sector; and
- a new governmental approach to the co-ordination of services that finds expression at the highest level in Cabinet committees and at national or local level in Crime and Disorder Reduction Partnerships (CDRPs), a National Criminal Justice Board (NCJB) and Local Criminal Justice Boards (LCJBs): see, especially, *Chapter 15*.

As described in *Chapter 5*, there will be a new Supreme Court from the autumn of 2009 as part of a tranche of reforms brought about by the Constitutional Reform Act 2005 and in the background to all public affairs there is a debate about the need for enhanced democratic involvement at all levels: *Chapter 15*.

---

[2] The Probation Service existed in local form from the early-1900s until 2001. By 2008, following the creation of local Probation Trusts and other contemporary developments, official statements again began to refer to 'The Probation Service', not the NPS: see further re these events in *Chapter 13*.

Other contextual factors

The above and many other developments—all of which are dealt with in their own setting within the chapters that follow—are in addition to a major restructuring of ministerial and departmental responsibilities described under the heading *Ministry of Justice*, below, a more polarised politics of crime and punishment in the wake of September 11, 2001, a global context for organized crime, an escalating UK prisoner population, concerns about internal[3] security and border controls and continuing developments in the contrastingly enlightened fields of restorative justice and penal reform. Indeed, a good deal has changed since the first edition of this work appeared in 1995, including, as noted in the *Preface* the fact that there is now a more recognizable Criminal Justice System (CJS) as opposed to a more disparate collection of component parts. At a time of such far-reaching change it seems ever more important to reiterate the importance of the values and principles on which justice ultimately rests: integrity, decency, fairness, openness, visibility and accountability.

CJS Online

For some years, a web-site has existed under the designation 'Criminal Justice System' or 'CJS'. The CJS home page states that the purpose of the CJS:

> ... is to deliver justice for all, by convicting and punishing the guilty and helping them to stop offending, while protecting the innocent. [It] is responsible for detecting crime and bringing it to justice; and carrying out the orders of courts, such as collecting fines, and supervising community and custodial punishment.

CJS Online also notes that the key goals of the CJS are:

- to improve the effectiveness and efficiency of the CJS in bringing offences to justice;
- to increase public confidence in the fairness and effectiveness of the CJS;
- to increase victim satisfaction with the police and victim and witness satisfaction with the CJS;
- to consistently collect, analyse and use good quality ethnicity data to identify and address race disproportionality in the CJS; and
- to increase the recovery of criminal assets by recovering (i.e. confiscating) £250m of assets acquired through crime by 2009-10.[4]

Under the heading 'Working Together to Cut Crime and Deliver Justice' the authors refer to the Criminal Justice Strategic Plan 2008-2011 against

---

[3] The term 'homeland security' is an Americanism, but the concept also resonates in Europe.

[4] Confiscating these via the criminal and civil courts, freezing assets pending the outcome of court proceedings when appropriate, and using powers conferred by the Proceeds of Crime Act 2002.

which the development of criminal justice provision now takes place and which sets out how the CJS agencies 'will work together to deliver a justice system which:

- is effective in bringing offences to justice, especially serious offences;
- engages the public and inspires confidence;
- puts the needs of victims at its heart; and has
- simple and efficient processes.'

These broadly stated and powerful sentiments are at times hard to relate to the myriad day-to-day responsibilities discharged by the various bodies and individuals described in this handbook. Nonetheless, the strategic plan and its associated links are nowadays fundamental to developments and they demand study by anyone seeking a complete understanding of the topic.[5]

Front line services

In the everyday front line of the CJS are police officers, police community support officers (PCSOs), Crown prosecutors, defence lawyers, forensic scientists, judges, prison officers, probation officers, criminal psychologists and a range of other 'actors' as described in later chapters. Many of them work within the CJS for a living, often for their entire careers. Other roles are performed by volunteers, such as magistrates (also known as justices of the peace) (JPs), members of the Parole Board, Independent Monitoring Board (IMB),[6] Victim Support and the Witness Service, or belong to groups which are directly involved in crime prevention initiatives (such as Neighbourhood Watch or Safer Communities). Any citizen aged 18 or over can be required to carry out jury service in the Crown Court after being chosen at random from the electoral roll and summoned to attend court for that purpose. After listening to witnesses and studying other relevant evidence, he or she will take part in critical decision-making concerning the guilt or otherwise of an accused person who is on trial for (what is likely to be) a serious offence. Certain CJS functions may involve the private sector, as with privately managed prisons, prisoner escorts (who convey, or 'transport', prisoners to and from court premises, or between prisons), scientific or technological services and security guards.

---

[5] These plans can be accessed at www.cjsonline.gov.uk, a government sponsored web-site, but whose exact provenance and capacity to speak for the CJS as a whole are somewhat unclear. CJS Online lists as constituent parts of the CJS, the MOJ, Home Office and Office of the Attorney General. It omits the courts (which the government cannot speak for, but which form a substantial part of the CJS and are, in effect, its 'hub': see the next heading in this chapter) as well, e.g. as the non-statutory, voluntary and private sectors. Its sweeping, sometimes disembodied, assertions reflect many modern-day public pronouncements and bringing 'crime' or 'offences' to justice (see the quotes in the text above), e.g. is a somewhat novel use of English.

[6] There is an IMB for each prison: see *Chapter 14*.

THE CRIMINAL COURTS: THE HUB OF THE CJS

The criminal courts stand at the centre of the CJS.[7] It is:

- with an eye to the demanding standards of the criminal courts and the ever-present possibility that there could be a need to provide evidence at a trial that investigators, prosecutors and defence lawyers act; and
- it is the outcomes of court decisions that set the tone, direction and parameters of what follows, whether, e.g. in terms of probation officers or psychiatrists providing pre-sentence reports (PSRs) or those on an offender's mental state, or prison governors, psychiatrists and other qualified individuals providing longer term risk assessments during a prisoner's sentence that may affect when and for how long he or she will be held in prison (if allowed back into the community at all).[8]

That said, there are aspects of criminal justice which operate independently of the courts. At a given stage in the criminal justice process, it may be the imminent decision, e.g. of a Crown prosecutor or the Parole Board, on which attention is focused. Other examples are cautioning by the police, diversion schemes that seek to avoid the need for formal action (*Chapter 7*), prison discipline or recall to prison following release on licence. The police also have an increasing and sometimes controversial role and accompanying range of powers to deal with situations, mostly involving aspects of public disorder, by means of 'on the spot' fines. But in general terms and for the general run of cases, it is the court that remains the primary focal point.

The criminal courts and the separation of powers

The courts are in a relatively isolated position due to the constitutional doctrine of the separation of powers—the principle that the Legislature (Parliament), Executive (Government) and Judiciary (courts) should be independent of one another. Neither Parliament nor Ministers can dictate to the courts what a particular law means or how it should be interpreted or applied in an individual case. Similarly, what sentence should be imposed on an offender (in the absence of express statutory provision for what are known as mandatory sentences of which there are few, if increasing in number). Determination of the facts of a case is for jurors or magistrates; interpretation of the law and its application to

---

[7] There have been intermittent references to other services moving 'centre stage': as with the then locally-based Probation Service in the 1990s. Describing courts as at the hub of the CJS is less about importance than useful in terms of exposition. All services are interdependent: *Chapter 2*.

[8] There are some 40 prisoners, known as 'natural lifers', who will never be allowed out of prison.

the facts in a given situation is a matter for the judge when directing a jury or magistrates acting on guidance from a qualified court legal adviser.

This is not to say that judges and magistrates may not share the wider aims and purposes of the CJS as a whole. Court user groups facilitate some dialogue, but largely on administrative matters, whilst the involvement of the judiciary in a range of cross-agency or multi-agency forums, committees and training events has tended to change the stance of the judiciary in modern times, but with due safeguards to prevent undue or improper influence. Central in bringing the courts into the 'criminal justice fold' was the creation of a National Criminal Justice Board (NCJB) together with Local Criminal Justice Boards (LCJBs) in various areas of the country (see, also, later in the chapter).

When the Ministry of Justice (below) was created in 2007 and the courts brought within its remit alongside HM Prison Service (HMPS) and the National Probation Service, judicial independence was reinforced by what is called 'The Concordat', an accommodation agreed by the Lord Chancellor with the judiciary via the Lord Chief Justice and the Judicial Office (see, further, *Chapter 12*). Even before that time, the Constitutional Reform Act 2005 had placed a duty on the Lord Chancellor to protect the independence of the judiciary. The relationship between Government and its aspirations for such boards remain to be fully worked through in the light of these competing, if essential, considerations.

The interdependent nature of the CJS as a whole—and the underlying rationale for this—is noted later in the next chapter.

The criminal courts in summary

The criminal courts currently comprise:

- magistrates' courts: *Chapter 3*;
- the Crown Court: *Chapter 4*;
- the High Court, Court of Appeal and House of Lords, soon to become the Supreme Court (known as the higher courts): *Chapter 5*; and
- the youth court—a part of the magistrates' court with special responsibility for people below the age of 18 years: a note on which also appears at the end of *Chapter 3*.

There is also the Courts Martial network of military tribunals to deal with service personnel. These are part of a parallel system of law and order for servicemen and servicewomen and there is analogous provision for the Navy and Royal Air Force. They are governed by many of the same rules and principles as the ordinary courts (often in this context referred to as the 'civil courts')[9] but their precise workings are beyond the scope of this book.

OTHER KEY CRIMINAL JUSTICE SERVICES

Each of the criminal justice services has its own status, culture and traditions in terms of independent decision-making, both in relation to government departments and vis-à-vis one another, but although this is sometimes specifically embraced by the law it is not part of the same high constitutional doctrine that applies in relation to the courts of law.[10] Some services can be seen as closer to the centre than others and thereby more susceptible to the edicts of the Executive or cross-agency influences,[11] but individual officers still have to use their own discretion within whatever framework exists in their own field. The reality is that police officers, Crown prosecutors, probation officers and prison governors all discharge their duties subject to a mix of personal judgement, training, 'career upbringing' and working cultures against a backdrop of policy requirements, codes, 'standing orders', instructions, standards and Best Practice as these apply to their own service.[12] The main participants include:

- **the police** as the preventers, detectors and investigators of crime. Many police forces have an 'administration of justice department' or 'justice unit' to deal with court-related matters. Other key functions include those of local custody sergeants and gaolers. Whilst relatively local forms of policing have survived in the face of Government moves aimed at rationalisation and amalgamation, some aspects of police work do now occur on a nationwide basis: *Chapters 6* and *11*;
- **the Crown Prosecution Service** (CPS) which is now responsible for most prosecution decisions (other than the most minor or urgent) and can take over a case from other public prosecutors or a private prosecutor. It is the CPS that since 2003 has decided on the appropriate charge following police investigations. All CPS files are reviewed on a continuing basis applying the twin test described in *Chapter 7* and cases can be discontinued or withdrawn by the CPS. It employs solicitors, barristers and what are known as 'designated case workers': *Chapters 7* and *12*;

---

9   Not to be confused with civil courts that deal with civil as opposed to criminal matters.

10 But it is reinforced by human rights law, especially re a fair trial: see *Chapter 2*.

11 Both HMPS and the NPS would appear to have been moved in that direction. In 2008, MOJ links to the Parole Board were held by the higher courts to be too close: *Chapter 14*.

12 But there have been commentators who see an emergent 'police state'. The arguments, debates and intricacies of this are beyond the scope of this work. ·

- **other law enforcement agencies** include the Serious Fraud Office (SFO); Serious and Organized Crime Agency (SOCA); Revenue and Customs; Department for Work and Pensions; Health and Safety Executive; Trading Standards; TV Licencing (TVL); National Society for the Prevention of Cruelty to Children (NSPCC) and Royal Society for the Prevention of Cruelty to Animals/Birds (RSPCA) and Royal Society for the Protection of Birds (RSPB): *Chapter 11;* [13]
- **the Criminal Defence Service** (CDS) which provides state funded legal representation under the auspices of the Legal Services Commission (LSC): *Chapter 12;*
- **legal representatives,** i.e. solicitors and barristers who can appear to represent (or 'speak for') either side (or 'party') in a criminal case as advocates and subject to rules about rights of audience: *Chapter 12;*
- **the Probation Service** which manages and supervises offenders and provides a range of related services to courts. Probation officers are subject to National Standards, e.g. for the 'Supervision of Offenders in the Community'; 'Preparation of Pre-sentence Reports' (PSRs); and 'Release on Licence' (i.e. from prison). The NPS also provides or facilitates a range of centres, hostels, programmes and schemes for offenders/ex-offenders as well as bail schemes for people who are awaiting trial or sentence. Additionally, probation officers work in or alongside prisons including in relation to 'throughcare', sentence planning and early release schemes: *Chapters 8, 9, 13;* and *14;*
- **HM Prison Service** (HMPS) that provides secure and controlled environments in some 140 establishments operating a range of prison regimes for different categories or kinds of offender, from those for short-term offenders (often in local prisons) to life sentences for dangerous, high-risk or long-term prisoners: *Chapter 14;*[14]
- **the Youth Justice Board, youth offending teams** (YOTs) and **youth offending panels** (YOPs) to provide for juveniles: see within *Chapter 3;*
- **local authorities** who have various responsibilities for vulnerable adults and children as well as community safety, crime prevention and prosecution duties, including with regard to the environment, bye-laws, consumer protection, school attendance and the formulation of an annual youth justice plan: see, in particular, *Chapters 3* and *13.* They use various secondary methods of crime prevention, e.g. in relation to tenancies, contracts, planning permission and other environmental responsibilities.

---

[13] Each of these organizations has a web-site that can readily be found on the internet.

[14] Special hospitals (i.e. secure hospitals) exist for the detention of mentally impaired people who may have committed serious crimes, some of whom are 'guilty but insane' or 'unfit to plead'. See further and generally, *Mental Impairment: A Note* in *Chapter 13.*

- **doctors** and **psychiatrists** who work in prison healthcare centres or in the community and may be called upon to provide reports on the physical or mental condition of an offender or alleged offender for use by a court or for other risk-assessment purposes: *Chapters 13 and 14;*
- **the non-statutory, voluntary and charitable sectors** which provide services to various parts of the CJS or direct to offenders, victims or their families, including through Nacro,[15] Victim Support (VS), the Witness Service (WS), research, information and penal reform: *Chapter 13;* and
- **the private sector** which provides services for purchase by the public sector part of the CJS, such as drug or alcohol treatment schemes, prison building, finance and management (i.e. 'private prisons'), prisoner escort services (which transport prisoners to and from court) and a wide range of resources for the security industry: see, especially, *Chapters 9 and 14.*

Those people directly affected by CJS processes and outcomes
Increasingly, CJS processes have been designed to be 'user friendly' with regard to those most directly affected by decision-making or CJS arrangements:

- **accused people** (or 'defendants') when even the most outwardly undeserving people must be guaranteed a fair trial (below);
- **witnesses** and other people who assist the process of justice who must be treated in a proper manner at court and in certain cases protected by the police under witness protection schemes. Note also the reference to the Witness Service above: *Chapter 13;* and
- **victims of crime** who although not directly involved in criminal proceedings, except when they appear as witnesses, should be kept informed about the progress of their case, treated with sensitivity and consulted concerning certain matters. The extent to which courts may now receive information concerning the position, concerns and views of victims has altered quite significantly in modern times from the former situation whereby, apart maybe from giving evidence in court, they were relegated to the sidelines: see, also, *Chapter 15.*

The wider criminal justice family
Beyond the formal parts of the official CJS lies what is sometimes styled 'the wider criminal justice family'. This includes people or services involved in the work of organizations such as Nacro, the Howard League for Penal Reform, Prison Reform Trust and Unlock[16]—together with a rich assortment of people with less visible roles, such as those who befriend offenders or act as mentors[17]

---

[15]   The crime reduction charity.
[16]   The National Association for Ex-offenders: see, further, *Chapters 13 and 14.*
[17]   For juveniles, especially, but also and increasingly other people at-risk of offending.

to people who are set on 'going straight' following a term in prison, or citizens engaged in local crime prevention projects, schemes or charities. Some such organizations are sponsored or receive other support from official channels.

THE MINISTRY OF JUSTICE (MOJ)

The network of official, formal, contracted or approved 'justice-based' arrangements was formerly somewhat less well-suited in terms of its links or connections to particular government departments and occasionally quite misplaced in terms of expected allegiance. The disparate and disjointed nature of criminal justice began to diminish during the 1980s and especially following Lord Woolf's report into prison disturbances in 1991,[18] which led to the creation of the then national Criminal Justice Consultative Council with its area committees comprising leaders of the different agencies.[19] It continued through initiatives such as 'working together' and 'partnership' whereby the various separate services aimed for a more coherent or 'end-to-end' approach which sought to understand and allow for the distinctive roles, responsibilities and problems of those making decisions at other points in the criminal process.

The move towards an MOJ

An extension of these events were the various forums, meetings, committees and similar groupings—at various levels of responsibility within the then national, regional, area or local CJS hierarchy—which reflected a varied mix of centralisation, delegation, multi-agency, multi-service or multi-departmental participation. Another logical step was the move to an MOJ.[20] Whilst certain constitutional issues remain to be fully resolved, mainly in relation to the judiciary (and so far as adults[21] are concerned), that part of criminal justice provision which touches on matters of *justice* as opposed, e.g. to policing (or what is sometimes termed maintaining *law and order*) can be traced to the MOJ, which as already indicated was created in 2007. In contrast, matters such as 'homeland security' and 'border controls' connect to the Home Office (which was re-structured at the same time in 2007): see the separate section, below. Seemingly in recognition that juveniles remain children—with regard to whom parents and schools have certain responsibilities—many aspects of youth justice passed to the new Department of Children, Schools and Families, but often in conjunction with the MOJ.

---

[18] This 1991 report represented a watershed in CJS thinking in that it looked behind prison riots and tensions to underlying and contributory causes.

[19] Which morphed into the NCJB and LCJBs mentioned in various parts of the text.

[20] See, e.g. *Crime, State and Citizen: A Field Full of Folk* (2nd edn, 2006), Faulkner D, Waterside Press.

[21] People aged 18 and over. Ministerial demarcation disputes were reported at certain stages.

These two key departments[22] have separate roles, functions and areas of responsibility, but are linked to Parliament via ministerial responsibility and to No 10 Downing Street via a number of Cabinet Committees, including a Cabinet Committee on Crime and the Criminal Justice System (CCCCJS). Civil servants also liaise at various levels within the MOJ, Home Office and other departments.

MOJ responsibilities summarised

The MOJ draws together various strands of activity, responsibility and duty under a broad remit encompassing 'matters of justice' and 'constitutional affairs'. In the context of criminal justice these can be summarised as follows:[23]

- working 'trilaterally' with the other departments that make up the central government strands of the CJS, chiefly the Home Office and Office of the Attorney General (the latter noted in *Chapter 14*);
- HM Courts Service (HMCS) (see, mainly, *Chapters 3* and *4*);
- support for the judiciary, including:
  - a Judicial Office in place of the former negligible administrative support for the Lord Chief Justice and senior judiciary;
  - appointments via a new Judicial Appointments Commission (JAC);
  - an independent Office for Judicial Complaints (OJC); and
  - a Judicial Communications Office (JCO)(all noted *Chapter 12*);
- the National Offender Management Service (NOMs)
  - Probation Service (*Chapter 13*);
  - HM Prison Service (HMPS) (*Chapter 14*);
- sponsorship of:
  - HM Inspectorates of Prison and Probation;
  - Independent Monitoring Boards (IMBs) (*Chapter 14*);
  - the Parole Board (*Chapter 14*); and
  - the Prisons and Probation Ombudsman (*Chapter 13*);
- legal aid and the Community Legal Service (CLS), through the Legal Services Commission (LSC) (*Chapter 12*);
- sentencing policy, including sponsorship of:
  - the Sentencing Guidelines Council (SGC); and
  - the Sentencing Advisory Panel (SAP) (both dealt with in *Chapter 9*);
- sponsorship of the Law Commission (concerned with law reform;
- hosting the Office for Criminal Justice Reform (OCJR)(this chapter);

---

[22] Certain other government departments have power to levy administrative penalties and undertake in-house law enforcement and prosecutions. They too connect to the Legislature and to the heart of Government via Parliamentary responsibility and various Cabinet Committees.

[23] Developed from a list of MOJ responsibilities provided at www.justice.org.

- the Privy Council Secretariat and the Office of the Judicial Committee of the Privy Council (*Chapter 5*); and
- human rights (*Chapter 2*).

Apart from the restructuring of the Home Office (below), responsibility for youth justice is now shared between the newly-created Department for Children, Schools and Families and the MOJ, including in relation to funding and policy concerning the Youth Justice Board (YJB) (noted in *Chapter 3*). A list of all the organizations that are sponsored by the MOJ can be found at the MOJ web-site.[24] In this handbook it is only possible to provide a bare outline of these matters. For a full treatment and 'top down' perspective, see the companion to this work, *The New Ministry of Justice: An Introduction.*[25]

The Office for Criminal Justice Reform
The Office for Criminal Justice Reform (OCJR) (noted in the list above) is sponsored by the MOJ. This key cross-departmental team supports all criminal justice agencies 'in working together to provide an improved service to the public'. As a cross-departmental organization, OCJR reports to ministers in the MOJ, Home Office and Office of the Attorney General. Its goal is 'to deliver the National Criminal Justice Board's (NCJB's) vision of what the CJS will look like in 2011'. It does so by providing Local Criminal Justice Boards (LCJBs) with 'an overall framework and guidance to facilitate reform at a local level'.

The Lord Chancellor
In 2007, the ancient role of Lord Chancellor, an office whose origins can be traced back for around 1,000 years, was combined with that of Justice Secretary at the head of the new MOJ. Until this and other developments in the Constitutional Reform Act 2005, and somewhat uniquely under the British constitution, the role required the occupant to play a part in all three arms of state (see the reference to the doctrine of the separation of powers elsewhere in this chapter). He[26] was formerly a senior member of the Cabinet, speaker of the House of Lords and head of the judiciary—a function sometimes performed in practice by sitting in the House of Lords as a Lord of Appeal, i.e. as a judge (*Chapter 12*). The Lord Chancellor was also responsible for ensuring the efficient administration of justice and the courts (as well as for promoting certain reforms to the *civil* law). Since the MOJ and the 2005 Act, the tri-partite nature of the role has come to an end along with responsibility for the selection and appointment,

---

[24] www.justice.gov.uk
[25] *The New Ministry of Justice: An Introduction* (2007), Gibson B, Waterside Press. All later such references in this work are to that publication which serves as a useful companion volume.
[26] All Lords Chancellor to date have been men.

or recommendation for appointment, of virtually all judges, judicial officers and magistrates in England and Wales (and Northern Ireland). The Justice Minister (the new and alternative name for the Lord Chancellor) is now a departmental Minister like any other.[27]

THE HOME OFFICE

Following the changes of 2007, the basic Home Office can be broadly described as being responsible for maintaining law and order and its remit summarised as follows:

- public safety and the protection of the public;
- the police and policing via independent local police forces and local police authorities (*Chapter 11*);
- crime prevention and crime reduction as the lead department but in partnership with other government departments;
- terrorism and other emergencies, including through an Office for Security and Counter-Terrorism that provides advice to ministers, develops policy and provides security measures;
- border controls, asylum and immigration via a unified Border Agency or 'Border Force' as it is sometimes described;
- safeguarding personal identity, e.g. through the development of identity cards and associated developments; and
- a range of miscellaneous responsibilities linked to the above such as the pursuit of scientific development and research.

The Home Office retains pre-existing links with MI5 and (along with the Foreign Office) the government listening station GCHQ.[28] There are further links to the Cabinet Office and its committees. In this handbook it is only possible to provide a bare outline of its reponsibilities. For a fuller treatment and a 'top down' perspective, see *The New Home Office: An Introduction.*[29]

The Home Secretary
The office of Secretary of State, like that of the Lord Chancellor, is of ancient origin. It was formalised in 1377 and its holders became powerful figures under

---

[27]   For consistency, the description 'Lord Chancellor' is used throughout this work even though departmental or media reports now veer towards 'Secretary of State for Justice', 'Justice Secretary' (especially when referring to prison-related or probation-related duties), or maybe 'Justice Minister'. For the background and nuances, see *The New Ministry of Justice, Chapter 9*.

[28]   The Security Services have themselves been in transition: a specialist area of study.

[29]   *The New Home Office: An Introduction* (2007), Gibson B, Waterside Press. All later such references in this work are to that publication which serves as a useful all round companion volume.

the Tudors. In 1782 the office was divided between the Secretary of State for the Home Department (or Home Secretary) and the Secretary of State for Foreign Affairs (Foreign Secretary). The Home Secretary occupies a key role in relation to public safety and protection (including from terrorism), policing, UK borders, deportation and related aspects of criminal-justice policy-making.[30] In recent years and post-Human Rights Act 1998 the Home Secretary has found himself in conflict with the judiciary on a number of occasions concerning who should set tariffs for life sentence prisoners (*Chapters 9* and *14*).

OTHER KEY NATIONWIDE ARRANGEMENTS

Apart from ministerial responsibility and the existence of key government departments, CJS Online (see earlier in this chapter) points to the National Criminal Justice Board (and its associated local boards) as 'a radical new initiative' under which the heads of each agency have been held collectively responsible for the performance of the system as a whole: 'As well as being accountable to the Government, [the NCJB and each LCJB] is accountable to YOU, the public, whom it serves . . . The result is a far more integrated system which is already starting to show major improved performance'. As already noted, the NCJB has been a major mechanism for involving the judiciary in particular in the wider issues that affect whether a service is being properly provided—or 'delivered'. Like the Sentencing Guidelines Council (*Chapter 9*), the NCJB is now a well-established and respected national institution. The Government itself also plays a key role through Cabinet committees. This is further noted in *Chapter 15* under the section on *Partnership and Working Together*.

UNDERSTANDING THE CJS

Knowledge of each CJS stage and the way in which it relates to others is fundamental to a sound understanding of the CJS and allows the reader to view it from varying perspectives. It is also necessary to view the individual roles of the services (or agencies) and 'actors' described in *Parts III* and *IV* of this book both individually and as parts of a coherent whole. The relationship is sometimes described as one of 'interdependence', a term first coined in the mid-1980s and that has gone hand-in-hand with the idea that the CJS as a whole is responsible for the efficient and effective delivery of a key public service.

---

[30] Many statutes give the Home Secretary power to make delegated legislation of a procedural, regulatory or technical nature. He or she is no longer, post-MOJ, primarily responsible for criminal justice legislation, but remains a partner to this via Cabinet committees: *Chapter 15*.

Interdependence

A certain level of fragmentation of responsibilities acts as a considerable restraint on the abuse of power, coercion or improper pressure to achieve a particular outcome. The validity of concerns expressed by some commentators in the past may now seem more sound and less radical in an era in which a Prime Minister has been interviewed by the police as a witness and key aides placed under investigation. Add to this continuing concerns about the legality of the Iraq War or events in relation to the dropping of an investigation of a prosecution in relation to BAE Systems (now BAES) and Saudi interests on the pretext of national security and it is easy to see why there is a need to be meticulous in such matters. In a liberal democracy there may be strengths in a process in which the constituent parts—some of which operate more closely alongside the interests of the state (or are more susceptible to influence from the centre or from political interests) than others—function independently of one another. Yet, as also noted in the first edition of this book and subsequently reiterated in the 2002 White Paper, *Justice for All*,[31] it can also be a weakness.

Throughout this book there are examples of a broad shift towards a nationwide agenda for participants in the CJS, including in relation to key aims such as crime reduction and crime prevention. Virtually all the criminal justice agencies now experience some degree of strategic direction at national level,[32] whilst decisions about day-to-day implementation are generally taken at area, local or what is sometimes described as operational level. Services have been progressively reorganized, and new organizations have been created to operate within the broad remit but at one remove from government. The judiciary is the exception to this as already noted but is now also playing its part through the NCJB, LCJBs, the SGC and a range of linked mechanisms.

The underlying rationale of interdependence is that each of the constituent parts of the CJS is unavoidably—and to a greater or lesser degree—reliant on other services to properly discharge its own, more specific role. Thus, e.g. the Crown Prosecution Service (CPS) relies on sound information from the police (or other law enforcement agencies) upon which to make a decision about whether there should be a prosecution at all or whether the prosecution tests described in *Chapter 11* are satisfied. In turn the police often require legal advice from the CPS concerning the exact legal scope of an offence. Courts cannot sentence in serious cases without the benefit of a pre-sentence report (PSR) from the Probation Service which, in turn, needs to understand the sentencing guidance issued to judges and magistrates and the factors and concerns that

---

[31] (2002) Cm 5563. For some developments in relation to BAES, etc., see *Rule of Law* in *Chapter 2*.

[32] Judicial decision-making is not in itself amenable to 'management' in the normal sense, national or otherwise—but there have been moves to monitor the performance of judges and magistrates. Since 2001, all criminal courts (including magistrates' courts, where many strategic decisions are also still made locally) have been linked via the Court Service (*Chapter 2*).

courts regularly take into account in arriving at their sentence decisions (see, mainly, *Chapter 12*). End-to-end sentencing involves close co-operation between the NPS and HMPS, whilst a whole chain of communications or risk-assessments may be involved in ensuring that everyone concerned has adequate and up-to-date information about any dangers presented by an offender, or knows that he or she is a risk to other people or at risk of self-harm or of committing suicide.[33]

What may seem to be an obvious statement at first sight is not so when viewed against the somewhat autonomous and often self-contained arrangements of the past as already hinted at under the heading *Ministry of Justice*, above. Nowadays, the trend is for the services to work towards better information, sound communications, improved performance, compatible working systems, agreed targets, protocols and understandings and there have been various moves towards geographical compatibility in terms of units or levels of operation. Practice standards are a high priority within each organization and other mechanisms include, e.g. codes of practice, working manuals, guidelines, liaison arrangements, multi-agency teams, task forces and *Partnership and Working Together* as described separately in *Chapter 15*.

COSTS AND CRIMINAL JUSTICE: A NOTE

The criminal justice system is one of the country's major programmes of public expenditure, and there is inevitable pressure to find savings or to limit the growth in costs as procedures have become more sophisticated and the needs of security have become more demanding. Court delays, uneconomic court houses and procedures, prison regimes, community-based resources, the expensive deployment of police officers as opposed, e.g. to police community support officers (PCSOs) or the use of private sector security guards at sporting events, legal aid and ways of funding research have for many years been targets for efficiency savings, and there has been concern that economies in such areas might sometimes prejudice bringing offenders to justice, including through the conduct of criminal trials and ultimately the integrity or quality of justice itself.

The most difficult area has, however, been the relationship between the sentencing practices of the courts and the capacity of the prison and probation services to give effect to the sentences imposed. Governments have never compromised the courts' independence by seeking to influence their decisions in particular cases, but have at times encouraged courts to use less expensive, non-custodial penalties rather than imprisonment, typically by making non-custodial penalties more 'demanding' or 'effective'. But this encouragement has

---

[33]   Similar examples of essential communications appear throughout this handbook.

been intermittent and its impact has often been counteracted by that on the sentencing climate of government Ministers' rhetoric, on other occasions, concerning the need for 'toughness' in dealing with offenders.

From time-to-time, there has been an emphasis on greater and better use of financial penalties rather than those outcomes which are more severe within the sentencing framework (see, generally, *Chapter 9*). Such attempts have, however, been fraught with difficulty: no government can afford to be seen as 'soft' on crime, and the Judiciary always and rightly resist any appearance of interference by the Executive (see also, generally, under *Criminal courts and the separation of powers* above). The situation is especially difficult when the issue is not about cost but about the system's immediate physical capacity. Some further comments concerning costs and the financial implications of criminal justice decision-making appear in *Chapter 15*.

CHAPTER 2

General Matters: A Selection

Criminal justice is a wide-ranging, multi-faceted topic touching on everything from the initial investigation of an offence—through the various stages of prosecution and trial—to the sentencing of offenders and beyond. Its further reaches encompass aspects of criminology and penology as well as of the criminal law, proper, rules of evidence and criminal procedure. Each of these is a discrete and specialist field. Criminal justice also has more down to earth, pragmatic, dimensions, including in relation to crime prevention, crime reduction and bringing offenders to justice—three key aims of the CJS. There are often perceived to be 'urgent' pressures and demands from the general public, the media and politicians for 'something to be done'. It is a constantly changing topic in terms of its preoccupations, priorities, targets and general content.

THE RULE OF LAW

The rule of law is a constitutional principle which has come to be recognised in Great Britain and the USA through the work of jurists and philosophers from the 18th century onwards. As a fundamental concept, it continues to evolve, especially in relation to human rights and international law. The Constitutional Reform Act 2005 includes a requirement for the Lord Chancellor to swear an oath (or affirmation) to 'respect the rule of law and the independence of the judiciary'. There is no standard definition of the rule. Essentially, it ensures that no-one is above the law, everyone is bound by the law and entitled to its protection, and that the law should be observed and enforced equally and universally. There should, e.g. be no such thing as 'no-go' areas whether controlled by criminal gangs, sectarian groups or, by the same token, the rich and powerful, including the Government. Everyone is bound by the law of the land in the same way as anyone else.

Appeals to the rule of law are sometimes made when the Government or powerful institutions are challenged in the courts in politically sensitive cases, e.g. where they involve an abuse of human rights or allegations of corruption. Even the UK Prime Minister, Tony Blair MP, was interviewed by the police in 2007 as a potential witness in connection with allegations of corruption in his political party[1] and in the BAE Systems case the High Court expressed

---

[1] The so-called 'cash for honours' investigation. There is no doubt that he could have been charged with an offence had the investigation moved in that direction. The Crown Prosecution ultimately

considerable disquiet about the way in which government pressure was brought to bear on the Serious Fraud Office to drop a prosecution on the pretext that this was 'in the national interest'. Ideas associated with the rule of law include the clarity and accessibility of the law, justice being done and seen to be done in public, and 'equality of arms' as between the prosecution and the defence.

THE ADVERSARIAL SYSTEM OF JUSTICE

In contrast to many European continental systems of justice but in common with those such as the USA where the same method has been adopted, the UK has an adversarial system. By this is meant that the parties oppose each other by seeking by lawful means, rules, procedures and legitimate forensic and other techniques to defeat the case of the other. The notion is of being on different sides, prosecution or defence and, in relation to the latter, there are a whole battery of different kinds of individual—from socially-minded practitioners and committed exponents of human rights to those lawyers who specialise in representing wealthy 'white collar' businessmen against allegations of fraud or involvement in organized crime—who seek every opportunity to undermine a prosecution. From time-to-time this may have led to underhand techniques, e.g. by police officers who were determined to obtain a conviction at all costs as to which certain miscarriage of justice cases over the years bear witness. In the setting of the courtroom, this 'battle' between opposing parties takes on a highly structured form and many of the rules by which the courts operate—including the rules of evidence—take their shape historically from the fact that each party operates from a premise of conflict.[2] Notoriously, the situation is perhaps at its worst when an accused dispenses with legal representation and insists on a prosecution witness such as a child abuse or rape victim being called to give evidence and cross-examines him or her in a way that involves 're-living the offence' and thus adding to the trauma.

It is partly in response to adversarial methods, which encourage the divide between victims and offenders that the restorative justice movement described in *Chapter 15* has arisen. The adversarial approach is also contrasted with the inquisitorial approach of certain European jurisdictions (and to an extent that in Scotland) in which a judicial officer (an 'investigating magistrate' or 'procurator

decided against any prosecutions whatsoever. Compare also the comments in relation to the role of the Attorney General in *Chapter 12*. In modern times a Lord Justice of Appeal stood trial on allegations of indecent exposure (of which he was acquitted by a jury) and a Crown Court judge was given a suspended sentence of imprisonment for downloading indecent images of children from the internet. There is a long history of people in power 'falling from grace' over the years and being tried by the courts, extending to the imprisoning of members of the House of Lords.

[2] For a highly absorbing account, see *Fighting for Justice: The Origins and History of Adversary Trial* (2006), Hostettler J, Waterside Press.

fiscal') looks into matters at an early stage and tries to discern not just whether there is evidence of an offence, or whether sufficient evidence might be found, but also what direction the case should take. This is not to say that the English system is devoid of agreement based measures or less divisive approaches, as with such items as formal admissions (which dispense with the need for something to be proved by evidence in court), agreed witness statements (similarly) and relatively modern duties placed on the parties to disclose their evidence or the nature of their case (*Chapters 8* and *9*) are examples. It would also be wrong to suggest that all people who are accused of a criminal offence are actively obstructive or given to exacerbating the harm already done. Many show remorse, contrition and may never offend again. Similarly, certain responsibilities of prosecutors and defence lawyers can be enforced by regulatory bodies if not adhered to as a matter of professional integrity. It is also the case that there must be even-handed treatment of both parties, a fair opportunity to put each side of the case, and 'equality of arms'.

CRIMINAL LAW AND CRIMINAL PROCEDURE

The criminal law is contained principally in those Acts of Parliament which define individual offences, such as theft, criminal damage or assault. There are also some common law offences, the most striking being murder. There is nothing pre-ordained about what constitutes a criminal offence: it is quite simply any matter that is prohibited (or 'proscribed') by law and to which criminal sanctions attach. The criminal law is also generally regarded as encompassing such matters as the general principles of criminal liability. These include the nature of an *actus reus* (prohibited actions or events) and the extent to which *mens rea* (a guilty mind, intention, knowledge, etc.) may need to exist, as well, e.g. as aiding and abetting, general or special defences to allegations and the law as it concerns 'inchoate crimes' such as conspiracy, incitement or attempts to commit offences. By contrast, criminal procedure (which is a topic of study in its own right) covers the very many different arrangements for processing or dealing with cases, such as how criminal proceedings can be commenced or what documents must be served on parties and according to what timescales. Such provisions are normally contained in rules or regulations—also known as Statutory Instruments (SIs) or delegated legislation. *Practice Directions* may also be issued from time-to-time by the Lord Chief Justice who heads a Criminal Procedure Rules Committee (CPRC) (*Chapter 8*).[3]

---

[3] Classic texts exist on all such topics, e.g. Smith and Hogan's *Criminal Law*, Archbold's *Criminal Pleadings* and *Stone's Justices' Manual*. An excess of new criminal laws, some 3,000 between 1998 and 2008, have had a criminalising effect whilst anti-social behaviour (ASB) provisions have ultimately done the same. There is also a sense in which the criminal law has become uncertain.

'CRIMINAL JUSTICE ACTS'

The term 'Criminal Justice Act' is used in two senses: (a) to describe an Act of Parliament (or 'statute') that is so designated in its own title, such as the Criminal Justice Act 1948, 1991 or 2003; or (b) in a looser sense to describe any Act that deals with aspects of criminal justice, such as sentencing or other powers or duties that are cast on component parts of the Criminal Justice System (CJS). Thus, e.g. the Crime and Disorder Act 1998, Police and Criminal Evidence Act 1984 (PACE), Offender Management Act 2007 or Criminal Justice and Immigration Act 2008[4]—which quite apart from changes to immigration law contains new powers to deal with anti-social and violent behaviour, make sentencing decisions clearer and introduce a new community sentence for young offenders—would all normally be described as Criminal Justice Acts. So too might statutes creating offences or introducing new frameworks or procedures as being germane to the work of the CJS. By contrast, statutes dealing with constitutional reform or human rights would not usually be so styled, but may nonetheless have significant effects on CJS functions.

A cautionary note for readers of this handbook

Historically, Criminal Justice Acts were something of a rarity and regarded as major pieces of legislation justifying wide-ranging prior consultation and debate. A modern complaint is that there has been a proliferation of such Acts,[5] several a year at times, with further changes of the kind that would formerly have merited a high level of visibility being contained in delegated legislation which might, in turn, involve uncertain implementation schedules. This, accompanied by a plethora of new criminal offences, claim some commentators, has made the law itself uncertain—to the extent that even experienced practitioners (or the courts on occasion) have commented that they do not always know exactly where matters stand. This cautionary note should encourage readers to carefully check the present status of any given procedure and whether there are imminent or latent changes. The Government has expressed itself as being committed to greater levels of consultation and declared its preparedness to listen to those concerned with the CJS (and other walks of public life as well as the public generally): see, generally, the note on the White Paper, *The Governance of Britain* in the closing chapter of this work.

---

[4] Still a Bill at the time of writing. Embryonic Acts are called 'Bills' during their Parliamentary progress throughout which time their contents are usually styled 'proposals'. For some indication of the extremely wide-ranging level of reform that has been occurring, see, e.g. *The Criminal Justice Act 2003: A Guide to the New Procedures and Sentencing* (2004) Gibson B, Waterside Press.

[5] A development that has been described as 'churning' and which has attracted the criticism that the UK is becoming a 'non-participating democracy': as to which see, further, in *Chapter 15*.

CRIMINAL EVIDENCE

The law of evidence covers such diverse matters as the law affecting the testimony of witnesses, the admissibility or otherwise of particular kinds of assertions, exhibits, documents or expert opinion—as well as matters touching on the relevance of, or weight which ought to be given to a particular strand of evidence in a given situation.[6] Different and more stringent rules of evidence apply in criminal cases as opposed to civil ones; albeit that many longstanding rules have been altered in modern times including under the Criminal Justice Act 2003 in relation to hearsay, confessions by accused people, evidence about the 'bad character' of witnesses or defendants, the rules about when someone can refresh their memory in court, e.g. from an earlier statement made to the police, and so as to allow greater use of video-recordings and live TV links, e.g. between courts, prisons or a witness giving evidence from abroad. Similarly, there are revised provisions about when a court can, as a matter of discretion, disallow evidence as being prejudicial to the accused person. Evidential rules are closely linked to those concerning the presumption of innocence and the burden or standard of proof (below). So to the role of a judge in guiding a jury on such matters (*Chapter 12*). Ultimately, they are of relevance not just to judges, magistrates and lawyers in a courtroom, but police officers during an investigation (*Chapter 6*) or Crown prosecutors when they are considering whether there is sufficient evidence to justify a prosecution (*Chapter 7*). They are also a primary concern of lawyers acting for an accused person (*Chapter 12*).

Burden and standard of proof

In a criminal case the *burden* of proving guilt lies with the prosecutor who must establish the accused person's guilt to the required *standard* of proof, i.e. beyond reasonable doubt. A classic statement is that of Lord Sankey in 1935 in the case of *Woolmington v. DPP*,[7] an appeal to the House of Lords on a point of law against a murder conviction (see, generally, *Chapter 10*):

> Throughout the web of the English criminal law one golden thread is always to be seen—that is the duty of the prosecution to prove the prisoner's guilt subject to ... insanity and ... to any statutory exception . . . If, at the end of and on the whole of the case, there is a reasonable doubt, created by the evidence given by either the prosecution or the prisoner . . . the prosecution has not made out the case and the prisoner is entitled to an acquittal . . . No matter what the charge or where the trial, the principle that the prosecution must prove the guilt of the prisoner is part of the common law of England and no attempt to whittle it down can be entertained.

---

[6] A classic work here is Cross on *Evidence*.

[7] 1935 AC 462.

Exceptionally, the law does reverse the normal onus of proof and the defendant must establish something, e.g. where this is exclusively within his or her own knowledge, control or purview, such as the fact that he or she held a licence or was covered by insurance—matters that it is virtually impossible to draw proper conclusions about unless the person who is accused provides the answer. The standard of proof is then the lesser civil standard, 'on a balance of probabilities'.

Right to silence

Closely associated with the above and an integral part of the adversarial system of justice that exists in England and Wales is the so-called right to silence. This is the equivalent of the American 'Fifth Amendment', the notion that a citizen should not be obliged to convict himself or herself out of his or her own mouth. Equally historically, this has been a feature of criminal justice in England for hundreds of years. But whereas in the past that was the end of the matter, an accused person who, since 1995, fails to give an explanation, e.g. to the police, that he or she later relies upon in court may find that adverse inferences are drawn by a jury or magistrates. This has become an integral part of the police caution when an officer 'reads his or her rights' to an alleged suspect during an investigation of the kind described in *Chapter 6*.

CRIMINOLOGY AND PENOLOGY: A NOTE

Criminology is the science of criminal justice and penology that of punishment. Both are extensive subjects in their own right, but also tend to overlap with each other and with criminal justice itself. They range from highly refined philosophical issues to purely practical or applied varieties, e.g. those concerned with statistical analysis, data gathering, research and evaluation. There has in modern times been a predilection for what is sometimes called 'evidence based practice', i.e. that which has been proved to have, or which has been shown to be more likely to have, a particular outcome, e.g. in terms of crime prevention or preventing re-offending due to a particular type of sentence or intervention. There is thus an overlap between these sometimes grandiose aspects of criminal justice and everyday issues, policies and strategies. However, the subject of criminal justice *per se* is generally regarded as involving more directly practical issues, such as the day-to-day arrangements, rules and mechanisms via which the CJS operates and the powers that exist in relation to sentencing.[8]

---

[8] Even the parameters of criminology/penology are open to debate! For examples of the subject matter, see, e.g. *The Oxford Handbook of Criminology* and the *Sage Dictionary of Criminology*. For a beginner's guide to criminology, see *Introduction to Criminology* (1999), Pond R, Waterside Press.

FAIRNESS AND HUMAN RIGHTS

It would be impossible in modern times to describe criminal justice or the CJS without reference to the Human Rights Act 1998 and European Convention On Human Rights and Fundamental Freedoms, not least the fair trials provisions of Article 6 of the Convention. One particularly important offshoot of Article 6 has been the growth of a duty to give reasons and explanations for decisions. Traditionally, criminal courts have always been guided by principles grounded in 'natural justice' whose twin pillars are: no-one can be a judge in his or her own cause (or the rule against bias); and always hear both sides. The first 'pillar' emphasises the need for courts to be impartial. If bias exists on the part of the judge or magistrate he or she is disqualified from sitting to hear the case— except when bias can properly be waived by the parties. A *financial* interest in the outcome of a case cannot be waived and neither should someone adjudicate if there is a close personal relationship or other interest. A further requirement of natural justice is that each party must be given a full and proper opportunity to put his or her case and with proper explanations by the court. This aspect is sometimes put by saying that the court must act fairly. This thinking is now subsumed with human rights law alongside a whole range of other fundamental rights and freedoms. In a directly criminal justice context, these include the right not 'to be punished without law' and various rights of assembly, association, expression, thought, conscience and religion.

Other examples from the Convention are its focus on the idea of proportionality in terms of actions and responses, the absolute right in Article 3 not to be subjected to torture, or inhuman or degrading treatment or punishment, a limited right under Article 5 whereby 'Everyone has the right to liberty and security of person' and 'No-one shall be deprived of his liberty' except as described in the article, including by 'lawful detention . . . after conviction by a competent court' or under various forms of 'lawful arrest or detention'. Article 8 also contains a qualified right to respect for private and family life which may feature in criminal cases but that can, e.g. be restricted by the state in the interests of preventing disorder or crime.

Right to a fair trial

As already intimated, central to the work of the criminal courts is the right to a fair trial. Article 6 provides, among other things, that everyone charged with a criminal offence has certain minimum rights, including to be informed promptly, in a language he or she understands and in detail, of the nature and cause of any accusation against him or her; to have adequate time and facilities for the preparation of a defence; to defend himself or herself in person or through legal assistance and, if without sufficient means to pay for this, to be given it free when the interests of justice so require; to examine and call witnesses; and to have the free assistance of an interpreter where necessary. The concept of a fair trial is much wider than establishing guilt or innocence by way of a trial in court and affects all stages of the criminal process, from investigation right through to sentence, prison discipline and the opportunities that an offender is given at the 'back end' of that process to progress with his or her eventual release plan (*Chapter 14*). Article 6(1) of the Convention provides:

> In the determination of his civil rights and obligations or of any criminal charge against him, everyone is entitled to a fair and public hearing within a reasonable time by an independent and impartial tribunal established by law. Judgement shall be pronounced publicly but the press and public may be excluded from all or part of the trial in the interests of morals, public order or national security in a democratic society, where the interests of juveniles or the protection of the private life of the parties so require, or to the extent strictly necessary in the opinion of the court in special circumstances where publicity would prejudice the interest of justice.

The article continues by stating that everyone charged with a criminal offence is to be presumed innocent until proven guilty according to law (see, further, below) and that anyone charged with an offence has the certain minimum rights:

- to be informed promptly, in a language he understands and in detail, of the nature and cause of the accusation against him;
- to have adequate time and facilities for the preparation of his defence;
- to defend himself in person or through legal assistance of his own choosing or, if he has not sufficient means to pay for legal assistance, to be given it free when the interests of justice so require;
- to examine or have examined witnesses against him and obtain the attendance and examination of witnesses on his behalf under like conditions;
- to have the free assistance of an interpreter if he cannot understand or speak the language in court.

The idea that such extreme concepts as torture or unlawful detention are things of the past or no longer live issues would appear to be dispelled, e.g. by allegations concerning so-called USA 'rendition flights' whereby suspects are transported to countries whose human rights protections are less well developed, if at all, in which the UK may be implicated by its acquiescence at least, or the treatment of prisoners of war or other terrorism suspects whilst being held in detention. Various organizations exist whose remit includes monitoring such events, such as Liberty, Justice, Statewatch and Fair Trials Abroad.

DISCRIMINATION AND DISADVANTAGE

Section 95 Criminal Justice Act 1991 requires the Lord Chancellor[9] to publish:

> . . . such information as he considers expedient for the purposes of . . . facilitating the performance by [persons engaged in the administration of criminal justice] of their duty to avoid discriminating against any person on the ground of race, sex or any other improper ground.

This provision applies to all people engaged in the CJS, whether as judges, magistrates, administrators, police, Crown prosecutors, probation officers, social workers and so on. Booklets and materials have been published annually ever since the 1991 Act. The European Convention on Human Rights does not contain a free-standing right not to be discriminated against but Article 14 requires all human rights to be applied without discrimination. Discrimination is often (but not always) associated with other forms of disadvantage and social exclusion and hence a Cabinet-level committee on the latter and the government's Social Exclusion Unit (SEU). In turn, disadvantage and exclusion tend to be directly associated with certain kinds of crime.

Ethnic and other monitoring

Since the 1991 Act each of the criminal justice agencies has taken steps intended to guard against discrimination, e.g. police monitoring of the use of stops and search powers, Crown Prosecution Service monitoring system to assess the number of cases identified by the police as containing an element of racial motivation and to review decisions taken by Crown prosecutors, monitoring of court decisions in relation to bail and sentencing, a national system for race and ethnic monitoring within the probation service whilst the HM Prison Service also has procedures to ensure equality and consistency of treatment across minority groups. Similar initiatives have extended across vulnerable groups who might suffer from hate crime (below). Yet, monitoring statistics continue to show disproportionate outcomes for black and minority ethnic (BME) defendants and offenders at various stages of the criminal justice process. An iconic reference point for concerns about the treatment of minority groups by the criminal justice system continues to be the Stephen Lawrence case of 1994.

Institutional racism

Stephen Lawrence was a young black man killed by a group of white youths in South London. The inadequate police investigation of his death led to the

---

[9] Formerly a duty cast on the Home Secretary.

Stephen Lawrence Inquiry, chaired by Sir William Macpherson of Cluny, into the death and its investigation by the Metropolitan Police service (MPS). The report was severely critical of the MPS, which it characterised as 'institutionally racist', and made a large number of recommendations for reform addressed both to the police and to central government. Almost all of them were immediately accepted. The report can be said to have significantly altered the attitude of the police, and the criminal justice services generally, to race and racism and the character of the debate at every level. The report did, however, attract severe criticism from some newspapers and certain sections of the police service. The Stephen Lawrence case was also one of the triggers for changes to the historic double jeopardy rule of English law noted later in this chapter.

Hate crime
Modern times have seen two particular legislative departures directed against discrimination or what have become known as 'hate crimes'. First, there are a growing number of offences aimed specifically at attacks or other aggressive or 'aggravated' behaviour that involves a racial, religious or similar element, such as gender or sexual orientation. Similarly, certain offences are, by statute, aggravated and attract higher penalties where there is such an element. This is reinforced by sentencing guidelines and the work of the Sentencing Guidelines Council (SGC) (see, generally, *Chapter 9*).[10]

MAPPAS AND RISK ASSESSMENT

In modern times there has been an emphasis on improving detection and ultimately conviction rates with the underlying aim of long-term crime prevention and crime reduction, both of which are essential tenets of present-day criminal policy. This begins with sound investigation techniques. There is an increased reliance on monitoring groups of offenders, e.g. via Multi-agency Protection Panels (known as MAPPAs) and making associated risk-assessments. These seek to identify and manage dangerous and high profile offenders in local communities in a concerted effort to stop them committing offences at the outset or further crimes. In addition there is, e.g. a Persistent Offender Task Force comprising senior representatives from the various CJS agencies and that is linked to a Persistent Offender Project aimed at 'catching, bringing to justice and rehabilitating offenders who are responsible for a disproportionate amount of crime'. The project began as a first step towards the Labour Government's manifesto commitment in 2001 to 'double the chance of persistent offenders

---

10   For some further details of this approach, see *The Criminal Justice Act 2003: A Guide to the New Procedures and Sentencing* (2004), Gibson, B, Waterside Press.

being caught and punished by 2011'. Often such approaches work in conjunction with referral schemes involving a wide range of provision, including services or resources provided by the voluntary sector. Enhancements in policing and law enforcement techniques are noted in *Chapter 11* and *Partnership and Working Together* in *Chapter 15*. MAPPAs operate alongside Crime and Disorder Reduction Panels (*Chapter 1*).

REASONS FOR DECISIONS

One key development of modern times is the increased extent to which all public authorities now explain themselves as a part of daily routines unless there is some sound reason not to do so. The underlying position under UK domestic law was that criminal courts need not, as a matter of course, give—i.e. announce publicly—the reasons for their decisions. Courts were expected to have valid reasons (otherwise cases would be decided on a mere hunch) and explanations were often given to the parties in practice. Reasons had to be disclosed, e.g. if there was an appeal by way of case stated, and the practice of the higher courts has been to give reasons when deciding on appeal or judicial review (*Chapter 10*). But the routine giving of reasons by judges or magistrates at 'first instance', immediately following a conviction or sentence, is of relatively, largely post-Human Rights Act 1998, origin. Gradually, the situation was affected by statute so that there was increasingly an obligation to give reasons in specific situations, initially, e.g.

- if not awarding compensation when it could be ordered;
- when sending someone to prison;
- when not activating a suspended sentence when someone re-offended;
- when refusing bail or granting conditional bail (*Chapter 3* and *6*).

Human rights obligations (above) extended the situations in which reasons were required so that, in effect, an explanation must now be given which is sufficient to allow the parties to understand the outcome of a case or determination, or any point or issue which arises during the hearing of a case. This is part of the fair trial implications of Article 6 of the European Convention under which 'judgements [must be] pronounced publicly'. The Criminal Justice Act 2003 contained a general provision placing a duty on courts, except where a sentence is mandatory, fixed or otherwise required by law, to give reasons for their sentencing decisions and to explain sentences in ordinary language. It also added quite substantially to the individual statutory situations in which reasons must now be given.[11] The obligation to explain outcomes in ordinary language can be viewed as part of a more general move away from the use of technical and sometimes confusing terminology by public institutions in general.

THE PRESUMPTION OF INNOCENCE

It may seem trite to state that an accused person is presumed innocent unless and until proved guilty—following a decision by a jury or magistrates. Again, this is now reinforced by Article 6 of the European Convention. The presumption affects the way in which accused people are dealt with at all stages of the criminal process prior to conviction and unless and until their status changes because they are found guilty. It is the reason why someone who is interviewed by the police should be described as 'a suspect' rather than 'an offender', the person standing trial is 'the accused' and the charge remains 'an allegation'. Similarly, although someone may be described as a prisoner, it is important to distinguish between a 'remand prisoner' who is awaiting trial and a 'convicted prisoner' who is awaiting or serving his or her sentence. Only following conviction by a competent court is the presumption of innocence treated as rebutted.

TRIAL BY PEERS

Trial in the Crown Court by a jury of ordinary people selected at random (*Chapter 4*), or by lay magistrates (*Chapter 3*), is sometimes described as trial by peers, the principle—said to stem from Magna Carta—being that people accused of crime should, so far as the key question 'guilty or not guilty' is concerned, be dealt with by ordinary members of the community, not by the state or a professional corps of judges. The one practical exception to this is that around 100 district judges (paid professionals) sit to hear cases in magistrates' courts: *Chapters 3* and *12*. Trial by peers has a somewhat different connotation in relation to peers of the realm who are members of the House of Lords. Theoretically, they are entitled to be tried by 'their peers' in that House, but the practice has been redundant for many years. It is unlikely that it would survive human rights or other legal challenges today.

The Criminal Justice Act 2003 made certain inroads into the principle so as to allow trial in the Crown Court by a judge alone in relation to fraud or jury tampering and there has been pressure for these limited situations to be added to or made more general. By definition, a judge only (or 'judge-alone') trial

---

[11]   See section 174 of the 2003 Act. The full list is set out in *Appendix I* to *The Criminal Justice Act 2003: A Guide to the New Procedures and Sentencing* (2004) Gibson B, Waterside Press.

(*Chapter 9*) is not 'trial by peers' and thus contravenes historic, democratic principle. Nonetheless, supporters of such developments would argue, e.g. that it is possible to adopt a more efficacious approach without diluting the quality of justice delivered.

DUE PROCESS

The principle of 'due process' is less developed in England and Wales than it is, e.g. in the USA, where it rises to the status of a high constitutional principle. Nonetheless the requirements of English law are such that people can only be interviewed, arrested, tried and sentenced if proper procedures and processes are followed at whatever stage. Similarly, public officers, whether judges or administrators must not abuse or misuse their powers: something which can be tested by way of judicial review (*Chapter 10*). This is now further protected by a raft of human rights considerations. At a less grandiose level, many instances of material failure to follow correct procedure will prevent a conviction or form grounds for an appeal in the normal way—unless, e.g. it is possible to deal with the case without resort to the evidence or item affected by the irregularity. There have, however, been disturbing moves that would prevent the taking by lawyers of 'mere technicalities' and suggestions that the higher courts should no longer be bound to hold in favour of a convicted appellant on that basis alone. Due process is something that might be expected to feature in any written Constitution for the UK as outlined in *Chapter 15*.

DOUBLE JEOPARDY

A legal rule that goes back many centuries is that someone who is convicted or acquitted of an offence may not be tried again for the self-same matter. Depending on the situation (and adopting the ancient terminology) this is styled *autrefois convict* or *autrefois acquit*. Notoriously in modern times, debates concerning the appropriateness of the rule have been linked to events flowing from the murder of Stephen Lawrence in 1994.[12] The rule is said to be grounded in the need to have some known finality of proceedings, a further argument being that if an investigator or prosecutor knows that he or she may have multiple 'bites at the cherry' he or she may well prepare less thoroughly (and thus less fairly) than ought to be the case. But with advances in technology including DNA testing and the ability to examine documents and materials more closely it has become possible to revisit cold cases and their related files

---

[12]   See earlier in the chapter.

many years on, including long after someone has been acquitted (or never proceeded against). Part 10 of the Criminal Justice Act 2003 changed the rule so that people can now be tried twice in relation to certain serious matters where there is 'new and compelling evidence'.

OPEN COURT

Members of the public (and the press: see further below) are entitled to observe court proceedings, subject to there being available space and no interference with the proceedings (which may amount to contempt of court). This can be seen as an example of the need for visibility in matters of justice. In exceptional circumstances, the criminal courts can decide to sit *in camera* (i.e. completely in private), e.g. in the interests of national security or where life and limb are at risk. This is a somewhat rare event in practice. A common statutory exception to the open court rule and where a court hearing *is* held in private is when a magistrates' court is considering whether to issue a warrant of further detention during a police investigation (i.e. before anyone has been charged with an offence) under the Police and Criminal Evidence Act 1984 (PACE) although, in such a case, the suspect will usually be present: see further *Chapter 6*. There are also now special rules whereby judicial oversight of control orders in relation to terrorist suspects occurs in private and also, since the Criminal Justice Act 2003, in relation to certain evidentiary and other rulings by judges in relation to a trial (*Chapter 9*). Youth courts (*Chapter 5*) are not open to the public but the press can attend. However, there has been a more sympathetic view towards admitting victims and other people with a legitimate interest in observing such proceedings in recent years.

Press restrictions
Broadly speaking, the press can report whatever they wish of court proceedings except in those few situations where an Act of Parliament restricts this, e.g. committal proceedings before magistrates (*Chapter 8*) (when only a bare outline of the case can be reported at that stage unless the defence applies for this restriction to be lifted because, say, the accused person hopes that other witnesses will come forward in support of his or her defence case), or where the law allows the court to restrict publication at its discretion. Publication may be postponed by order of the court to avoid a 'substantial risk of prejudice to the administration of justice' which accounts for those sometimes strange newspaper reports in which some quite newsworthy case first meets the public gaze following the conviction or acquittal of the accused person. Other legal restrictions on what can be reported exist in relation to the youth court, children (the court can make a direction preventing identification whenever a child appears in court, including, e.g. as a witness) and a limited range of other matters. Seats are normally reserved for the

press in court and representatives are entitled to be present except in those rare instances when proceedings are held *in camera*, above.

Photography
Photographing, drawing[13] or tape-recording court proceedings is punishable as a contempt of court—but a court can give leave for the use of a tape-recorder, e.g. to an advocate who wishes to record complex evidence for transcription. The Crown Court takes its own shorthand note, however, which an advocate might be expected to rely on. Many hearings relating to the adjournment of cases and the remand of offenders are now conducted via video links.

CONTEMPT OF COURT

Both the Crown Court and magistrates' court have power to punish for contempt, including, where applicable, under the Contempt of Court Act 1981. This extends to anyone who wilfully insults the court, a judge, magistrate, juror, officer of the court, lawyers or witness—whether in court or whilst going to or returning from court. Similarly, if anyone wilfully interrupts court proceedings or misbehaves in court. Offenders can be detained until the end of the proceedings and, if the court thinks fit, can be committed to custody (limited in the case of magistrates to committal to prison for up to one month) or can be fined (again limited in magistrates' courts to £2,500), or both. Committal to custody can be revoked at any time, e.g. where the offender asks to apologise (thereby showing contrition and 'purging' his or her contempt).

CATEGORIES AND CLASSIFICATIONS OF OFFENCE

It is impossible to fully understand the CJS without at least an outline knowledge of the three categories of offence. All criminal cases—from unlawful parking to murder—start out in the magistrates' court (*Chapter 3*). But a distinction must first be drawn between allegations which magistrates' courts can try (i.e. decide upon guilt or innocence, then pass sentence) and those where they may only deal with the preliminary stages of a case before the matter is passed to the Crown Court (*Chapter 4*). In simplest terms, these categories are:

---

[13] The drawings regularly seen in newspapers or on TV screens are created from memory by an artist who observed the proceedings. For an outline of media law in general, including justice-related aspects, see *Media Law for Journalists* (2006), Smartt U, Sage Publications.

- summary;
- either way; and
- indictable[14] only.

Summary offences

In the normal course of events, summary offences can *only* be tried—and, if convicted, the offender can *only* be sentenced—by magistrates. Everyday examples of such 'purely summary' or 'summary only' matters are:

- speeding and some other road traffic offences such as careless driving, defective brakes, lights or steering, driving with excess alcohol in the blood or urine, and taking a vehicle without consent;
- using a TV set without the necessary licence;
- some lesser public order offences;
- common assault;
- criminal damage—where the value of the damage is low;[15]
- certain social security offences; or
- offences against local bye-laws.

If the defendant pleads guilty, such a case may only take up a few minutes of court time. Lesser offences are often dealt with by way of a written plea of guilty as 'paperwork cases' (*Chapter 9*). Nonetheless, a plea of not guilty will attracts the full panoply of the criminal law and associated procedures. The trial of a summary offence observes the same general rules of procedure and evidence as one for the most serious of offences. Maximum penalties for summary offences are laid down by the Act of Parliament creating the offence. This is often a fine although some more serious summary offences attract imprisonment. Many minor matters are now dealt with by way of fixed penalty notices that are issued by the police or other authorised people, or, where appropriate, as anti-social behaviour (see later in this chapter). Such matters are styled as 'non-convictions' in certain quarters, including on the Police National Computer (PNC).

Either way offences

The next level of offence is styled 'triable either way'—often simplified to 'either way'. Such offences can be tried in the magistrates' court or the Crown Court. depending on the outcome of a procedure known as allocation and sending (or sometimes 'mode of trial'). This is described in *Chapter 9*. Commonplace either way offences include:

---

[14]   Technically speaking, the umbrella classification 'indictable' includes both indictable only and either way matters—hence the sub-classifications 'indictable *only*' and 'either way'. The significance of this is for the experts and beyond the scope of this handbook.

[15]   Currently below £5,000.

- theft;
- handling stolen property;
- various kinds of deceptions;
- burglary;[16]
- criminal damage where the value is high;[17]
- assault occasioning actual bodily harm (ABH); or
- possession or supply of certain prohibited drugs.

Quite apart from mode of trial, either way offences may involve other procedures such as 'plea before venue', 'committal for trial' and 'committal for sentence'. All of these are noted in *Chapter 9*.

Indictable only offences

Indictable only offences *must* be tried in the Crown Court before a judge and jury. Such cases are now sent to the Crown Court from the outset once the accused has appeared in the magistrates' court on remand, following arrest by the police and being charged: *Chapter 3*.Indictable only offences include:

- murder and other homicides;
- rape;
- causing grievous bodily harm with intent (GBH);
- robbery;
- aggravated burglary (see earlier footnote);
- blackmail;
- conspiracy by two or more people to commit a criminal offence.

RECORDED CRIME AND REPORTED CRIME

There is a difference between the volume of crime which actually occurs, or crime reported to the police, and crime which is recorded by them in compliance with standard police practice or legal requirements. The amount of crime which survives the entire process from commission to sentence is sometimes put as low as three or four per cent of all crime, the difference being known as the 'justice gap'. Various initiatives have been mounted from time-to-time with a view to narrowing this gap, but some commentators point to there being what they regard as a futile exercise. No-one can really know with certainty the full extent of crime and enforcement strategies can sometimes have unintended or unexpected effects, such as displacing crime to another area, or replacing it with other kinds of offences that may not be so easily detected. It is,

---

[16]   Unless it is an 'aggravated burglary', e.g. with a firearm or weapon.

[17]   Currently £5,000 or more.

however, important to consider precisely what it is that is being referred to or described when criminal statistics or assertions about crime levels are at issue.

LAW REPORTS

Where a point is a difficult one—or argued in depth by lawyers in a case—they are likely to refer a court to reports of rulings of the higher courts for it to consider the comments and remarks of senior judges. Such reports—known as 'law reports'—are normally authenticated by a barrister and are the mechanism by which the law of precedent operates: see *Chapter 10*. They are published in various formats and series. Those in regular use in the criminal courts include, e.g. the *All England Law Reports, Weekly Law Reports, Criminal Appeal Reports* (together with a separate series of those reports which deals exclusively with sentencing), *Justice of the Peace Report* and *Road Traffic Reports*. Practitioners also keep abreast of developments regular authenticated law reports that appear in *The Times* and *Independent* newspapers. Such reports relate as much to the work of the courts as they do to government departments, local authorities, the police, the Crown Prosecution Service or HM Prison Service.

ANTI-SOCIAL BEHAVIOUR (ASB): A NOTE

A modern dimension to 'criminal justice' is the development of anti-social behaviour orders (ASBOs) (and other kinds of what are termed 'civil behaviour orders'). ASBOs were first introduced under the Crime and Disorder Act 1998 to deal with relatively minor, nuisance-type behaviour (not necessarily of a criminal kind). An application to a court for an ASBO is a *civil* matter and results from liaison and discussion between the police and local authority. Once an ASBO is granted, then if it is not complied with (i.e. 'breached') this is treated as a criminal matter punishable in the case of an adult by up to five years in prison.[18] Human rights issues then arise, such as Article 6 ('fair trial') and Article 10 ('freedom of expression'). Civil remedies linked to criminal sanctions can also be seen in relation to harassment and football banning orders (*Chapter 9*) whilst the Police Reform Act 2002 allows 'on the spot fines' for a range of (admittedly in this particular case criminal) behaviour loosely categorised as 'anti-social'.

The theme of tackling anti-social behaviour has been a central if sometimes controversial plank of the Government's 'Respect Agenda' and this aspect of law enforcement has, within a few short years, become an integral part of the CJS. There are those commentators and organizations, such as ASBO Concern,[19] who

---

[18]   Two years in custody in the case of a juvenile aged 14 to 17.

[19]   Other organizations, details of which can readily be found on the internet, include ASBO Watch.

see something unsatisfactory in the notion that a wide range of somewhat vaguely defined behaviour can be criminalised in this way. For similar reasons, such organizations object to the proliferation of ASBO-related methods of law enforcement, their questionable, somewhat elastic scope and the ease with which orders with such potentially momentous affects in the event of a low-level breach may be obtained. ASBOs can also now be made in the county court.

The CRASBO
The ASBO should be contrasted with the criminal anti-social behaviour order (CRASBO) that can be made in criminal proceeding following conviction for any offence. Once made it has similar consequences to the civil ASBO.

PUTTING THE PROCEEDS OF CRIME TO WORK

Punishment apart, there are various methods by which a convicted offender can be required to make reparation or pay compensation to a victim, or in which he or she can be deprived of the proceeds of crime (see, in particular, *Chapters 9*). The Proceeds of Crime Act 2002 introduced a short lived Assets Recovery Agency (ARA) to investigate and recover wealth accumulated through criminal activity. It also consolidated and strengthened pre-existing powers of confiscation and civil recovery and powers and requirements in relation to money laundering. ARA responsibilities are now subsumed within the arrangements for the Serious Organized Crime Agency (SOCA) that was created under the Serious and Organized Crime and Police Act 2005. It is now virtually impossible for any citizen to conduct any substantial financial transactions without there being some trace of that activity, certainly if suspect, without professional advisers, banks, businesses and the like falling under some duty or obligation to alert either the police or revenue authorities. Proceeds have been channelled into a wide variety of crime reduction initiatives and projects.

COMMUNITY JUSTICE

An interesting innovation in local justice has been the North Liverpool Community Justice Centre, established in 2005, and similar, smaller schemes in other parts of England and Wales which began in 2007. Based on the Red Hook Centre in New York, USA, the Liverpool Centre is described as a community resource providing both a court function and a range of preventative and social services for the wider community. A single judge has charge of the centre, holding a joint appointment as both a district judge and circuit judge (i.e. Crown Court judge). Much of the work of the centre is focused on what can be described as low-level offending, anti-social behaviour (ASB) and compliance with court orders, but the court is also able to deal with some non-criminal matters and the judge can try more serious criminal cases when it is convenient for him to do so. The co-ordination of local services and involvement of the local community are important features of this departure. Along similar lines, some prisons now describe themselves as 'community prisons'.

Other uses of the term 'community justice'
The term is sometimes used in a different and more general sense to refer to local efforts to promote, e.g. the use of generic community sentences (*Chapter 9*), the employment of offenders to do unpaid work for the benefit to local communities, and the involvement of local communities and especially voluntary organizations in providing various kinds of support for offenders, victims and their families.

INSPECTION, MONITORING AND SCRUTINY

A further way in which the integrity of the CJS is protected is through independent arrangements to audit its activities. Increasingly the criminal justice process has come to rely on inspectorates including:

- HM Inspectorate of Constabulary;
- HM Inspectorate of Court Administration;
- HM Inspectorate of Prisons;
- HM Inspectorate of Probation; and
- HM Crown Prosecution Service Inspectorate.[20]

Various inspectorates are noted in the chapters which follow along with the arrangements, e.g. for an Independent Police Complaints Commission (IPCC) (*Chapter 11*), Prisons and Probation Ombudsman (*Chapter 13*) and Independent Monitoring Boards (IMBs) for each prison (*Chapter 14*). Scrutiny also occurs at other levels, as when the Audit Commission is asked to examine a particular area of the work of the CJS or an individual travels as an independent observer in relation to a prisoner who is being deported. Scope for scrutiny also exists within organizations due to their own working methods, Best Practice and the standing arrangements that exist for reporting abuses.

---

[20]   In 2007, an attempt to create a combined Criminal Justice Inspectorate was defeated in the House of Lords having been criticised as to great a cross-agency intrusion and influence.

CHAPTER 3

Magistrates' Courts

For the most part, magistrates' courts are served by ordinary members of the public who sit on the court bench two or three times per month as a form of voluntary and unpaid public service. Magistrates, or 'justices of the peace' (JPs) (terms which are interchangeable), are appointed for their character, integrity, capacity for sound judgment and fair-mindedness. They are often described as 'lay' magistrates,[1] to signify that they are not qualified specifically for this role in terms of their education. The receive expenses plus a modest allowance if their usual earnings are affected by attending court or carrying out related duties.

Part of a democratic and constitutional process

Magistrates usually sit 'in threes'[2] and receive legal advice from their own legal team comprising a justices' clerk and other court legal advisers.[3] This accords with the notion that the law is made and enforced on behalf of citizens and, in this respect, the arrangement is not dissimilar to that in the Crown Court where 12 members of the public—the jury—listen to the evidence and determine whether to convict or acquit the accused person; what is sometimes called 'trial by peers' (*Chapter 2*). But unlike jurors, magistrates also pass sentence, within their summary powers (below). In addition to the 30,000 or so lay justices there are some 100 district judges, who are salaried and usually full-time legal professionals, and who can sit alone (see further below and in *Chapter 12*).

SUMMARY JUSTICE

Magistrates' courts are courts of summary jurisdiction, the word 'summary' serving to emphasise the relatively straightforward and inexpensive nature of the response to crime that such courts provide when compared with the more elaborate arrangements in relation to the Crown Court (*Chapter 4*).

---

[1] The use of the term 'lay' has been discouraged by the Ministry of Justice as implying some shortcoming and undervaluing the training arrangements noted in *Chapter 12*.

[2] See, also, later in the chapter.

[3] See, further, in *Chapter 12*.

Summary offences must normally be prosecuted within six months and the outcome is thus comparatively immediate, albeit generally for more minor offending behaviour or, in modern times, forms of anti-social behaviour (ASB). Many summary cases amount to little more than transgressions or contraventions as opposed to crimes in the full sense and some occupy only minutes, or even seconds, in court. But magistrates do also deal with many matters which are serious, complex and of considerable import, including many either way offences.[4] At whatever level, the same high criminal standards of law and procedure apply even if there are sometimes special mechanisms whereby, e.g. summary justice can occur in the absence of the offender under 'paperwork' or 'written plea of guilty' arrangements (*Chapter 8*). Increasingly, by legislation, many lesser offences have, sometimes controversially, been turned into matters that can be dealt with by the issuing of a fixed penalty notice by the police or other law enforcement agents, with an appeal to magistrates if the offender disagrees with such action.

Origins of the magistrates' court

The description 'justice of the peace' first appeared in the 14th century (when the function was fused with that of carrying out various forms of local administration), although its origins can be traced back at least to the 'keepers of the peace' appointed by Simon de Montfort in 1264. The Justices of the Peace Act 1361 built upon emerging powers to arrest suspects and investigate offences. Three or four of 'the most worthy in each county' were commissioned to dispense justice locally. Powers to punish offenders were added before the end of that century. Property qualifications were abolished in 1905 in favour of seeking out people with the personal qualities and suitability for the role. Since then, the bench has slowly become more broad-based and representative of the community that it serves, more balanced as regards social background, age, gender, race and ethnicity.[5]

The mechanism for legal guidance

The system of summary justice relies for its effectiveness on the unique nature of the relationship between magistrates and their legal advisers. The chief advisers are known as justices' clerks, whilst everyday advice in court is usually provided by one of a team of court legal advisers (who sit below the magistrates,

---

[4] See *Chapter 2* for allocation and sending and *Chapter 4* for magistrates' historic role as 'examining justices' where an either way case is prospectively to be sent to the Crown Court.

[5] For information about the appointment of magistrates see *Chapter 12*.

often in front of them or to one side). Historically, they were known as 'court clerks'. The legal adviser is not party to the decision of the court whether concerning guilt or sentence and legal rules dictate the extent and kind of advice which can be given. The adviser can intervene, or can enter the magistrates' private quarters (known as the 'retiring room') for certain purposes. Many magistrates do in fact become highly experienced and the relationship with the adviser tends to adjust and adapt accordingly.

Management of the magistrates' courts

For administrative purposes, magistrates' courts now, since 2005, fall under HM Court Service, some further details of which appear in the next chapter. For many years before that, the justices' clerk was also the manager of his or her court—but, following the Police and Magistrates Courts Act 1994, each of the former local magistrates' courts committees (MCCs) (then responsible for oversight of administration) had to appoint a justices' chief executive with overall responsibility for the day-to-day matters in its area. Since 2005 and with HM Court Service a part of the MOJ, this function is discharged within and subject to the management structure and hierarchies that have since developed. Non-statutory innovations include such developments as Judicial Interest Groups (JIG) and Area Judicial Forums (AJF)—the former an interface between judges, magistrates, justices' clerks and administrators, the latter, where implemented, a forum for judicial interchanges. As with the Crown Court, magistrates' courts are inspected by HM Inspectorate of Courts Administration.

JURISDICTION

The word 'jurisdiction' is used to describe the extent of authority to deal with a given type or level of case. In the criminal justice context, magistrates' courts have a wide range of responsibilities, including:

- dealing with around 98 per cent of all prosecuted crime in England and Wales, from start to end—the remaining cases being sent by magistrates to the Crown Court for trial or sentence. Virtually all criminal cases begin in the magistrates' court, but 'indictable only' matters (such as murder, rape and robbery: see *Chapter 1*) are now sent directly to the Crown Court;
- deciding in many other cases whether or not an accused person is guilty of an offence, i.e. holding a summary trial: *Chapter 8*;
- sentencing offenders (with powers of up to six months' imprisonment for a single offence in many instances or 12 months in aggregate where

sentences for two or more either way offences (*Chapter 1*) are imposed to run consecutively (i.e. one following on in time after the other). A list of the available sentences appears in *Chapter 9;*[6]

- authorising further detention by the police of a suspect during an investigation under the Police and Criminal Evidence Act 1984 (PACE): *Chapter 6;*
- deciding whether someone ought to be released on bail or kept in custody pending the next stage of court proceedings: *Chapter 8;*
- dealing with people under 18 years of age in the youth courts: *Chapter 3;*
- issuing warrants of arrest, to search premises, seize illicit money, property or substances, or in other authorised situations;
- discharging a range of linked administrative duties, either at a courthouse or in some instances in a magistrates' private home.

Magistrates' jurisdiction is sometimes limited in time, e.g. proceedings for a purely summary offence must be commenced within six months of that offence being committed or coming to the notice of the prosecutor; and certain errors can be rectified by the court itself within 28 days (see, also, *Chapter 10*).

LOCAL JUSTICE

Magistrates' courts developed as local courts and remain so, even if, as in other walks of life, modern-day developments have tended to stretch the meaning of 'local'. The number of locations where such courts are held has fallen from over 1,000 in the 1960s to some 360 today. Often, now, magistrates sit in combined court centres in the same set of buildings as the Crown Court. Magistrates still deal principally with matters arising in their own court area even though, again strictly speaking now, they are no longer restricted to cases arising in their immediate area. The workload varies. A busy city court is likely to see a greater proportion of serious (or 'heavy' crime) than a remote rural area. A 'motorway court' will see a high percentage of road traffic cases; ports and airports generate HM Revenue and Customs prosecutions, smuggling cases and those involving various forms of cross-border trafficking or evasion; country areas often deal with agricultural crimes, poaching and those relating to the welfare of animals or movement of livestock. Offences linked to or triggered by drugs are

---

[6] Provisions exist in the Criminal Justice Act 2003 for these powers to be increased together with a new sentencing regime. But these have not been brought into force.

increasingly all-pervasive in terms of where they arise. Cases and court lists are often streamed into, e.g. 'remand courts', 'traffic courts', 'not guilty hearings' and 'non-police matters' (or what are sometimes called private prosecutions[7]).

Units of operation

Again historically and emphasising the intrinsic nature of summary justice, the geographical unit of operation of the magistrates' court was the 'petty sessional division' (PSD), later renamed the 'petty sessions area' (PSA)—which has now become known simply as a 'court area'. This has also become of decreasing significance due to magistrates' less geographically constrained jurisdiction. The largest centres of the magistracy outside London are in cities such as Birmingham, Liverpool and Manchester, which have over 500 magistrates each. The former miniscule and ultra-local arrangements, sometimes based on as few as five magistrates in a small town or large village, disappeared long ago under administrative restructurings, amalgamations and regroupings of magistrates' courts so as to create ever larger administrative centres. The politics involved in a town having or retaining its own magistrates' court and symbolic public building are still a live issue in many places.

Bench chairs and deputy chairs

Each bench has an overall chair whose role it is to oversee the general affairs of his or her local bench, as well as to sit in judgement alongside his or her bench colleagues and to act as the senior magistrate when he or she is on duty. The bench chair is influential in shaping bench policy (e.g. the local starting points for sentences for particular offences; preferred ways of conducting court proceedings; modes of address in court; and general housekeeping[8]). He or she will also act as a sounding board for the views of members of the bench, who as ordinary members of their own communities are exposed to various shades of public opinion and concern. This is also the context within which magistrates must somehow retain a degree of judicial detachment.

A secret ballot for the post of chair takes place at a private bench Annual General Meeting—when the successful candidate must obtain more than 50 per

---

[7] There is still a right to bring a private prosecution, although rarely used and subject to the right of the Crown Prosecution Service (CPS) to take over the case: *Chapter 7*. Now rarely used, prosecutions based on events arising out of quarrels between neighbours are probably nowadays more likely to be dealt with under legislation to deal with anti-social behaviour (ASB). But private prosecutions do occur, a notorious instance being that brought against the alleged killers of Stephen Lawrence in 1994 after the CPS declined that opportunity.

[8] A frequently quoted, if nowadays spurious, example concerns whether or not women magistrates should wear hats. Until the 1960s, the country was divided fifty-fifty on this issue.

cent of the votes cast. The term of office is one year but, if re-elected, the successful candidate may serve up to five consecutive one-year terms. Local practice may mean that, e.g. a voluntary three year rule is observed.

Each bench will usually have one or more deputy chairs (sometimes called vice-chairs) who are appointed in a similar way, but without any requirement to obtain a given percentage of the votes cast. A bench can, if it so wishes, adopt a special statutory open nominations procedure, otherwise there is a secret ballot.

Presiding justices, court chairs and day chairs

According to local practice and custom, some benches appoint what are termed 'court chairs', 'day chairs' or 'presiding justices'. A busy centre may have a dozen or more courts sitting simultaneously each day of the week, all needing someone other than the bench chair or one of his or her elected deputies to take charge. Since 1996, only those magistrates whose names appear on a list approved by a local bench selection panel are eligible to act in this way (except under supervision during training). Similarly, no-one can preside unless they have undertaken a dedicated course of instruction.

HEARINGS BEFORE MAGISTRATES

The general picture across England and Wales is one of lay magistrates (above) sitting to hear cases, but with district judges (below) sitting additionally in London, other urban centres and also, nowadays, in many rural areas.

Court sittings

Magistrates normally sit 'in threes' to decide the outcome of cases. Three is the legal maximum: the minimum is two justices, except when, by legislation, powers are conferred on a single justice. The core functions of magistrates in terms of decision-making are noted earlier in this chapter. Those magistrates who belong to a specialist youth court panel or family court panel have equally demanding additional duties in relation to those spheres of the work. [9]

Evidence, argument and representations

According to the situation, magistrates listen to evidence, legal argument, representations and speeches from prosecutors, lawyers or defendants. They

---

[9] Special rules apply altogether to those specialist jurisdictions as to which other works should be consulted. Responsibilities which were formerly discharged by a Licensing Panel, concerning, e.g. public houses and off-licences have been transferred to the local authority.

might then adjourn, i.e. leave the courtroom to discuss matters and arrive at a decision in the privacy of their retiring room. If legal advice is required, they can call upon the court legal adviser (above) for this part of their discussions. Once the magistrates have arrived at their decision this is formally announced in court by whoever is the court chair. An explanation must be given of any significant aspects of the magistrates' private discussions and an opportunity must be given to the parties to comment or make representations before the final outcome is announced. There is also an obligation under certain national laws, but also more generally under human rights law, to give reasons or explanations in ordinary language (see, also, *Chapter 2*).

In practice, straightforward cases are often dealt with—and justice thereby dispensed without adjourning—'on the bench'. The court chair simply consults with his colleagues who sit to either side (and are hence known as 'wingers') and gives the decision of the court there and then. In contrast, complex cases might need to be considered for a significant period of time in the privacy and calm of the retiring room. For some years, the trend has been towards the giving of advice out loud and making decisions in open court whenever possible.

Decisions by a single justice

Some decisions can be taken, or other functions can be performed, by a single lay magistrate. One example is whether to allow bail or to place an alleged offender in custody pending his or her next appearance before the court (called a 'remand': *Chapter 8*). Just one magistrate is often used for out-of-hours or stand-by courts, this being permissible under longstanding arrangements to ensure that there is emergency cover out-of-hours or at weekends. Cases may then be adjourned to a time during normal court sitting times to be heard by a 'full court'. A range of out-of-court duties, such as signing documents or certificates, can also be carried out by a single justice.

District judge (magistrates' courts)

As well as lay magistrates, there are some 100 district judges.[10] They are salaried professional lawyers and empowered to act alone. Whilst mostly located in London and the larger urban centres, district judges have also been appointed to serve many counties sitting in different places as required. A district judge can be called in by any bench, e.g. at times of abnormal pressure, or to deal with a

---

[10] Formerly known as stipendiary magistrates or 'stipes'. The novelist Sir Henry Fielding was one of the earliest such magistrates in the 1750s at what became the (historic but since 2007 defunct) Bow Street Magistrates' Court. There is also the district judge (county courts).

legally taxing or locally sensitive matter. He or she has all the powers of a lay bench and will tend to work quickly by comparison—being a trained and often experienced professional, and with no need to retire for consultation. The issue of the extent to which the magistracy should be professionalised in this way (as it is in many other countries, so far as such foreign arrangements can be compared) arises from time-to-time, but successive Lords Chancellor have always intimated that wholesale replacement of the lay magistracy by professionals has never been part of the government's criminal justice agenda. Indeed, it would almost certainly be an expensive exercise, quite apart from its seemingly less democratic nature.

RELATED ORGANIZATIONS

Influential in relation to the work of the magistrates' courts are two key membership organizations, the Magistrates' Association and the Justices' Clerks' Society. The role and nature of these bodies is noted in *Chapter 12*. Also under the umbrella of the magistrates' court is the youth court: see next section.

THE YOUTH COURTS AND YOUTH JUSTICE SYSTEM

The youth court was established in 1991 when it took over the work of the former juvenile court. The youth court still deals with juveniles or what are sometimes termed 'youths'. It consists of specially trained magistrates who belong to a statutory youth court panel.[11] Juveniles fall into two different age bands and there are often different powers, procedures or considerations in relation to each. By law these are:

- children aged ten (the age of criminal responsibility) to 13 years; and
- young persons aged 14 to 17.

The investigation, processing and outcome of cases involving juveniles follows a similar pattern to that in relation to adults as described in *Chapters 6 to 10*, subject to additional safeguards, procedures, sentencing powers and interventions. Notably, all first time offenders are now dealt with:

---

[11]   Not to be confused with the youth offending panel: see later in this section.

- by the police under a scheme of reprimands and warnings; or, where they do appear in court,
- by way of a referral order to a youth offending panel (YOP) (below), thus avoiding a sentence in the normal sense, unless the offence is too serious.

Special provisions in the PACE Codes of Practice (*Chapter 6*) for investigating police officers include a duty to ensure that someone concerned with the welfare of the juvenile is informed about the latter's arrest, etc. and to secure the involvement of an 'appropriate adult'.

A specialist area that has seen a number of changes

The arrangements for youth justice were heavily revised by the Crime and Disorder Act 1998, including by their being placed under the overall auspices of a national Youth Justice Board (YJB).[12] That Act also placed duties on local authorities to formulate an annual Youth Justice Plan for its area alongside new, multi-agency youth justice teams (or YOTs) which since that time have played a crucial role in dealing with juveniles. They included a new regime of youth offending panels (YOPs) that were later introduced and to which, as already noted above, virtually all first-time offenders whose cases do reach the courts are referred by courts for an action plan or intervention plan to be devised in relation to the offender rather than his or her being sentenced by the court in the ordinary sense. This applies in the case of all but the more serious offenders. Juveniles may still find themselves being sentenced if they offend again or fail to comply with the arrangements made by the YOP and YOT.

Separately, the anti-social behaviour Order (ASBO) (*Chapter 2*) can be used against anyone who is ten years of age or over and has behaved in a manner that has caused or was likely to cause harassment, alarm or distress to anyone who does not live in their own household. An acceptable behaviour contract may be used when a local authority and YOT identify a young person who is behaving anti-socially at a low level. With the young person and their parents or guardians, the juvenile agrees a contract under which he or she agrees to stop the patterns of behaviour that are causing nuisance to the local community and undertake activities to address their offending behaviour. If he or she breaches the terms of that contract, the local authority can use this to obtain an ASBO.

Some outline information is contained here, youth justice is a specialist and rapidly developing field concerning which readers should consult specialist

---

[12]   Except for the continuing and quite independent role of the youth courts.

works. The YJB comes under the Ministry of Justice (MOJ)[13] for formal purposes, but work across much of the youth justice field is now, since 2007, a primary concern of the Department of Children, Schools and Families (DCSF). Since 1998, there has been a strong emphasis on parenting, including by making parents or guardians responsible for fines and compensation ordered to be paid by juveniles and also through the development parenting orders that can require parents or guardians to attend related courses and schemes. A significant proportion of work with juveniles is informed by restorative thinking and some areas of the country have been to the fore in involving offenders in restorative and other victim-oriented schemes (see, generally, *Chapter 15*).

The welfare principle
Many of the developments that have occurred over the years stem from the welfare principle contained in section 44 Children and Young Persons Act 1933 and which still operates (and whether, e.g. the person concerned appears as a defendant or as a witness and in any court, not simply the youth court):

> Every court in dealing with a child or young person ... either as an offender or otherwise shall have regard to the welfare of the child or young person.

This welfare principle must now be reconciled with both the principle statutory purpose of youth justice contained in the Crime and Disorder Act 1998, which is to prevent offending, and with official sentencing guidance and practice.

Grave crimes
Generally speaking the youth court deals with all criminal offences, whatever their level of seriousness. [14] However, there *is* power to commit a young person (i.e. aged 14 or over: above) to the Crown Court for trial in respect of certain grave crimes. It can—at the outset of a case—and in respect of certain very serious (what are termed 'grave') crimes, such as rape, wounding, aggravated burglary or sexual assault—decline to deal with the matter altogether and commit the accused to the Crown Court for trial. The nature of the individual offence, the age of the offender and other relevant considerations are weighed by the youth court to determine whether it should exercise this power pursuant to

---

[13]   Until then, the relationship was with the Home Office.

[14]   Although—the grave crimes provisions apart—a juvenile can appear in the magistrates' court for remand purposes or if charged alongside an adult, as he or she may also be in the Crown Court. Efforts are nowadays made to avoid either of these possibilities, following criticisms flowing from the Bulger case mentioned in a later footnote.

section 53 Children and Young Persons Act 1933. Certain cases *must* be sent to the Crown Court under this provision, i.e. where homicide (murder, manslaughter, causing death by dangerous driving, etc) is involved. Following the landmark Bulger case,[15] the grave crimes provisions attracted criticism from the European Court of Human Rights in that the formal setting of the Crown Court was deemed inappropriate when dealing with young children, however serious the allegation (the murder of a child in that case). Since that time, the Crown Court has adopted procedures designed to reduce formality when dealing with juveniles.

The Youth Justice Board

The Youth Justice Board for England and Wales (YJB) is an executive non-departmental public body. Its twelve board members are appointed by the Lord Chancellor but which now operates largely in conjunction with the Department of Children, Schools and Families that was created in 2007 at the same time as the MOJ. The YJB oversees the youth justice system and works to prevent offending and reoffending by children and young people under the age of 18, 'ensuring that custody for them is safe, secure, and addresses the causes of their offending behaviour'. The board also:

- advises ministers of state on the operation of, and standards for, the youth justice system (it has no powers in relation to the youth court);
- monitors its performance;
- purchases places for, and places, children and young people remanded or sentenced to custody;
- identifies and promotes effective practice;
- makes grants to local authorities and other bodies to support the development of effective practice;
- commissions research and publishes information.

The YJB bases its work 'on evidence, where this exists'.[16] Its vision is (summarised) of an effective youth justice system, where:

- more offenders are caught, held to account and stop offending;

---

[15] This seminal case from 1993–known by the name of the victim, James Bulger, aged two—with its much publicised, grainy and hence iconic CCTV images of the victim being led away by his killers, themselves children, may have distorted public attitudes towards youth justice and crime and punishment generally and put back progress at a time when sections of the media were looking for excuses to attack liberal reforms or more innovative thinking.

[16] See, further, the details given at www.yjb.gov.uk

- juveniles receive the support they need to lead crime-free lives;
- victims are better supported; and
- the public has more confidence in the youth justice system.

Everything the YJB does is based upon certain core principles of sound leadership, partnership, teamwork, openness, respect and trust.

Youth offending team (YOT)

Central to work with juveniles is the YOT, which concentrates on specialist work with young offenders including writing special, youth-based pre-sentence reports (PSRs) (see, generally, *Chapter 13*). YOTs (and YOT members through their own agencies) co-ordinate youth justice services locally including, e.g. rehabilitation schemes, community sentences, crime prevention and reduction initiatives, bail schemes and reparation schemes for victims. Reprimands and warnings (above) are the exclusive province of the police. Each youth offending team (YOT) should include a:

- social worker;
- probation officer;
- police officer;
- someone nominated by the health authority; and
- someone nominated by the local authority's chief education officer.

The team may also include individuals from other quarters where this is appropriate, or for special purposes. Apart from its co-ordinating role, a YOT must carry out any functions assigned to it pursuant to an annual Youth Justice Plan which each local authority must formulate, publicise and implement.[17] The YOT also organizes and co-ordinates the youth offending panel or YOP.

The youth offending panel (YOP)

The YOP operates under the auspices of the local YOT and is comprised of YOT members and other people appointed to the panel, either generally or in an individual case. Its responsibilities include devising an intervention plan for the juvenile, and counselling him or her with the aim of preventing future offending. This may, in appropriate cases, involve input by the victim and measures such as the making of reparation, as part of a restorative justice approach (*Chapter 15*).

---

[17]   This is now their only direct involvement in the youth justice system: an important feature in promoting co-operation between the various agencies undertaking work with young people.

National Association for Youth Justice

A National Association for Youth Justice (NAYJ) membership organization was established in 1994 following the merger between the former National Intermediate Treatment Federation (NITFed)[18] and former Association for Youth Justice. Members of the NAYJ work in relation to both the youth court and the Crown Court, with strong links to youth offending teams and other professional youth workers, educationalists and child specialists. Since the youth justice reforms of the late-1990s (referred to above), the NAYJ undertook a major review of its overarching philosophy and policy regarding the youth justice system. The first stage of this was the formulation of, 'Working with Children: The Philosophical Base' which was offered as a set of values and beliefs that should underpin legislation, policy and practice. As a second stage, the NAYJ's manifesto built upon this foundation and is compliant with human and children's rights.[19] The NAYJ also publishes *Youth Justice: An International Journal*.

---

[18] Intermediate treatment (IT) was a form of supervision of juvenile offenders that predominated from the 1980s onwards and which laid the foundations for much work with juveniles today, especially its multi-agency facets. 'IT' was amongst the first initiatives to employ what is now an everyday approach at all levels and that will be of interest to anyone wishing to trace the rise of *Partnership and Working Together* into mainstream use as noted in *Chapter 15*.

[19] Both documents can be found at www.nayj.org.uk

CHAPTER 4

The Crown Court

The Crown Court sits to hear cases at around 90 locations—known as 'Crown Court Centres'—across England and Wales. It replaced the historic system of Assize Courts and Quarter Sessions in 1972 following the Beeching Report which led to the Courts Act 1971. Ever since that time the Crown Court has been administered by what is now HM Court Service, part of the Ministry of Justice.

A national institution

The Crown Court is usually named after its location, e.g. Liverpool Crown Court, Leeds Crown Court or Winchester Crown Court[1]—although each such venue may deal with cases from a wider catchment area under powers that allow cases to be transferred from one place to another for all manner of reasons, including those of security, local sensitivity, or convenience for the parties, witnesses and legal representatives. Typically, the Crown Court is accommodated in a fine public building—but, equally, premises can be modern, functional, somewhat anonymous-looking and constructed in the interests of cost-effectiveness. The Old Bailey or Central Criminal Court is the Crown Court for central London. This world famous court, which is associated with many a *cause celebre* or notorious offender, deals with cases arising in the capital as well as many high profile ones transferred there from other parts of England and Wales.[2]

JURISDICTION

In broad terms, the Crown Court deals with what can be termed serious offences, the two or three per cent of prosecuted crime that filters beyond the magistrates' court (*Chapter 3*). There are several strands to its criminal jurisdiction:

- the trial of criminal cases before a judge and a jury, i.e. involving:
  - those very serious offences which can be tried *only on indictment* such as murder, manslaughter, rape or robbery (*Chapter 1*). These cases are now sent straightaway to the Crown Court as soon as the

---

[1] Strictly speaking, the Crown Court, a statutory creation, is one institution, with separate locations, venues or centres where the Crown Court sits. It is thus normally referred to in the singular.

[2] For an interesting history, see *The Old Bailey: Eight Centuries of Crime, Cruelty and Corruption* (2003), Murphy T, Mainstream Publishing. See, also, www.online.oldbailey.org

accused person has been charged with the offence and has appeared in the magistrates' court for preliminary matters such as immediate bail and legal aid to be settled. There is no opportunity nowadays, as there once was, to test the evidence in a murder case before magistrates in committal proceedings (*Chapter 8*);

— either way matters where a magistrates' court declines its own jurisdiction at the allocation stage or the accused person elects trial by jury as is his or her right in such a case (*Chapters 2 and 8*)

— certain summary matters which can be dealt with whenever either of the above kinds of case are involved;

— allegations of 'grave crimes' against accused people below the age of 18 where these have been sent to the Crown Court for trial by youth court magistrates;[3]

- committals for sentence by magistrates in respect of either way offences, i.e. where the offender has been convicted in the magistrates' court but the justices consider that their powers of sentencing are insufficient;[4]

- appeals against conviction or sentence by magistrates, or against both of these. This may relate to summary or either way matters that have been dealt with by magistrates (see *Appeal and Review* in *Chapter 10*); and

- appeals against conviction or sentence by magistrates, or against both of these. Such convictions may be in respect of summary or either way matters (see generally *Chapter 10*).

In contrast to the position in the magistrates' court where a time limit affects summary cases (*Chapter 2*), the jurisdiction of the Crown Court is not limited in time and it often deals with cases many years after the offence was committed, especially since the onset of DNA-testing which has led to an increasing number of serious crimes and 'cold cases' being solved (and, correspondingly, miscarriages of justice being corrected) 20 or more years after the events concerned and also under war crimes legislation, the very nature of which may contemplate a significant period of time between offence and prosecution. There is, however, a longstanding common law and now human rights principle

---

[3] This aspect is not further dealt with. Ever since the Bulger case of 1993 noted in a footnote in *Chapter 3*, the fact that quite young children may be arraigned in or be required to appear as witnesses in over-bearing surroundings has been critcised—but the Crown Court now goes to lengths to reduce formality on such occasions and may, e.g. place a screen around a child witness or use a 'live link' from another location from where he or she can give evidence (*Chapter 9*).

[4] So long as this power and arrangement subsists. It has been abolished by statute but the relevant provisions have not yet been brought into force. The situation arises less frequently nowadays due to other venue-related changes in the practices and procedures of both courts.

whereby a long-delayed trial may be judged unfair (see, generally, Article 6 of the European Convention On Human Rights in *Chapter 1*).

In terms of the place where an offence is alleged to have been committed, the jurisdiction of the Crown Court extends across the whole of England and Wales. The court can also deal with various offences committed in territorial waters, on British ships and with treason, the murder of a British subject, terrorism-related matters and an increasing number of offences wherever in the world they were allegedly committed. Decisions about where someone is to be prosecuted, i.e. in which country, may also depend on the actions, outcomes and decisions occurring within the criminal justice systems of other countries.

SENDING A CASE FOR CROWN COURT TRIAL

The process via which cases reach the Crown Court is known as committal for trial. As already indicated, where an offence is *indictable only* the case is sent straightaway to the Crown Court at the outset. With either way offences (*Chapter 2*) there will be a committal to the Crown Court for trial if the magistrates' court has determined that trial at the Crown Court is more appropriate or, even where it has determined that summary trial is appropriate, if the defendant has elected (i.e. chosen) trial by jury.[5] The proceedings before the magistrates then automatically metamorphose into proceedings with a view to committal for trial at the Crown Court. In cases of serious fraud or certain offences against children a special process known as 'transfer for trial' comes into play so that supporting evidence does not have to be submitted or rehearsed at the magistrates' court level. Various initiatives to extend this process more widely have foundered.

The nature of 'sending'

Historically at what was formerly a 'committal for trial', the magistrates have always been styled 'examining justices', i.e. they examine the evidence to see whether there is a case for such a committal. Since 1967, there has been a general power to conduct a 'paperwork committal' without consideration of the evidence and the huge majority of committals now follow this route. The defendant must be legally represented and agree to the procedure and not wish to make a submission that written statements and other documents (all of which must be

---

[5]   This stage of the proceedings in the magistrates' court is known as 'mode of trial', i.e. when the magistrates decide which mode is more suitable, or 'determining venue'. As part of moves aimed at avoiding delay and encouraging a timely guilty plea (for which credit should be given: *Chapter 9*), the accused person can, before the mode of trial stage is reached, indicate that he or she wishes to plead guilty (known as 'plea before venue'). In the event of an indication of a guilty plea, the magistrates can then decide whether to sentence the offender themselves or to commit him or her to the Crown Court for sentence (see text).

served on him or her in advance) plus any exhibits do not disclose sufficient evidence for the case to be committed to the Crown Court. Sending may be on the charge initially put to the accused or any amended or substituted charge disclosed by the evidence. In due course, the accused will answer to the Crown Court indictment (below). If he or she is allowed bail but fails to appear at the Crown Court, a bench warrant will be issued by that court, with or without bail.

VOLUNTARY BILL OF INDICTMENT

It remains possible for cases to start out in the Crown Court rather than in the magistrates' court—by way of a historic procedure known as the voluntary bill of indictment. Here, a written application, supported by other documentation, is made direct to a High Court judge who may, after considering the papers and any representations, order a trial in the Crown Court. In cases where magistrates have refused to commit or transfer a case to the Crown Court this is the only route open to the prosecutor if he or she wishes to pursue the matter further.

JUDGE AND JURY

The business of the Crown Court is arranged according to the upper level of seriousness of criminal offences with which a given Crown Court centre will normally deal and, correspondingly, the rank of the most senior judges who normally preside at that centre. The most serious cases are dealt with before a High Court judge (or, in future, a judge of the Supreme Court). The bulk of offences—sometimes and historically described as second and third tier matters—are dealt with by a circuit judge or recorder.[6] All Crown Court trials take place before a judge and a jury of 12 ordinary members of the public empanelled at random from the electoral roll if a plea of 'not guilty' is entered. The same jury of 12 people may deal with several cases in succession where these are short and heard over a relatively short time span, although this may nowadays be less usual. Given that a criminal trial may involve complex issues of law or fact, trial by jury—the dispensing of justice through the deliberations of ordinary citizens—is achieved via a careful and longstanding separating of the functions of the judge and the jury:

- **the judge** has general charge of the course of the trial and deals with all matters of a legal nature, such as purely technical submissions or legal argument (often in the absence of the jury so that they are not 'tainted' by

---

[6] Judicial personnel and juror eligibility and disqualification are noted in *Chapter 12*.

knowledge of matters which do not become part of the evidence proper). The judge is responsible for ruling on the admissibility of evidence and on the practice and procedure of the Crown Court. He or she also decides certain questions of mixed fact and law, such as whether the jury should hear about an alleged confession said to have been made by the accused person but which it is now claimed was obtained by duress or oppression, or whether other evidence should similarly be excluded because it is prejudicial. The judge must withdraw a case from the jury if there is insufficient evidence to support a conviction.

Before the start of a case, the judge is responsible for matters of a preliminary nature and can make orders affecting the progress of the case—known 'directions' or 'criminal directions'. Since 2003, certain such evidentiary or other rulings may result in a special form of expedited appeal to the Court of Appeal (*Chapters 5, 9* and *10*). At the conclusion of a jury trial, he or she must sum up to the jury, i.e. remind them of and guide them through the evidence and point out to them its potential weight and possible effect. At the end of a trial he or she will ask the foreman of the jury (who is elected by a simple vote of all the jurors) whether the jury has considered its verdict, whether that verdict is unanimous and whether they find the accused person guilty or not guilty. In the event of a conviction, the judge will pass sentence—usually after obtaining and considering a pre-sentence report (PSR) (*Chapters 9* and *13*) and in many instances a medical or psychiatric report.

- **the jury** decides whether the accused is guilty or not guilty, by considering all the evidence and weighing-up this in the light of the factual matters which are relevant to whether the accused committed the offence with which he or she stands indicted. This will include listening to any admissible expert opinion (e.g. in relation to forensic evidence). Subject to procedural safeguards, the judge can accept a majority verdict (below) and a jury can return an 'alternative verdict': *Chapter 8.*

As mentioned in *Chapter 2,* trial by jury represents the purest form of 'trial by peers'. The Auld Report of 2002[7] suggested that an accused person might be denied his or her present unfettered right to jury trial in certain cases when the decision about the appropriate venue for trial would become a matter for either the magistrates' court or Crown Court alone. That report also suggested that some cases might be tried by a judge alone. Except for the limited arrangements for judge-only trials described in *Chapter 12,* neither of these suggestions has come to fruition.

---

[7] Review of the Criminal Courts (2001): see www.criminal-courts-review.org.uk

ARRAIGNMENT

Whereas an accused person is 'charged' in the magistrates' court if he or she is remanded there or is to stand trial in that court, he or she is 'arraigned' in the Crown Court, i.e. the clerk of the Crown Court calls upon the accused by name, reads over the indictment (below) and asks whether he or she pleads 'guilty' or 'not guilty'.

THE INDICTMENT

'Indictment' is the name given to the formal Crown Court document in which the allegation or allegations against an accused person is or are set out in writing. It is also the name given to the processes involved. Indictments may contain several different allegations or 'counts', as they are known, each setting out a separate offence. But each individual count can only allege a single offence. Several people can be charged in the same indictment. These basic rules are supplemented by others affecting the circumstances in which offences or offenders can be tried alongside one another (known as 'joinder'). Drawing up indictments is a skilled legal task. Applications may need to be made to a judge to settle any matters affecting the indictment which remain at issue.

TRIAL

The course of a trial follows the same broad pattern in both the magistrates' court and the Crown Court.[8] The accused person is asked to plead to each count or charge in turn. The data indicate that many cases turn into guilty pleas once the accused has been arraigned, but that until this time many accused people prefer to maintain their innocence.[9] Initiatives have emerged to counter such events, as with the plea before venue procedure[10] and the rule that an offender should be given credit for a timely guilty plea (*Chapter 9*). Every attempt is made by the Crown Court to expedite cases, but in some areas of the country it is still possible to spend a long period on remand awaiting trial. Where a plea is one of 'not guilty', the trial follows the general pattern outlined in *Chapter 8*. A judge only (or judge-alone) trial can occur in certain situations, see *Chapter 9*.

---

[8] Subject to certain differences of context that do not affect the description given here.

[9] Possibly due to a wish to remain a remand prisoner rather than become a convicted offender, but also tactics designed to test whether the prosecution will go ahead; or there may be a 'cracked trial': see the *Glossary*.

[10] See the explanation given earlier in an earlier footnote.

Re-trial

As noted in *Chapter 2* the longstanding and historic rule until 2003 was that an accused person could not be charged a second time with an offence of which he or she had already been acquitted. Modern-day inroads in relation to that rule are noted in that chapter. Re-trial has always been possible, in normal circumstances, where ordered by the Court of Appeal or High Court.

VERDICT

The initial outcome of a criminal case is the verdict, i.e. of 'guilty' or 'not guilty', as further elaborated upon in *Chapter 8*. The basic rule is that the verdict of the jury must be unanimous. However, it is possible for the judge to accept a majority verdict provided that at least ten of the 12 jurors are of the same mind. This can only occur after the jury has been allowed time for consideration (at least two hours, or longer in a complicated case) to arrive at a unanimous verdict and where the judge is satisfied that this cannot be achieved.

SENTENCE

The powers of the Crown Court range up to life imprisonment, which is mandatory for murder and in certain other situations, but discretionary, e.g. for manslaughter or rape. Many of the more serious offences carry a maximum sentence of 14 years in prison, a life sentence or an indeterminate sentence for public protection (ISPP) (*Chapter 9*). Sentences can be made consecutive to one another or concurrent and the Crown Court has a wide range of powers with regard to ancillary order—including with regard to compensation for victims of crime, destruction of contraband goods and the seizure, confiscation or forfeiture of property and assets representing the proceeds of crime (*Chapter 2*). The main principles and considerations which affect sentencing and a note of the changing nature of the Crown Court's powers are set out in *Chapter 9*.

RIGHTS OF AUDIENCE

In general terms, rights of audience (i.e. the right to address the court on behalf of a client) in the Crown Court are restricted to barristers (sometimes called 'counsel') and those solicitors in private practice who are licensed to practice in that court. Employed solicitors, such as members of the CPS are not allowed to represent their employers in the Crown Court so that, as a case progresses from the magistrates' court to the Crown Court, its conduct must be handed over from the CPS to a barrister (aka 'counsel') if this has not already occurred. A move which would have allowed Crown prosecutors their own statutory rights of audience foundered in 1995. Barristers retained by the Crown are known as 'Treasury counsel'. Senior barristers or Queen's Counsel (QCs) appear in the more serious cases. The Courts and Legal Services Act 1990 enabled a wider range of people to acquire rights of audience in the Crown Court—either generally or in a given case, whilst European obligations may eventually come to have a significant impact on the structure of the legal profession and consequently such rights as a whole. A general note about barristers and solicitors is contained in *Chapter 12*.

CROWN COURT CIRCUITS

For administrative purposes the Crown Court is divided into circuits serving different regions of the country and based closely on the historic Assize Court or Bar circuits which preceded the creation of the Crown Court. These are the Midlands and Oxford Circuit (based on Birmingham); Northern Circuit (Manchester); North Eastern Circuit (Leeds); South Eastern Circuit (London); Wales and Chester Circuit (Cardiff); and the Western Circuit (Bristol).

MANAGEMENT OF THE CROWN COURT

As already indicated, for administrative purposes, the Crown Court functions as part of HM Court Service (HMCS) (within the MOJ). Each Crown Court Circuit (above) is headed by an administrator and each Crown Court by a manager (formerly known as a 'chief clerk'). The latter is responsible among other things for the running of his or her Crown Court centre, including such matters as the listing and scheduling of cases and the care of witnesses[11] (subject in the case of items affecting judicial matters to the direction of the judge). One former function of HMCS, the calling and swearing-in of jurors has been transferred to a nationwide Jury Central Summoning Bureau (JCSB).[12] In court, a member of HMCS staff acts as a court clerk, calling on cases, swearing in jurors and witnesses, reading out the indictment to the accused and generally dealing with day-to-day matters affecting the course of a case. Unlike the situation in the magistrates' court (*Chapter 3*), the court clerk in the Crown Court does not have to be a lawyer (though some are), nor does he or she perform advisory, legal or judicial functions in relation to the trial (there being no need with a professional judge). There are however some functions for court managers of a quasi-judicial

---

[11] A nationwide Witness Service offers support to witnesses: *Chapter 13*.
[12] Not to be confused with the Judicial Studies Board (also JSB).

nature, such as taxing bills of costs (i.e. the assessment of claims by legal representatives where costs have been ordered by the judge to be paid from public funds or between the parties), with power to disallow questionable items.

HM INSPECTORATE OF COURT ADMINISTRATION

The Courts Act 2003 provided for the setting up of HM Inspectorate of Court Administration (HMICA) which occurred in 2005. The remit of HMICA is to:

- inspect and report to the Lord Chancellor on the system that supports the carrying on of the business of the Crown Court and the magistrates'
- courts (and also the county court) and the services provided for those
- courts; and
- discharge any other particular functions which may be specified in connection with the above courts.

All inspection activity excludes the work of 'persons making judicial decisions or exercising any judicial discretion'. HMCIA is independent of all CJS service providers. It provides 'assurance to Ministers and the public about the safe and proper delivery of court services', contributes to their improvement and reports publicly in its aim to deliver value for money In order to inspect court administration not subject to review by other bodies, the inspectorate has identified key areas for inspection which include:

- promoting diversity and that working arrangements ensure that diversity is promoted and achieved;
- public governance and accountability as regards the actions and activities of HMCS to confirm transparency, responsibility and fairness;
- leadership and strategic management to see that key strategic issues are identified and effective action plans are implemented and evaluated;
- finance so that funds are used cost effectively;
- buildings, information technology and equipment to see that these cost effectively and meet the needs of all court users;
- court administrative processes which should support the business of the courts and deliver appropriate services for all court users;
- enforcement to ensure that prompt and effective action is taken to ensure compliance with orders of the court;
- quality of service as this affects all court users.

HMICA's work also covers measurement against targets, priorities and performance as well as monitoring improvement action taken.

CHAPTER 5

The Higher Courts and European Court

The vast bulk of criminal cases end with conviction and sentence, or acquittal, in either the magistrates' court or the Crown Court as described in the foregoing chapters. However, there are various routes by which a case may go to appeal at a higher level of judicial decision-making. These avenues are described in *Chapter 10, Appeal and Review*. This chapter looks at the underlying structure of each of the higher courts involved in such processes. It also looks at the arrangements for a new Supreme Court from 2009 and the role and import of the European Court of Human Rights.

REFORM OF THE HOUSE OF LORDS

This chapter is written at a time of impending change. There has, for many years, been a 'Supreme Court', so called. Broadly speaking, this is the description that has been given to the High Court and Court of Appeal (below) as an entity. The UK's first Supreme Court proper and in a wholly new sense of that term, in the sense of its being the highest court in the land, was created by the Constitutional Reform Act 2005. That court is scheduled to begin its work in October 2009.[1] It will take over the judicial function of the House of Lords as described below and become the final court of appeal for England, Wales and Northern Ireland with regard to criminal cases.[2] Centrally, it will hear appeals on arguable points of law where these are of general public importance.[3] Everything said in the remainder of this chapter must be understood in the light of these developments, some further details of which appear below.

Management of the Supreme Court
It is anticipated that the new-style Supreme Court will be supported not by HM Court Service (HMCS) (*Chapters 3* and *4*) nor, as is currently the case at this level, the staff of the Houses of Parliament but by a members of a new and dedicated service currently designated by the working title 'Supreme Court

---

[1] This is the latest of a series of dates that have been announced, but would now seem to be reasonably firm in the light of construction and renovation work starting. The court has its own web-site at www.justice.gov.uk/whatwedo/supremecourt.htm

[2] And also with regard to civil matters (including, with regard to the latter, in relation to Scotland).

[3] The MOJ has UK-wide responsibilities, whereas HMCS covers England and Wales.

Staff'. However, as with HMCS staff, they will be civil servants. It will be housed in Middlesex Guildhall, Westminster.[4]

Judicial oversight and the judges of the Supreme Court

The President of the Supreme Court (initially a senior Law Lord)[5] and its chief executive will have responsibility for the day-to-day administration of the court, staffing, resources and operation. In balancing independence with ministerial accountability for the expenditure of public money there will be certain links with the Lord Chancellor and Ministry of Justice (MOJ) of the kind envisaged by 'The Concordat' (see *Chapters 1* and *12*). The court will also assume the jurisdiction of the Judicial Committee of the Privy Council (below).

At the start, the existing Law Lords (*Chapter 12*) will become the first Supreme Court Justices (as they will be known). The court will initially have 12 such justices. Existing Law Lords will, technically speaking, also remain non-debating members of the House of Lords, but any new justices will be appointed directly to the Supreme Court and they will not, by virtue of that fact alone, be or become members of the House of Lords.

The Constitutional Reform Act 2005

These developments form part of a package of measures contained in the Constitutional Reform Act 2005 that are designed to separate out further the Executive and Legislature from the Judiciary (*Chapter 2*) whilst retaining lines of democratic accountability. The need for the changes arose not just to satisfy the modernisation needs of UK institutions but also European obligations. Together with other contemporaneous reforms (some of which are described in *Chapters 1* and *12*) and developments, the changes mark a significant watershed in the evolution of the legal system as a whole.

Transition

Consultation on rules for the Supreme Court is being carried out in accordance with the terms of the 2005 Act (and associated legislation)[6] under senior Law Lord, Lord Bingham of Cornhill, with a view to formulating new Supreme Court Rules. Until the new Supreme Court is in being, the existing appeal structure is as outlined in the remainder of this chapter.[7]

---

[4] Off Parliament Square and directly opposite to the Houses of Parliament.

[5] It has been announced that the first president will be Lord Phillips, the serving Lord Chief Justice.

[6] See Statutory Instrument 227 of 2006.

[7] A description of the judges who serve in the higher courts is contained in *Chapter 12* in accordance with the general scheme of the handbook.

JURISDICTION OF THE HIGHER COURTS

The higher courts have no 'first instance' jurisdiction, except theoretically and for the time being to the extent that in the House of Lords a peer of the realm (i.e. a member of that House) may opt to be tried by the House (i.e. by his or her peers, see generally under *Trial by Peers* in *Chapter 2*). This procedure has not been invoked for some long time and is unlikely to be again. Where members of the House of Lords have been charged with criminal offences in modern times they have invariably opted for trial in the ordinary courts and any other course would undoubtedly now attract political condemnation. It is also likely that such an attempt would invite challenge in the European Court of Human Rights (below). Pending implementation of the 2005 reforms, the jurisdiction of the House of Lords is noted below alongside that of other courts in the hierarchy. In each of the courts described, geographical jurisdiction extends nationwide across England and Wales (with certain added or separate powers as described in relation to the House of Lords and Privy Council).

THE HIGH COURT OF JUSTICE

The High Court deals predominantly with the more important civil disputes and is split into three divisions: the Queen's Bench Division (QBD), Chancery Division and Family Division. It is centred in London at the Royal Courts of Justice in The Strand (often referred to by practitioners simply as 'The Strand'). It may also sit in designated towns and cities across England and Wales from time-to-time as the need arises. In terms of its criminal jurisdiction, the QBD is the most significant division. It is presided over by the Lord Chief Justice and, although it has a broad remit to deal with civil actions for damages arising, e.g. from breach of contract and libel, commercial disputes and Admiralty cases, a Divisional Court of the QBD deals with appeals from magistrates' courts and possibly Crown Courts by way of case stated which is a special, largely legally-based form of challenge (see further in *Chapter 10*).

Additionally, the High Court has a general supervisory jurisdiction in relation to a wide range of courts, tribunals and public bodies and their officers—including, e.g. the criminal courts, the police, law officers, government departments, their ministers, local authorities, elected or appointed members of public authorities and relevant staff. This function is known as 'judicial review'. It is designed to ensure that decisions made by such bodies or individuals are arrived at in a proper manner, that they do not exceed the powers conferred by Parliament or the Common Law, involve only relevant considerations and that people discharging responsibility in the public domain act reasonably. The High

Court can compel or prohibit lower courts to act or refrain from acting in a given way. It can quash decisions and require matters to be reconsidered.

COURT OF APPEAL

As its title implies, the Court of Appeal has an exclusively appellate jurisdiction. Also commonly referred to as 'The Appeal Court', it comprises two divisions, criminal and civil. It is again housed in the Royal Courts of Justice in The Strand (but may occasionally sit elsewhere). Decisions are by a majority of the three judges of whom the court is composed (or sometimes just two such judges). Both divisions of the court may refer cases involving points of law to the House of Lords the progress of which are also dependent on leave to appeal, a mechanism designed to weed out spurious, questionable or hopeless cases.

The Criminal Division of the Court of Appeal

This Criminal Division hears appeals from people convicted and sentenced in the Crown Court. Its senior judge is the Lord Chief Justice who is also responsible for the way in which the court is run and who sets the tone of the court and its stance towards the criminal law in general during his or her period of office. He or she may issue *Practice Directions* to be followed by other criminal courts.[8] Leave is required before there can be an appeal to the Court of Appeal.

A main significance for criminal justice practitioners is that the Court of Appeal gives rulings on appeal against sentence (see, generally, *Chapter 9*). Best described as judicial guidance on sentencing, such rulings inform and in many instances liberate or constrain, the sentencing practices of the Crown Court and magistrates' courts—although this aspect now falls to be described and assessed in the light of the work of the Sentencing Guidelines Council (SGC) (see, further, in *Chapter 9*). The signs are that the SGC still looks to the Court of Appeal to provide sentencing indicators and advice through its judgements. Indeed, a number of Court of Appeal judges have been tasked with providing advice to the SGC on specific aspects of sentencing.

Key rulings of the Court of Appeal are referred to as 'guideline judgements' (or in some instances 'sentencing guidance'[9]). Most rulings of the court are published in the form of law reports (*Chapter 1*) and there are special series of law reports on criminal law and sentencing. They are often eagerly awaited and digested by criminal practitioners and become a central and particularly

---

[8]   The intriguing history of the office of Lord Chief Justice is ably described by Anthony Mockler in *Lions Under the Throne* (Muller, 1983).

[9]   But distinguish sentencing guidance of this kind from that issued in recent times by the SGC itself or, e.g. the Magistrates' Association (*Chapter 12*).

influential component of the law of precedent (below). A judge of the Court of Appeal is called Lord Justice (*Chapter 12*) and is automatically a Privy Counsellor. Court of Appeal law reports are often signified by the letters CA.

HOUSE OF LORDS

Pending the birth of the Supreme Court under the Constitutional Reform Act 2005, the House of Lords is the final court of appeal in the UK for both criminal and civil cases decided by lower courts in England and Wales. The appeal may be from the Court of Appeal or High Court (both above) depending on the circumstances. Leave is required before there can be such an appeal. Scottish criminal cases have no right of appeal to the House of Lords. Appeals are heard by an Appellate Committee of the House. This committee was formerly presided over by the Lord Chancellor (who sometimes sat as a judge in that court) but this is one of the constitutional anomalies that were cured by the Constitutional Reform Act 2005 and the accompanying overall revision of the that role. Since the 2005 Act, the presiding judge is usually a senior Law Lord. The Appellate Committee is made up of Law Lords (otherwise called Lords of Appeal in Ordinary) as further described in *Chapter 12*. This committee sits apart from the main business of the House of Lords in what many people consider to be a somewhat undersized, if intimate, committee room.

There is a convention that Law Lords do not engage in political debate on the floor of the House of Lords except where this is of direct judicial concern, e.g. in relation to the courts, justice or related constitutional matters. Even this constitutional anomaly will evaporate once new Supreme Court Justices take up their positions. As already noted, newcomers will not be Law Lords.

Rulings of the House of Lords—the judgements of the Law Lords, known as 'speeches'—are of considerable importance in relation to the day-to-day proceedings of all courts and as an instrument of the Common Law (as will also be the case with rulings of the Supreme Court). As precedents, they carry great weight. Frequently a rule of criminal law or criminal justice comes to be known by the name of the case concerned or by the shorthand for some principle that was formulated during a particular case. They are also likely to have an equivalent impact on future Parliamentary legislation and debates. Thus, e.g. when, in 1995, the House of Lords had to deal with the question whether the longstanding *doli incapax* rule[10] should be abolished, the House, whilst acknowledging the need for a review of the law, declined to alter the existing

---

[10] Whereby, in the case of a defendant below the age of 14, the prosecutor had to establish—over and above the essential ingredients of the offence—that the defendant knew that what he or she was doing was 'seriously wrong'.

law. Such a fundamental change, it was stated by the Law Lords, was something more appropriately dealt with by Parliament itself—following which Parliament, as the Legislature, duly abolished that rule by Act of Parliament. But there have been instances where what the House decided altered the way in which courts applied the criminal law (e.g. by 'creating' the crime of conspiracy to corrupt public morals and when marital rape was first held to be a crime).[11]

THE PRIVY COUNCIL

A Privy Council (PC) or its Judicial Committee (in effect the Appellate Committee of the House of Lords 'wearing another hat', but possibly supplemented by foreign judges) sits as a final court of appeal from some Dominion territories, or former such territories who have opted to continue with this last avenue of appeal as an adjunct their own national appeals systems, in effect countries which have retained an appeal to Her Majesty in Council or, in the case of republics, to the Judicial Committee. Rulings of the PC or its Judicial Committee are 'persuasive' under the English doctrine of precedent (see the note below) rather than binding within England and Wales. The Judicial Committee sits in the Privy Council Chamber in Downing Street. The Privy Council itself also advises on matters pertinent to the exercise of the royal prerogative and, e.g. in relation to devolution issues. Its secretariat comes under the auspices of both the Cabinet Office and Ministry of Justice.[12]

THE DOCTRINE OF PRECEDENT: A NOTE

Rulings of the higher courts are published in the law reports (*Chapter 2*) in the form of verbatim accounts of the judgements or speeches of the judges, including any dissenting opinion or opinions. They contain the facts and outcomes of the cases concerned, the reasons for the judges' decisions or rulings and deal, in particular, with any matters of law arising in the case. They represent something of an art form and are the subject of minute study and subsequent argument amongst legal practitioners and students alike.

The sum total of the law reports comprise a vast library or databank of common law and legal interpretation from which lawyers seek to understand the exact nature of the law on any given topic. These rulings should be distinguished from legislation, i.e. laws passed by Parliament in the form of

---

[11] Scope for judicial creation or extension of crimes may be narrower due to Article 6 of the European Convention on Human Rights: 'no punishment without law' (*Chapter 2*). The debate about whether judges sometimes make law rather than interpret is historic and enduring.

[12] For further information, see www.privy-council.org

Acts of Parliament (also known as 'statutes'), or associated delegated legislation. Judges purport to interpret statutes, not to make new law and the doctrine of precedent is the vehicle by which such interpretations are communicated both to lawyers and to the public at large.

The lower courts (Crown Court and magistrates' court) do not themselves set precedents and they are bound by (i.e. must follow) the rulings of the higher courts, whilst within the upper courts hierarchy of House of Lords/Supreme Court, Court of Appeal and High Court, a lower court is bound by a higher court. The entire process is much more subtle than this: certain rulings may be persuasive only, others accepted as of considerable weight and authority. Lawyers 'cite' rulings or extracts from them in court as either supporting or detracting from a given proposition. Part of their daily routine involves unravelling such matters as well, e.g. as seeking to 'distinguish' cases, i.e. highlight differences between the facts of one case as opposed to another, or to put forward reasons as to why the law impacts differently in relation to the facts of their client's case: sometimes described as 'a matter of mixed fact and law'. Or they may try to argue that some exception or reasons for departing from a given rule applies in particular circumstances, sometimes described as 'pleading an exception'.[13] These and other forensic techniques are part of the everyday routine of courts of law. In sheer practical terms, a great deal may depend on the status of a judge within the judicial hierarchy whose judgement has been reported as part of the law of precedent and his or her general standing, record and reputation as a lawyer. This aspect also represents something of an art form.

RELATED MECHANISMS

The Criminal Cases Review Commission (CCRC) has power to examine a suspected miscarriage of justice and to refer this back to the Court of Appeal; whilst the Attorney General has power to refer a case to that court in certain situations including where he or she believes there to have been an 'unduly lenient sentence' (see, further, the role of the Attorney General in *Chapter 12*).

THE EUROPEAN COURT OF HUMAN RIGHTS

As noted in *Chapter 2*, implementation of the Human Rights Act 1998 has had a considerable impact on the criminal courts in relation to the backdrop of European law against which all proceedings now take place. There is also a

---

13 'Pleading the exception' is also used where a fixed statutory exception may apply.

general right of appeal to the European Court of Human Rights (ECHR)[14] in Strasbourg and English courts are under a duty to apply English law compatibly with the European Convention On Human Rights and Fundamental Freedoms, if not compatible already. Various mechanisms exist to deal with situations where this is not the case and, in general, UK courts have continued to apply domestic law in a human rights context without constant resort to appeals.[15]

Further, English judges must accommodate European jurisprudence more generally, which is sometimes at odds with English methods, as, e.g. with the doctrine of precedent (above). Unlike English law, e.g. the Convention is regarded as a 'living instrument' which allows the law to adapt as time passes and surrounding events and circumstances change—this without any new legislation or legal rulings. In contrast, the English doctrine of precedent is relatively static in the sense that a rule is deemed to hold good unless overturned by a better rule in the light of legal argument and interpretation and considerations. In a sense European law now takes precedence—and these dynamics continue to unfold. Naturally, the situation depends on the strength of the European law or ruling in question, the scope for domestic variation (what is known as the 'margin of appreciation') and the scale and import of the issues arising.

---

[14]   Note that ECHR may also be used to signify the European Convention on Human Rights.

[15]   Any court (but in practice one of the higher courts) can make a declaration of incompatibility with the European Convention in relation to domestic legislation. This compels a UK Minister of State to consider fast track amending legislation. The practice has been for Ministers to certify that all new legislation is 'human rights friendly'. This is not definitive. In the last resort the courts are the arbiters of compatibility, if need be the European Court of Human Rights.

CHAPTER 6

Investigation, Arrest and Charge

The priorities of the Criminal Justice System (CJS) encompass crime prevention and crime reduction, including through such developments as Crime Reduction Partnerships (CDRPs), Multi-agency Protection Panel Arrangements (MAPPAS) and risk-assessment (*Chapter 2*). However, many CJS services will only be triggered once a crime happens, and only then if discovered by or reported to the authorities. Formal action against an individual on behalf of the state will only occur if the processes of detection and investigation lead to the identification of a suspect and a decision to charge him or her with an offence.

It should be reiterated that various public authorities other than the ordinary police have investigative and often prosecuting functions (see, further, e.g. in *Chapter 7*). Also, within the private sector, organizations may have their own fraud investigation teams, 'store detectives', security guards or intellectual property experts who will refer matters to the police as appropriate. Hence, there are various ways in which action may come about besides a direct report to the police by a victim or bystander. Once reported, investigations are prioritised and investigations and interviews conducted accordingly.[1]

A wide array of developments
Modern reforms and initiatives have sought to give the police and Crown Prosecution Service (CPS) the ability to bring more offenders to justice, in particular, by 'getting things right at the start'. Not least in this are arrangements to make sure that if a case does reach court—and there is a trial (*Chapter 9*)—there will be reliable and legally admissible evidence, whether the testimony of witnesses, 'hard evidence' such as weapons, drugs, stolen property, etc., or other items recovered by scene of crime officers (SOCOs). Advances in science and technology, especially in relation to DNA-testing have led to all-round advances in this regard, whilst the ease of access to databases has also moved forward means that information can be virtually instantaneous. Some such developments have been controversial, especially concerning surveillance and it is said that UK citizens are now the most 'watched' of all.

As to the management of criminal cases there are now likely to be, e.g. virtual case files, improved communications and more co-ordinated systems of record-keeping. The powers of the police have also increased significantly in

---

[1] Information about reporting and priorities can often be found on local police force web-sites.

terms, e.g. of their authority to intervene on the street, to stop and search people and to regulate particular forms of activity that is either potentially criminal or constitutes anti-social behaviour (*Chapter 2*), especially that which might lead to disorder. Various extra powers are a side-wind of increased powers to deal with terrorism.[2] But the police no longer decide upon whether a prosecution should take place or the nature of the charge to be brought, this responsibility having been passed to the CPS under the Criminal Justice Act 2003 (*Chapter 7*).

DETECTION

Crimes may be detected in a variety of ways including due to:

- information being received from the victim or member of the public;
- an offender being caught in the act, or 'red-handed';
- admissions by suspects when questioned (known as 'confessions');
- the results of analysis of forensic and/or circumstantial evidence;
- evidence being provided by an police informant; or increasingly
- forms of surveillance or access to electronic databases.

Information is frequently described as 'intelligence' and hence much police work as being intelligence-led, i.e. based on information provided to or collated by the police, e.g. in databases and other recording systems. Some crimes are cleared up when an offender who is charged with or convicted of an offence admits to other offences, i.e. beyond those that the police are primarily investigating. He or she may ask for these to be taken into consideration when sentence is passed (known as TICs: *Chapter 9*). An offence is 'cleared up' once:

- the accused has been charged with it by the police;
- someone has been cautioned for it;
- it is admitted in such a way that it could be taken into consideration when the offender is sentenced (above and *Chapter 9*); or in some cases
- where no further action is taken—provided that there is sufficient evidence to establish who the culprit was, e.g. where it is clearly admitted in a prison interview by somebody who is already serving a custodial sentence for another offence but it is pointless bringing extra charges that would not affect how long he or she is held in prison. Similarly, where the offender is under the age of criminal responsibility,

---

[2] Matters such as stop and search, the policing of demonstrations and protest and the potential for misuse of terrorism powers are all highly sensitive issues.

or suffering from mental impairment (*Chapter 9*), or the victim or other key witnesses are unable to give evidence for some valid reason.

In effect, the detection rate is the ratio of offences cleared up in a given period to the offences that are recorded in that same period. Overall and across the years, something in the order of 25 per cent of recorded crimes are cleared up; but for violent and sexual offences the rate tends to be higher, upwards of 75 per cent. Some types of offences have better clear-up rates than others, e.g. because there is a high likelihood of the victim being able to identify the offender (as with many sexual offences) or once an offence comes to light this may directly identify the offender (as with certain frauds, handling stolen goods, going equipped for stealing or where drugs, knives or guns are discovered during a search). Technology is increasingly dictating the course of certain investigations with databases and computer programmes generating lists of suspects.[3] Various specialist police investigation teams exist and the Serious Organized Crime Agency (SOCA) has an increasingly important role in relation to such crime (*Chapter 11*). The influential 2002 White Paper, *Justice for All*, drawing attention to fear of crime rather than crime itself, noted that:

> . . . the gap between recorded crime and the number of offenders brought to justice needs to be reduced. Our priority must be bringing more criminals to justice . . . Less than half the public believe that the CJS is effective in bringing people who commit crimes to justice. While crime overall has fallen since 1997,[4] the fear of crime is still too high: according to the [regular] *British Crime Survey,*[5] over 22 per cent of people have a high level of concern about violent crime and many also worry about less serious types of crime . . . Unfortunately, too many people do escape justice.

The same document expressed concern about under-reporting of hate crimes and domestic violence (later the subject of the Domestic Violence, Crimes and Victims Act 2004) along with public anxiety about how certain sexual offences with low conviction rates are responded to. These are ongoing concerns with various initiatives being mounted to improve matters.

THE COURSE OF AN INVESTIGATION

An investigation into a criminal offence may involve interviewing many prospective witnesses and assembling other evidence of the kinds outlined in *Chapter 8*, such as exhibits, documents, and forensic or other expert reports.

---

[3] A practice that is sometimes described as 'harvesting' or 'mining' data.

[4] Crime has continued to fall despite a fast growing prisoner population.

[5] An annual survey, supplemented by other, shorter-term ones. See the explanation in the *Glossary*.

Relevant information must only be obtained within the law and special legal provisions come into play as soon as there is a suspect—breach of which may result in evidence later being ruled inadmissible by a court. Certain evidence may also be ruled out as prejudicial on statutory grounds or the fair trials provisions of the European Convention On Human Rights (*Chapter 2*).

Arrest, search and seizure: and new ways of policing

The police enjoy wide powers of arrest[6] and search in respect of people suspected of criminal offences either under the general law or in relation to particular kinds of offence. The Police National Computer (PNC) records information on people arrested and prosecuted for criminal offences whilst the Criminal Records Bureau (CRB) stores further evidence of convictions. The police can impound property where they believe it to be the proceeds of crime, or where they believe it to have been the subject of a criminal offence or that it is or was intended for use in committing an offence, such as weapons, tools, keys, getaway vehicles, account books and forged documents—or any other item which might become evidence. Procedures exist for the return of property if ownership is later disputed and the court can, e.g. order restitution or compensation for victims of crime: *Chapter 9*. With some crimes it is an offence merely to possess certain items, e.g. in relation to terrorism, drugs offences or pornographic images involving children.

There is a modern emphasis on targeting the proceeds of crime, *Chapter 2*. Extensive duties have been placed on banks, lawyers, accountants and others to make suspicious activity reports (SARs), particularly in relation to potential money laundering, which has extensive connections to organized crime, illegal drugs, the sex industry (so-called) and trafficking of various kinds. Yet there is still concern that those who profit most from crime often escape detection or prosecution at the expense of people whose activities represent a softer target. Particularly since September 2001, police powers in relation to terrorism have been greatly increased under various Terrorism Acts[7] and there have been concerns about the use of such powers to confront crime on a wider front as well as about the impact of such legislation on civil liberties.[8]

The Criminal Justice Act 2003 introduced changes designed to 'rebalance' criminal justice and to enhance work at the 'front end' of the criminal process, including a power for police officer to grant street bail (to which the Bail Act 1976 does not apply) rather than take suspects back to the police station for that purpose, greater freedom to take fingerprints and non-intimate samples whilst a

---

6 Under the Police Reform Act 2002, community support officers (CSOs) will be able to detain an individual pending their arrest by the police.

7 Notably the Terrorism Act 2005.

8 See, in particular, the civil liberties web-site www.liberty-human-rights.org.uk

suspect is in detention, with a heavier onus being placed on people who commit further offences whilst on bail or who abscond whilst on bail.

In many instances, the police still require a warrant from a magistrate in order to search, e.g. for stolen goods or drugs—but powers exist to seize property where the police are already lawfully on premises or the level of seriousness of an offence justifies an immediate response, such as an emergency entry. Where a warrant is required, the application must normally be authorised by a senior officer before being made.

The police may now demand a DNA-sample from anyone who is arrested for a recordable offence and also to take fingerprints whether the suspect agrees to this or not, by force if need be. Previously such events could only happen following charge or conviction respectively. The first of these changes together with other shifts in police powers has been partly responsible for generating a national DNA-database containing over four million profiles. It is also true, on the basis largely of anecdotal evidence, media reports and documentaries, to say that the police are now more far more likely to raid premises without prior warning, often in the early morning, to carry out an arrest and search.[9] The police have also use the media extensively to get their message across, not least via regular 'fly-on-the-wall' footage of investigations, arrests, raids, 'hot pursuit' of vehicles and undercover surveillance.

Arrestable offences and serious arrestable offences

Certain offences are 'arrestable' by definition, i.e. as listed in the Police and Criminal Evidence Act 1984 (PACE)—irrespective of any free-standing power to arrest someone in relation to a given offence—i.e. principally those attracting a maximum sentence of imprisonment of five years or more. Where offences are arrestable other police powers may go hand-in-hand with this fact although the overall significance of this has reduced with various reforms. Other powers rest on an investigation being into a 'serious arrestable offence' (again see PACE), or where its commission has led to, or is intended or likely to lead to, serious harm to the state or public order; serious interference with the administration of justice or the investigation of offences; the death of, or serious injury to, someone; or substantial financial gain or loss to any person.

Bail by a police officer

An arrested person can be granted bail by a police officer during an investigation for re-appearance at a police station—or, after being charged with a criminal offence, for appearance before a magistrates' court at a fixed time and

---

[9]   Notoriously, this occurred in relation to the homes of staff at No 10 Downing Street during the cash for honours investigations of 2006-7. See the comments on the Rule of Law in *Chapter 2*.

place. Since 2003, the police can grant certain kinds of conditional bail and, as already noted, street bail. The Bail Act 1976 obliges a police officer to make a record of any bail decision and, if requested by the person in relation to whom the decision was taken, to give him or her a copy. Where bail is granted by endorsing a court warrant of arrest that is endorsed for bail the constable must also make a record: see, generally, the section on *Bail or Custody* in *Chapter 8*.

PACE and the PACE Codes

Investigation and arrest fall within an array of legal provisions and approved practice created by PACE and the various Codes of Practice made pursuant to that Act.[10] There is provision throughout the PACE procedures for the individual concerned or his or her solicitor to make representations at appropriate times. PACE or the Codes have the following effects in relation to certain key points in the process of investigation, arrest and charge:

Procedure on arrest

Where someone is arrested or taken into custody by a constable he or she must be taken to a police station as soon as is reasonably practicable (except, of course, when already there). Certain statutory powers of arrest are exempted and, as already indicated above, since 2003 it is possible for an offender to be granted bail at street level rather than after being taken to a police station for that purpose. Nonetheless, the full PACE procedures described in the remainder of this chapter still stand at the heart of this aspect of police work and are unavoidable if the situation is one where there is a need to hold an offender rather than to release him or her immediately following arrest.

The police station must be a 'designated police station' (i.e. designated by the chief constable) if it appears that it may be necessary to detain the person for more than six hours—unless the constable will be unable to take the individual to such a police station without injury and lacks the necessary assistance. Delay is authorised in certain instances. The person must be released if the constable becomes satisfied that there are no grounds for keeping him or her under arrest.

At the police station

If someone attends voluntarily at a police station or other place[11] or accompanies a constable there without being arrested, he or she is entitled to leave at any time unless he or she is arrested—when he or she must be informed at once of the arrest and the reasons for it. Someone brought to a police station under arrest or arrested at the police station should be informed by the custody

---

10   Since 2003 there have been streamlined procedures for amending the PACE codes.

11   Often euphemistically described as 'helping the police with their inquiries'.

officer of the following rights and that these need not be exercised immediately:[12]

- the right to consult the PACE Codes of Practice;
- the right to have someone informed of his or her arrest. Someone arrested and held in custody is entitled on request to have a friend, relative or other person who is likely to take an interest in his or her welfare told, as soon as is practicable, that he or she has been arrested and is being detained. An officer of at least the rank of superintendent may authorise delay in the case of someone in police detention for a serious arrestable offence (above) if he or she has reasonable grounds for believing that such contact will lead to interference with or harm to evidence relating to such an offence, or interference with or physical injury to other people, or that it will lead to the alerting of other suspects not yet arrested or hinder the recovery of property;
- the right to consult a solicitor. Someone arrested and held in custody in a police station or other premises is entitled on request to consult a solicitor privately at any time. Consultation must be permitted as soon as practicable except to the extent that delay is permitted by the codes. An officer of at least the rank of superintendent may authorise delay where there are reasonable grounds for believing such consultation would have a comparable effect to that described in the last paragraph. The right is to consult privately,[13] but an assistant chief constable or police commander may authorise consultation to take place only in the sight and hearing of a qualified uniformed officer where there is good reason for this.

Police detention of suspects

Where someone is arrested without a warrant from a court but the custody officer at the police station to which he or she is taken considers that there is insufficient evidence to charge that person and is not prepared to hold that individual for questioning, or cannot legally do so, the custody officer must release him or her. But this may be on bail subject to a requirement to return to a police station at a later time. Likewise, if a custody officer is conducting a review of detention (below) and he or she thinks that detention without charge can no longer be justified, the suspect must be released, with or without bail.

After 24 hours

Similar decisions must be made at the end of 24 hours detention without charge. The basic rule is that someone must not be kept in police detention for more

---

[12]   Special provisions apply to terrorism offences.
[13]   Difficulties have arisen over the bugging of such conversations in police cells or prisons.

than 24 hours without being charged (and, as indicated earlier, must be released before that time if there is no longer any justification for holding him or her). This 24 hour limit may be extended up to 36 hours by a senior police officer, something that can now be done by telephone. A police officer of the rank of superintendent or above who is responsible for the police station may authorise someone to be kept in police detention for the period up to 36 hours subject to certain criteria, including that detention without charge is necessary to secure or preserve evidence or to obtain evidence by questioning the suspect and that the investigation is being conducted diligently and expeditiously.

When detention for less than 36 hours is authorised, a further period expiring not later than the end of the initial 36 hours may be authorised, provided the relevant conditions are still satisfied.

Beyond 36 hours: further detention following an application to the court
Where continued detention *is* authorised by a senior officer, the detained person must still be released with or without bail at the expiry of 36 hours unless an application is made to a magistrates' court—sitting 'otherwise than in open court' (see *Chapter 2*)—and this results in a warrant of further detention being issued, thereby allowing the police to continue to detain the suspect. Warrants of further detention can be issued for up to 36 hours at a time, provided that the suspect is not detained for longer than 96 hours overall. He or she must then be released—although a fresh arrest is possible, e.g. if new evidence emerges, and provided that the provisions are not being abused.[14]

Application must be made by a constable on oath, supported by information specifying the offence, the general nature of the evidence on which the suspect has been arrested, what inquiries have already been made and what further inquiries are proposed; plus the reasons for believing that continued detention is necessary. The court must be satisfied that there are reasonable grounds for believing that further detention is justified under the same criteria that govern the superintendent's discretion (above). Application may only be made:

- before the expiry of 36 hours
- where it is not practicable for the magistrates' court to sit at the expiry of 36 hours but the court will sit during the six hours following the end of that period, before expiry of those six hours.

This six hour leeway is not limited to the situation where the 36 hour period expires and no court is sitting at all. Magistrates also have a discretion during the course of a court sitting whether to hear such an application straightaway or

---

[14]   Again, special provisions apply to terrorism when the limit is 28 days. Government attempts to increase this to 42 days have been the focus of much political dissent and Parliamentary delay.

to wait, provided they do so for no longer than six hours. Where the court is not satisfied that further detention is justified it must refuse the application (but can adjourn within the basic, initial, 36 hours). If the application is refused the arrested person must be released unless he or she is then charged. However he or she need not be released before the expiry of 24 hours detention, or of any longer period for which continued detention has been authorised by a superintendent, i.e. up until the end of the initial 36 hours.

Where application is made after the expiry of 36 hours and it appears that it would have been reasonable for the police to have made the application within that time, the court must dismiss the application.

AFTER CHARGE

As an alternative to prosecution, there are well-established mechanisms for police cautions where people admit an offence; and the Criminal Justice Act 2003 introduced 'conditional cautions', whereby requirements can be added to such a warning. This may involve referral to an agency, e.g. concerning a drugs problem, alcohol addiction or mental impairment. Referral schemes are increasingly a feature of the 'front end' of the criminal process: *Chapter 7.*

Once someone has been charged with an offence at a police station or elsewhere (above), the police custody officer must decide whether or not to grant bail to the accused for his or her appearance at court or to arrange for him or her to be kept in detention and brought before a court within 24 hours for it to take that decision. The custody officer must order release, with or without bail, unless one of a number of grounds is satisfied, e.g. that his or her name or address cannot be ascertained; that the custody officer has reasonable grounds for believing that the person will abscond, commit an offence or interfere with the administration of justice if released; or that detention is necessary for the person's own protection or, if a juvenile,[15] in his or her own interests.

Anybody who, after being charged, is kept in police detention must be brought before a magistrates' court. If he or she is brought before a court for the area in which the police station is situated this must be as soon as is practicable and in any event not later than the first sitting after being charged with the offence. If no magistrates' court is due to sit on the day when he or she is charged, or the next day, the custody officer must inform the justices' clerk who must consider whether to arrange for a court to sit specially. Thereafter the magistrates' court or, where applicable, the Crown Court to which the case is sent for trial will make all decisions about bail or custody.

---

[15] For this purpose meaning anyone under the age of 18.

CUSTODY OFFICERS AND THEIR DUTIES

As noted above, certain police stations must be designated by the chief officer of police to be used for detaining arrested people and one or more custody officers must be appointed for each designated police station. The custody officer must be of at least the rank of sergeant; but a non-involved officer of any rank may perform the function if a designated custody officer is not readily available.

It is the duty of the custody officer to ensure that all people in police detention are treated in accordance with PACE and its Codes of Practice. Special provisions cover the situation where an arrested person is taken to a police station which is not a designated police station, and to transfer between police stations. Where someone is arrested for an offence or returns to a police station to answer to bail, the custody officer must, as soon as practicable, determine whether he or she has sufficient evidence to charge that person with the offence. If there *is* sufficient evidence, the suspect must be charged or released without charge—with or without bail. Following a charge, the custody officer must order release, either with or without bail, of anyone arrested without a warrant and other than in limited circumstances which are set out in PACE.

Review of police detention

Periodic reviews of the circumstances of people in police detention must be carried out by the review officer who is, in the case of someone arrested and charged, the custody officer, and in the case of someone arrested but not charged, a non-involved officer of at least the rank of inspector. PACE sets out a timetable and the detained person or his or her solicitor is entitled to make representations at appropriate points.[16]

---

[16]   Special provisions apply to juveniles when the custody officer must, if practicable, ascertain the identity of the person who is responsible for his or her welfare and inform that person that the juvenile has been arrested, and the reason why he or she is detained. If the juvenile is known to be subject to a supervision order, reasonable steps must be taken to notify the supervisor. The custody officer must also, as soon as practicable, inform an 'appropriate adult' of the grounds for detention and the juvenile's whereabouts and ask the adult to come to the police station to see the juvenile. A custody officer who authorises an arrested juvenile to be kept in police custody must ensure that, after being charged, the arrested juvenile is moved to local authority accommodation unless he or she certifies either that it is impracticable to do so or, in the case of a juvenile aged 12 or over, that no secure accommodation is available and keeping the juvenile in other local authority accommodation would not be adequate to protect the public from serious harm from him or her. Similar provisions apply to mentally impaired people.

Charge and requisition

The new system for commencing criminal proceedings known as 'charges and requisitions' is explained in *Chapter 8*. Where a defendant is charged by the police (usually the custody sergeant) (*Chapter 6*) appropriately related documentation is completed, a copy is given to the accused person and another sent to the magistrates' court. Similarly, a formal bail notice will tell the accused person to appear at court at a given time and place (assuming that he or she is not kept in custody: below) and this is also notified to the court. Other changes introduced by the Criminal Justice Act 2003 affecting the charging process include a power for the Director of Public Prosecutions (DPP) to issue guidance for use by custody officers which they should have regard to when discharging this aspect of their duties under the PACE.[17]

REVIEW BY THE CROWN PROSECUTOR

The next stage and to many extents inter-related stage in the criminal justice process is for the case file to be reviewed by a Crown prosecutor where this has not already occurred at the time of the investigation under modern practices for joint working. The police and CPS are often now located in joint Criminal Justice Units (CJUs) or Trial Units in relation to the Crown Court. The work of the CPS is considered in the next chapter.

---

[17] See, e.g. the new section 37A to D of PACE as inserted by Schedule 2 to the 2003 Act.

CHAPTER 7

The Decision to Prosecute

Historically speaking, the decision whether or not to bring a prosecution was always a matter for the police (or other relevant law enforcement agency). From the beginnings of the first police forces it was the individual police officer who brought his or her own case to court. Over time, this became more systemised as 'prosecuting inspectors' took over the ordinary police officer's role in this regard. In the post-Second World War years, this began to pass to police prosecuting solicitors departments, with private sector firms of solicitors being brought in as necessary. This police prosecuting function passed to an independent nationwide Crown Prosecution Service in 1986 (*Chapter 12*).

The Crown Prosecution Service (CPS)
The decision to arrest someone with a view to formal action in relation to a specific offence (rather than simply as a suspect), still coincides with the decision to charge them or to launch proceedings by other means (*Chapter 8*). Since 2003 and with regard to the police, the decision whether or not to charge someone is a matter for the Crown Prosecution Service (CPS) in all but minor cases or where the situation is urgent. The police regularly consult with the CPS during the early stages of an investigation as described in the last chapter, particularly concerning matters of evidence, over legal technicalities, or if the case itself is complex or concerns a vulnerable individual. Further information about the court-based role of Crown prosecutors appears in *Chapter 12*.

Some cases require the consent of the Director of Public Prosecutions (DPP) (below) or may fall within the remit of the Attorney General (such as corruption trials or matters affecting the national interest), albeit that this latter requirement has fallen under intense scrutiny (see, further, in *Chapter 12*) These extra requirements do not prevent investigation, detention and arrest (*Chapter 6*) or, in most instances, someone being charged in court and remanded by the court on bail or in custody during the preliminary stages of a case (*Chapter 8*).

Other public prosecutors
Various other prosecuting authorities operate within the public domain and some also bring their own prosecutions, including the Serious Fraud Office (SFO) (see later in the chapter) which has both an investigative and prosecuting function, albeit that this involvement may often be triggered by information provided to the SFO by the police when a fraud is uncovered. A list in the

Criminal Justice Act 2003 includes HM Revenue and Customs and 'anyone specified in an order made by the Secretary of State to this end'. The CPS can intervene and take over cases brought by these other public prosecuting authorities as it can in the case of a 'private prosecution' (again, see later).

CAUTIONING AND DIVERSION

Even when an offence is discovered and a suspect identified, the police are not compelled to initiate proceedings.[1] This principle is carried over into the Code for Crown Prosecutors. The police have an inherent discretion whether or not to continue against an offender at all, i.e. to take 'no further action', or to formally caution him or her (below),[2] or to refer the matter to the CPS with a view to a caution, conditional caution or prosecution. The CPS, likewise, now has the same discretion in so far as such decisions fall to be made by that service. This said, prosecution is likely to follow as a matter of course where the offence is serious and even with regard to lesser offences in those geographical locations where there is a zero-tolerance approach to offending.[3] The Code for Crown Prosecutors contains advice on the selection of charges.

Cautions and conditional cautions

When an offender admits his or her guilt and there is sufficient evidence for a conviction, the offender consents, and it is not necessary in the public interest to institute criminal proceedings, a caution, i.e. a warning about future behaviour may be given. This is a formal warning administered by a senior police officer in uniform, normally at a police station, when 'advice' may also be given concerning the offender's future behaviour and his or her now enhanced liability to prosecution if he or she offends again.[4] A conditional caution has been available at the behest of the CPS since 2003, to which specific requirements can be added.[5] The Code for Crown Prosecutors now sets out guidance for Crown prosecutors in relation to cautioning.

---

[1] As established in *R. v. Metropolitan Police Commissioner, ex parte Blackburn* [1968] 2 QB 118 in which a member of the public unsuccessfully challenged a refusal to prosecute. A telling example of this also arose in relation to the 'Lambeth Experiment'—a 'softly, softly' approach to simple possession of soft drugs that spread to many police force areas at one time.

[2] In the case of a juvenile, to warn or reprimand within the statutory scheme: *Chapter 3.*

[3] Some low-level behaviour may now be dealt with as anti-social behaviour (ASB): *Chapter 2.*

[4] The practice of 'giving advice' or a 'talking to' goes much wider as part of everyday policing, including on the street. It is of a somewhat vague and self-proclaimed nature—and may, e.g. be judgemental, lack objectivity or involve matters that are legally or otherwise debatable.

[5] The conditional cautioning regime is more fully explained in *The Criminal Justice Act 2003: A Guide to the New Procedures and Sentencing* (2004), Gibson B, Waterside Press.

Cautioning has long been governed by guidelines and standards which allow less serious offenders a chance to reform their ways without the blight of a criminal record. This can be an effective alternative to (or means of diversion from) prosecution—in the sense that comparatively few people who are cautioned re-offend—especially those who committed relatively minor offences for the first time, for whom cautioning is today mainly reserved.

In the early days of cautioning, the Home Office advice to police forces encouraged greater use of cautions and the number of offenders dealt with in this way rose rapidly, as did the number of second and third cautions. Following a change of policy, a circular issued 1994 sought to regulate the level of cautioning, in particular by discouraging the use of 'repeat cautions', i.e. those where the offender has already been cautioned in the past. Cautioning is nowadays governed by nationwide guidelines, supplemented locally.

Cautions will be cited in court if the offender commits a further offence for which he or she is prosecuted and may have an affect on the sentence for his or her new offence as part of the offender's general character and antecedents, provided that the subject matter of the caution is relevant to the behaviour for which the offender is to be sentenced (see, generally, *Chapter 9*). In a sentencing context, a caution will tend to show that the offender at least understood the wrongfulness of his or her conduct, having been warned about it already.

Other forms of diversion from prosecution

Cautioning is one form of diversion from the more formal parts of the CJS. Various criminal justice strategies involve diverting offenders away so that they are dealt with 'out of court' (a term which some people prefer), into less formal networks.[6] Such schemes often involve referrals to specialists or agencies who can assist, support or assess people in relation to various underlying causes of offending behaviour, or arrange reparation to a victim, or some other form of remedial action. Also, e.g. under a vehicle rectification scheme an offender might be given the opportunity to repair his or her vehicle within a fixed timescale of, say, a couple of weeks and to return with it to a police garage for inspection. Some prosecuting authorities have the authority under particular Acts of Parliament to offer mitigated penalties. Acceptance avoids the need for a prosecution and serves as a form of diversion, or 'alternative to' it, as, e.g. in certain regulatory or revenue contexts.

A number of arrest referral schemes target different kinds of offenders, usually involving partnerships between the police and other agencies including multi-agency drug actions teams (DATs). Such groups exist to co-ordinate local

---

6   The term 'diversion' is also used, where there is a conviction, to describe the channelling of offenders towards community-based sentencing options rather than custody.

action on drug misuse and bring together senior representatives of various public services including from the CJS as well as health and social services. DATs function against a backdrop of various bail-related schemes and an amendment to the Bail Act 1976 contained in the Criminal Justice Act 2003 whereby an accused person will normally be refused bail if he or she tests positive for a Class A drug, refuses to undergo assessment or fails to adhere to follow-up action.[7] These and other schemes (e.g. those concerned with mental disorder) seek to identify a range of vulnerable and other people who should be referred for help, treatment, advice or participation in a particular programme and where prosecution might be counter-productive or serve little real purpose. Nonetheless, prosecution is likely to follow unless the person concerned co-operates in such crime reduction-based strategies.

THE CROWN PROSECUTION SERVICE (CPS)

The CPS is responsible for most public prosecutions in England and Wales and may take over any private or other public prosecution, except those requiring authority at a higher level, as with cases brought by the Attorney General. It has a duty to prosecute in relation to proceedings commenced by police forces (widely defined by statute). The governing provision is the Prosecution of Offences Act 1985, under which the CPS was established and that also places duties on the Director of Public Prosecutions (DPP) (below). Whilst the early days of the CPS were typified by chaos and criticism of the agency, it is nowadays possibly one of the more established, outwardly solid and least controversial of CJS institutions, nowadays strong enough to stand its ground in the face of considerable political, financial and other pressures. Also in a modern context, there are now often specialist prosecutors to deal with specific types of offences, especially in relation, e.g. to rape, other sexual offences, domestic violence, hate crime or those involving juveniles. The nature, organization and structure of the CPS is further outlined in *Chapter 12*.

The Director of Public Prosecutions
The DPP is the head of the CPS,[8] on whom various duties and responsibilities are cast by law, including to issue a Code for Crown Prosecutors 'giving guidance on general principles to be applied by them'. Certain offences can only be prosecuted by the DPP or with his or her agreement. However, in practice such decisions are taken on a daily basis by Crown prosecutors. The DPP is accountable to the government's chief law officer, the Attorney General.

---

7   See section 19 of the 2003 Act amending the Bail Act 1976, Section 3 and Schedule 1.

8   Although the historic office of DPP pre-dates CPS.

THE CODE FOR CROWN PROSECUTORS

The code is explanatory of the day-to-day functions of the CPS, the process of prosecution decision-making and that agency's role within the CJS.[9] The CPS maintains both a short form of the code and a detailed version for internal use and which, due largely to the sensitivity of some of the more intricate decisions which prosecutors have to make, is not available to the general public. The code is a public document. Although written for members of the CPS, it is widely used by other lawyers and agencies such as the police in order to understand the way in which the CPS makes decisions. The code begins with a number of general statements and principles as follows:

1. Introduction

1.1 The decision to prosecute an individual is a serious step. Fair and effective prosecution is essential to the maintenance of law and order. Even in a small case a prosecution has serious implications for all involved—victims, witnesses and defendants. The CPS applies the Code for Crown Prosecutors so that it can make fair and consistent decisions about prosecutions.

1.2 The code helps the CPS to play its part in making sure that justice is done. It contains information that is important to police officers and others who work in the criminal justice system and to the general public. Police officers should take account of the code when they are deciding whether to charge a person with an offence.[10]

1.3 The code is also designed to make sure that everyone knows the principles that the CPS applies when carrying out its work. By applying the same principles, everyone involved in the system is helping to treat victims, witnesses and defendants fairly, while prosecuting cases effectively.

2. General Principles

2.1 Each case is unique and must be considered on its own facts and merits. However, there are general principles that apply to the way in which Crown prosecutors must approach every case.

2.2 Crown prosecutors must be fair, independent and objective. They must not let any personal views about ethnic or national origin, disability, sex, religious beliefs, political views or the sexual orientation of the suspect, victim or witness influence their decisions. They must not be affected by improper or undue pressure from any source.

---

[9] For descriptions of personnel in the CPS and of its general running see *Chapter 12*.
[10] Now subject to the changes in responsibility described in the chapter.

2.3 It is the duty of Crown prosecutors to make sure that the right person is prosecuted for the right offence. In doing so, Crown prosecutors must always act in the interests of justice and not solely for the purpose of obtaining a conviction.

2.4 Crown Prosecutors should provide guidance and advice to investigators throughout the investigative and prosecuting process. This may include lines of inquiry, evidential requirements and assistance in any pre-charge procedures Crown Prosecutors will be proactive in identifying and where possible, rectifying evidential deficiencies and in bringing to an early conclusion those cases that cannot be strengthened by further investigation.

2.5 It is the duty of Crown prosecutors to review, advise on and prosecute cases, ensuring that the law is properly applied, that all relevant evidence is put before the court and that obligations of disclosure are complied with, in accordance with the principles set out in this code.

2.6 The CPS is a public authority for the purposes of the Human Rights Act 1998. Crown prosecutors must apply the principles of the European Convention On Human Rights in accordance with the Act.

The decision to prosecute

3.1 In most cases, Crown prosecutors are responsible for deciding whether a person should be charged with a criminal offence, and if so, what that offence should be. Crown prosecutors make these decisions in accordance with this Code and the Director's Guidance on Charging. In those cases where the police determine the charge, which are usually more minor and routine cases, they apply the same provisions.

3.2 Crown prosecutors make charging decisions in accordance with the Full Code Test [in Section 5 below], other than in those limited circumstances where the Threshold Test applies [see section 6 below].

3.3 The Threshold Test applies where the case is one in which it is proposed to keep the suspect in custody after charge, but the evidence required to apply the Full Code Test is not yet available.

3.4 Where a Crown prosecutor makes a charging decision in accordance with the Threshold Test, the case must be reviewed in accordance with the Full Code Test as soon as reasonably practicable, taking into account the progress of the investigation

The continuing duty to review cases

The High Court has held (in a judgement in a civil case) that the CPS owes a duty of care to people who are subject to its decisions. The high standards demanded by the duty to review cases and to make effective decisions as to whether a case should continue or be discontinued are encapsulated as follows:

4. Review

4.1 Each case the CPS receives from the police is reviewed to make sure that it is right to proceed with a prosecution. Unless the Threshold Test applies, the CPS will only start or continue with a prosecution when the case has passed both stages of the Full Code Test.

4.2 Review is a continuing process and Crown prosecutors must take account of any change in circumstances. Wherever possible, they should talk to the police first if they are thinking about changing the charges or stopping the case. Crown prosecutors should also tell the police if they believe that some additional evidence may strengthen the case. This gives the police the chance to provide more information that may affect the decision.

4.3 The CPS and the police work closely together, but the final responsibility for the decision whether or not a charge or a case should go ahead rests with the CPS.

The twin test

Crown prosecutors apply an evidential test (sometimes described as an 'evidential sufficiency test') and a public interest test both of which are self-explanatory from the following extracts, even though the terminology has moved on as can also be seen from the wording of the present code,[11] which intertwines these tests with a threshold test (e.g. for remand application purposes) and a 'full code test'.

5 The Full Code Test

5.1 The Full Code Test has two stages. The first stage is consideration of the evidence. If the case does not pass the evidential stage it must not go ahead, no matter how important or serious it may be. If the case does pass the evidential stage, Crown prosecutors must proceed to the second stage and decide if a prosecution is needed in the public interest ...

The largely technical evidential test is explained in more detail in section 5 of the code and the public interest test in section 6. The evidential test is sometimes summarised by saying that for a prosecution to be launched or continued there

---

[11] The emphases appear in the original.

must be a realistic prospect of conviction'. The Crown prosecutor must consider what the defence case may be, and how that is likely to affect prosecution— including whether the evidence can be used in court and whether it is reliable. As to the public interest test:

5.6 In 1951, Lord Shawcross, who was Attorney General, made the classic statement on public interest, which has been supported by Attorneys General ever since: 'It has never been the rule in this country—I hope it never will be—that suspected criminal offences must automatically be the subject of prosecution' (House of Commons Debates, volume 483, column 681, 29 January 1951.)

5.7 The public interest must be considered in each case where there is enough evidence to provide a realistic prospect of conviction. Although there may be public interest factors against prosecution in a particular case, often the prosecution should go ahead and those factors should be put to the court for consideration when sentence is being passed. A prosecution will usually take place unless there are public interest factors tending against prosecution which clearly outweigh those tending in favour, or it appears more appropriate in all the circumstances of the case to divert the person from prosecution (see section 8 below).

5.8 Crown prosecutors must balance factors for and against prosecution carefully and fairly. Public interest factors that can affect the decision to prosecute usually depend on the seriousness of the offence or the circumstances of the suspect. Some factors may increase the need to prosecute but others may suggest that another course of action would be better.

The code then lists some common public interest factors, both for and against prosecution, which it states are not exhaustive. Crown prosecutors must decide how important each factor is in the material circumstances of each case and go on to make an overall assessment, including the interests of the victim.

Some common public interest factors in favour of prosecution

5.9 The more serious the offence, the more likely it is that a prosecution will be needed in the public interest. A prosecution is likely to be needed if:

a a conviction is likely to result in a significant sentence;

b a conviction is likely to result in a confiscation or any other order;

c a weapon was used or violence was threatened during the commission of the offence;

d the offence was committed against a person serving the public (for example, a police or prison officer, or a nurse);

e the defendant was in a position of authority or trust;

f the evidence shows that the defendant was a ringleader or an organizer of the offence;

g there is evidence that the offence was premeditated;

h there is evidence that the offence was carried out by a group;

i the victim of the offence was vulnerable, has been put in considerable fear, or suffered personal attack, damage or disturbance;

j the offence was committed in the presence of, or in close proximity to, a child;

k the offence was motivated by any form of discrimination against the victim's ethnic or national origin, disability, sex, religious beliefs, political views or sexual orientation, or the suspect demonstrated hostility towards the victim based on any of those characteristics;

l there is a marked difference between the actual or mental ages of the defendant and the victim, or if there is any element of corruption;

m the defendant's previous convictions or cautions are relevant to the present offence;

n the defendant is alleged to have committed the offence while under an order of the court;

o there are grounds for believing that the offence is likely to be continued or repeated , for example, by a history of recurring conduct;

p the offence, although not serious in itself, is widespread in the area where it was committed; or

q a prosecution would have a significant positive impact on maintaining community confidence.

Some common public interest factors against prosecution

5.10 A prosecution is less likely to be needed if:

a the court is likely to impose a nominal penalty;

b the defendant has already been made the subject of a sentence and any further conviction would be unlikely to result in the imposition of an additional sentence or order, unless the nature of the particular offence requires a prosecution or the defendant withdraws consent to have an offence taken into consideration during sentencing;

c the offence was committed as a result of a genuine mistake or misunderstanding (these factors must be balanced against the seriousness of the offence);

d the loss or harm can be described as minor and was the result of a single incident, particularly if it was caused by a misjudgement;

e there has been a long delay between the offence taking place and the date of the trial, unless:

- the offence is serious;
- the delay has been caused in part by the defendant;
- the offence has only recently come to light; or
- the complexity of the offence has meant that there has been a long investigation;

f a prosecution is likely to have a bad effect on the victim's physical or mental health, always bearing in mind the seriousness of the offence;

g the defendant is elderly or is, or was at the time of the offence, suffering from significant mental or physical ill health, unless the offence is serious or there is a real possibility that it may be repeated. The CPS, where necessary, applies Home Office guidelines about how to deal with mentally disordered offenders. Crown prosecutors must balance the desirability of diverting a defendant who is suffering from significant mental or physical ill health with the need to safeguard the general public;

h the defendant has put right the loss or harm that was caused (but defendants must not avoid prosecution or diversion solely because they pay compensation); or

i details may be made public that could harm sources of information, international relations or national security.

5.11 Deciding on the public interest is not simply a matter of adding up the number of factors on each side. Crown prosecutors must decide how important each factor is in the circumstances of each case and go on to make an overall assessment.

The code notes the relationship between the victim and the public interest:

5.12 The CPS does not act for victims or the families of victims in the same way as solicitors act for their clients. Crown prosecutors act on behalf of the public and not just in the interests of any particular individual. However, when considering the public interest, Crown prosecutors should always take into account the consequences for the victim of whether or not to prosecute, and any views expressed by the victim or the victim's family.

5.13 It is important that a victim is told about a decision which makes a significant difference to the case in which they are involved. Crown prosecutors should ensure that they follow any agreed procedures.

The Threshold Test and the Full Code Test

Each of these are explained in the CPS code as follows:

6.1 The Threshold Test requires Crown prosecutors to decide whether there is at least a reasonable suspicion that the suspect has committed an offence, and if there is, whether it is in the public interest to charge that suspect.

6.2 The Threshold Test is applied to those cases in which it would not be appropriate to release a suspect on bail after charge, but the evidence to apply the Full Code Test is not yet available.

6.3 There are statutory limits that restrict the time a suspect may remain in police custody before a decision has to be made whether to charge or release the suspect. There will be cases where the suspect in custody presents a substantial bail risk if released, but much of the evidence may not be available at the time the charging decision has to be made. Crown prosecutors will apply the Threshold Test to such cases for a limited period.

6.4 The evidential decision in each case will require consideration of a number of factors including:

• the evidence available at the time;
• the likelihood and nature of further evidence being obtained;
• the reasonableness for believing that evidence will become available;
• the time it will take to gather that evidence and the steps being taken to do so;
• the impact the expected evidence will have on the case;
• the charges that the evidence will support.

6.5 The public interest means the same as under the Full Code Test, but will be based on the information available at the time of charge which will often be limited.

6.6 A decision to charge and withhold bail must be kept under review. The evidence gathered must be regularly assessed to ensure the charge is still appropriate and that continued objection to bail is justified. The Full Code Test must be applied as soon as reasonably practicable.

The code goes on to explain that deciding on the public interest is not simply a matter of adding up the number of factors on each side. Crown prosecutors must decide how important each factor is in the circumstances of each case and go on to make an overall assessment. It also stresses the relationship between the victim and the public interest: There are also special and often quite different considerations in relation to youths and juveniles. The modern-day Code for Crown Prosecutors contains advice on the selection of charges, diversion from prosecution, mode of trial (*Chapter 8*), when to accept a guilty plea and in relation to re-starting a prosecution following a change of mind.[12]

---

[12] These aspects, which are not reproduced in this chapter, are available at www.cps.gov.org

DISCONTINUANCE

Several other chapters of this book contain references to cases being discontinued by the CPS. This is a statutory function which allows a prosecutor to stop a prosecution during its early stages if the twin test referred to earlier in this chapter is no longer satisfied. It goes hand in hand with the duty of the Crown prosecutor to conduct regular reviews of the case file to see whether anything has changed since the original decision to launch a prosecution.

The procedure is available in all cases in magistrates' courts at any time before the defendant has pleaded guilty or the trial has started and, in some cases only, at the Crown Court up until the time when the indictment (*Chapter 3*) is brought in (see, generally, *Chapter 4*). In reviewing and deciding whether to discontinue a case, the Crown prosecutor is guided by code principles.

THE SERIOUS FRAUD OFFICE (SFO): A NOTE

The Serious Fraud Office is an independent government department that investigates and prosecutes serious or complex fraud. It is headed by a Director of Serious Fraud who is appointed by and accountable to the Attorney General. There are four investigation and prosecution divisions, each headed by an assistant director. They contain a number of multi-disciplinary case teams comprising lawyers, financial investigators and support staff. Each operational division covers cases of fraud committed in its own geographic area of the country and falling within SFO jurisdiction. Nonetheless, a large percentage of SFO cases originate in London and are then shared between the various divisions, including an Accountancy Support and Forensic Computing division that links among other things to the UK Internet Crime Forum. A Policy Division undertakes the monitoring of legislation and provides legal advice to the Director. It also provides a library and research services for investigators and case lawyers.

The key criterion used by the SFO when deciding whether to accept a case are whether the suspected fraud appears to be so serious or complex that its investigation should be carried out by those responsible for its potential prosecution. It focuses its resources on major and complicated fraud and considers factors such as whether, e.g.:

- the value of the alleged fraud exceeds £1 million;
- there is a significant international dimension;
- the case is likely to be of widespread public concern;

- the case requires highly specialised knowledge, e.g. of financial markets;
- there is a need to use the SFO's special powers, including to order disclosure of documents and information or to demand answers to questions posed by the SFO.

The work of the SFO has sometimes proved controversial, not least when significantly large sums have been expended on prosecutions that failed to secure convictions. However, other commentators would point out that the very nature of large scale fraud is such that such prosecutions involve an element of risk and are inevitably complex, demanding of time and may well involve legal and accounting niceties. This was part of the rationale behind the setting-up of the SFO to begin with, i.e. so that the work could take place separately and away from the everyday distractions faced by the CPS. Notoriously, and perhaps most controversially, the SFO became embroiled in the as yet unresolved BAE Systems case[13] in which a former Attorney General intervened such that a longstanding corruption investigation with links to a member of the Saudi royal family was ended 'in the national interest': see, further the section on the Attorney General in *Chapter 12*.

PRIVATE PROSECUTIONS

Except where expressly provided otherwise by law or where the consent or authority of a designated official or body is required by statute, any citizen can bring a private prosecution, i.e. commence criminal proceedings. There are hazards however. Among other things, a private prosecutor risks costs being awarded against him or her if the prosecution fails; an attempt to lay an information may be rejected as vexatious or an abuse of the processes of the court; a badly judged citizen's arrest[14] may result in an award of damages; or the matter can be taken over by the CPS as explained earlier in this chapter (when it may be discontinued or withdrawn whatever the wishes of the private prosecutor). Nonetheless, a number of such prosecutions occur each year, often in respect of quite serious matters, and sometimes where the CPS has already advised the police against prosecution or declined to continue with the case.

---

13 Similarly, other cases with high political implications in relation to foreign powers.
14 Private prosecutions are usually commenced by way of information and summons and without reference to modern-day methods of commencing proceedings as they apply to public prosecutors (*Chapter 8*). An applicant will need to convince a magistrate or justices' clerk of the *bona fides* of his or her application and special rules apply in relation to vexatious litigants.

Modern times have seen private prosecutions result in convictions, e.g. for manslaughter, rape and serious offences involving the abuse of children.[15]

The costs of a successful private prosecution fall to be met from the public funds but there is nothing in the nature of state funded legal representation for an individual to bring a prosecution rather than to defend one (*Chapter 8*).

Closely associated with the idea of private prosecutions is that of the 'citizen's' arrest whereby an offender can be apprehended by anyone and handed over to the police. There are considerable hazards attached to a citizen's arrest—where the lawfulness test for an arrest by a private citizen is more arduous than for a police officer, who is entitled to act on reasonable suspicion.

Somewhat confusingly, the term 'private prosecution' may also be used in relation to court listing arrangements to signify any matter that is brought by someone other than the CPS.

---

[15] But not in the Stephen Lawrence case mentioned in *Chapter 2* in which a private prosecution was unsuccessful, thereby giving the alleged culprits immunity from prosecution under the former rule against double jeopardy.

CHAPTER 8

Bringing a Case to Court

Criminal proceedings begin—or, to use the technical term, 'commence'—by way of arrest and charge as described in *Chapter 6*, by the new method for public prosecutors described in this chapter or following an information and summons being issued.[1] In practice, all the more serious cases begin by arrest and charge. Following an investigation in accordance with the requirements of the Police and Criminal Evidence Act 1984 (PACE), the accused person will appear at court, including where he or she is taken directly to court in custody.[2] By whichever route, he or she will be called upon to answer the allegation unless it is discontinued or withdrawn by the Crown Prosecution Service (CPS) (*Chapter 7*). Modern practices have focused on the effective management of case from an early stage through preliminary hearings of the kind noted below.

CRIMINAL PROCEDURE RULES COMMITTEE (CPRC)

Court procedure is laid down by Act of Parliament—or, more generally, under delegated legislation.[3] Since 2004, this has occurred via a national Criminal Procedure Rule Committee (CPRC) chaired by the Lord Chief Justice and comprising judges, magistrates and other interested parties. The central provision is the Criminal Procedure Rules 2005.[4] The CPRC acts as a single forum for the review of criminal court procedures in all criminal courts with the intention of creating rules that are 'modern and simply expressed'. It is responsible for the development of:

- rules governing the practice and procedure to be followed in the Crown Court (*Chapter 4*), Criminal Division of the Court of Appeal (*Chapter 5*) and magistrates' courts (*Chapter 3*) or, as applicable, by justices' clerks; and
- procedures which are designed to bring about 'the closer alignment of the criminal courts', the creation of a single code of procedure for criminal courts and the efficient running of criminal trials.

---

[1] The latter is being largely replaced by new procedures under the Criminal Justice Act 2003.

[2] Usually, if in custody, within 24 hours: Sundays and Bank Holidays excluded.

[3] Also called Statutory Instruments (SIs) but often referred to as 'rules' or 'regulations'.

[4] SI 2005/384. But see also subsequent amending rules. The CPRC has invited comments on proposals to further streamline aspects of the rules.

Engagement and commitment

The expression 'signing-up' to a particular method or approach has often been used in relation to aspects of CJS practice, e.g. where practitioners agree to discharge their responsibilities within a given time scale or that they will not object to something just for the sake of forcing an issue. One purpose of the CPRC is to eliminate the unnecessary delay that can affect the progress of cases if everyone concerned is not committed to its progress: the common wisdom being that 'justice delayed is justice denied'. A central rationale of the CPRC is to engage the commitment of the judiciary, legal profession, police and representatives of the wider community—as well as voluntary organizations who deal with victims of crime or work with ex-offenders—so that all are able to work in harmony. In 2007/8 and indicative of these modern-day aspirations, new rules were issued on 'Case Management' setting out, among other things, the general duties and powers of courts concerning the pre-trial preparation of a case. At the same time, many of the former provisions designed to tease out the issues in cases as they will arise in a trial or appeal were replaced by enhanced requirements.[5] Further changes introduced rules in relation to civil behaviour orders in criminal proceedings: see, generally, *Chapter 2*. Concurrent developments saw the extension of Trial Units within the Crown Prosecution Service (CPS) (often with police input) that are responsible for the preparation of Crown Court prosecutions; and complement the Criminal Justice Units (CJUs) in relation to the early stages of proceedings in magistrates' courts (*Chapter 3*).

Inherent jurisdiction

No purely 'black and white' rules can cover every conceivable or residual situation that may arise in a courtroom or during preparations for the hearing of a case. Under longstanding legal rulings, the formal rules are thus supplemented or made to work by the inherent jurisdiction of judges or magistrates—which arises by virtue of their office—to adapt their procedures to the potentially ever-changing circumstances and needs of individual cases.[6]

COMMENCING COURT PROCEEDINGS

Virtually all criminal cases begin life in the magistrates' court and are also dealt with there to their final conclusion. In the case of an either way offence, the

---

[5] The Criminal Procedure (Amendment No 3) Rules 2007 (SI 3662) effective from April 2008.
[6] Following rules of natural justice or, nowadays, principles of human rights: *Chapter 2*.

accused person may be sent to the Crown Court for trial (*Chapters 2, 3* and *4*) or for sentence (so long as this latter power continues to exist: *Chapter 9*). Indictable only matters—the most serious (again see *Chapters 2* and *3*)—are nowadays sent straightaway by magistrates to the` Crown Court, whilst streamlined allocation procedures ensure that either way cases arrive there without undue delay.

In conjunction with a raft of other related changes introduced by the CJA 2003, that Act introduced a new method of instituting court proceedings in criminal cases. The method applies to all public (but not to private) prosecutions.

Charges and requisitions
Under the new arrangements, a public prosecutor may institute criminal proceedings by issuing a document—a 'written charge'—alleging an offence. Where he or she does so, a further document—called a 'requisition'—requiring that the accused person appear before a magistrates' court at a given time and place to answer the charge must also be served on the person concerned. These procedures replace those whereby a prosecutor applies to a court by 'laying an information' with a view to a summons being issued (which a public prosecutor is barred from doing by the 2003 Act). In effect, the court is removed from this part of the criminal process altogether, the process is streamlined, and it is simply notified what has happened. The charge and requisition must be served on the person concerned and copies sent to the court named in the requisition. However, the prosecutors can still lay an information for the purposes of obtaining a warrant. Neither do the new procedures prevent someone who is already in custody being charged under pre-existing procedures.[7]

Meaning of 'public prosecutor'
'Public prosecutor' is defined by the 2003 Act as any of the following (or people authorised by them to institute criminal proceedings):

- a police force (as per the Prosecution of Offences Act 1985);
- the Director of the Serious Fraud Office;
- the Director of Public Prosecutions (in practice a Crown prosecutor);
- the Attorney General;
- a Secretary of State;
- HM Commissioners of Revenue and Customs; and
- anyone specified in an order made by the Lord Chancellor.

---

[7] See sections 29 and 30 Criminal Justice Act 2003.

Prosecutions brought by 'non-listed' prosecutors

The pre-existing procedure[8] (MCA 1980) continues in relation to any prosecutor not named above. The right of a private individual to lay an information etc. is similarly unaffected (subject to standard exceptions, e.g. where the right to start proceedings is limited to the Attorney General or DPP). Where a public prosecutor takes over a 'non-listed' prosecutor's case—as, e.g. he or she may do as a matter of discretion—that public prosecutor will be able to rely on a valid information already laid by the non-listed prosecutor.

Form, content etc. of charges and requisitions

The 2003 Act makes further provision concerning the new method, including so that rules under pre-existing legislation can also regulate 'the form, content, recording, authentication and service' of charges and requisitions. At the same time in relation to such matters, the Lord Chancellor can make 'such other provisions' as appear to him to be necessary or expedient.[9]

Use of the word 'charge'

The word 'charge' is used in various contexts where a defendant is confronted with an allegation, e.g. by a police officer (as in *Chapter 6*), a prosecutor (*Chapter 7*) or (in court) when the charge is put to the accused by a court legal advisor (*Chapter 12*). Words my be used such as, 'You are charged that on a certain date at a certain time you did such and such, contrary to a particular legal provision'. This may be accompanied by a warning or statement of the accused person's rights as applicable. The word charge also serves to distinguish events in the magistrates' court from those in the Crown Court hearing, when, with regard to the latter, the terminology is that of 'indictment' and 'arraignment' (*Chapter 4*). It is also, obviously, now used in the context of 'charges and requisitions' (above).

Warrant of arrest

Warrants with or without instructions to the police to bail a defendant to appear in court at a fixed time and place can be issued by magistrates or judges (the latter being known as 'bench warrants'), principally:

---

[8] See section 1 Magistrates' Courts Act 1980.

[9] One example of the wide-ranging powers now cast on departmental Ministers.

- instead of other forms of process if the offence carries a possible sentence of imprisonment and those other methods will not ensure attendance (e.g. where the address of the accused is not known);
- when the defendant has failed to attend court on a previous occasion; or
- when he or she has failed to surrender to bail after being charged by the police and released on bail by them to attend court, or following the granting of bail by a court where a case has been adjourned.

A warrant containing instructions to the police to release the accused person on bail after arrest is styled a warrant 'backed for bail'. Both the Crown Court and the magistrates' court can issue a warrant where the accused person does not remain at court throughout the proceedings. There are similar powers arrangements in relation to witnesses, albeit rarely relied upon, but sometimes necessary if there is a recalcitrant witness. Generally speaking, witnesses attend and give evidence voluntarily and there are enhanced schemes of witness care and where appropriate witness protection (*Chapters 4* and *12*).

Failure to surrender to bail

Failure by an accused person to surrender to his or her bail (or to remain at court throughout the relevant proceedings) is called 'absconding'. Quite apart from the fact that this means that the absconder is likely to be arrested, the failure will also be a ground for refusing bail in the future: see, generally, under *Bail and Custody*, below. Failure to surrender is a criminal offence in its own right, punishable by a fine and/or imprisonment in the magistrates' court or Crown Court

BAIL AND CUSTODY: DECISIONS BY COURTS

As explained in *Chapter 6*, once someone has been charged with an offence by the police, he or she must be released on bail by them or be brought before a magistrates' court in custody, usually within 24 hours. The courts and the general public have seemingly long been concerned about the extent to which some people commit further offences when on bail. Measures to deal with this situation include the development of bail support schemes (below) and legislative provisions in the Criminal Justice Act 2003. The latter provides that when sentencing an offender (see, generally, *Chapter 9*), an offence *must* be treated as more serious than it would otherwise have been if it was committed whilst the offender was on bail.

Court bail

The Bail Act 1976 guarantees a right to bail to people charged with a criminal offence, i.e. a right not to be held in custody unless one of several fairly strict legal exceptions applies. Where the court does find that an exception exists on the facts and merits of a particular case the defendant is remanded into custody, usually for not more than eight clear days at a time before conviction, i.e. with the case being adjourned a week at a time. Longer remands in custody are possible in certain circumstances for up to 28 days and also after the case has reached the Crown Court. After conviction and pending sentence (usually for reports to be prepared as described in *Chapter 9*), the limit on each such a remand is 21 days. Again, this can be repeated, but, consistent with a fair trial, the momentum is nowadays behind dealing with all stages of a case within the shortest time span that allows for all relevant procedures to be followed.

Someone who is refused bail by a court can appeal to a judge of the Crown Court or a judge of the High Court (often at a Crown Court centre). A prosecutor can appeal to the Crown Court against the grant of bail in certain cases.[10]

Young people

People aged 17 to 20 who are refused bail are held in a remand centre[11] or prison. Below the age of 17, a refusal of bail operates as a remand to local authority accommodation but during the remand period, a court can order or authorise the use of secure accommodation. If the defendant is aged 15 or 16 and male a court can remand him to a remand centre or prison if strict statutory criteria are met.

Grounds and reasons

Apart from in exceptional situations, bail can only be refused if a court is satisfied that a statutory exception to the general right to bail exists. Exceptions are known as 'grounds'. Bail can be refused before conviction in relation to any offence that carries imprisonment but only where there are *substantial grounds* for believing that if bail were to be allowed to the defendant he or she would:

- fail to surrender to custody (i.e. abscond);
- commit an offence; or
- interfere with witnesses.

---

10   Assuming that bail was opposed by him or her in the first place.

11   In effect a special form of prison or prison wing (i.e. part of a prison) for unconvicted or unsentenced male prisoners aged 17 to 21, or for women of any age.

The scope for refusing bail is greater after conviction and less where the offence does not carry a possible sentence of imprisonment. However, defendants can be held in custody for any offence for their own protection (e.g. to prevent them being harassed, placed in fear or physically attacked, or where they are personally vulnerable or likely to harm themselves). Similarly, where there has been a previous breach of bail by absconding and the court believes that the defendant would abscond again if released on bail. Among other special situations, an offender need not be granted bail if the offence is indictable only or triable either way (*Chapter 2*) where he or she was already on bail for an earlier offence when the later, i.e. new offence was allegedly committed.

The Bail Act 1976 requires that where a court or constable grants or withholds bail a record should be made of that decision and the reason for it. Magistrates are obliged to announce the grounds for refusing bail in open court (e.g. that the defendant might interfere with witnesses) and, as a distinct item, their reasons for this conclusion (e.g. that the defendant has already made threats towards such witnesses). This was one of the very first situations in which courts were obliged to explain their reasoning and the statutory position is now reinforced by fair trial considerations under human rights law (*Chapter 2*).

A copy of the decision must be given to the defendant on request. In practice, pro forma are used with grounds and reasons already pre-printed and boxes available for ticking, or adding to if the decision does not fit a standard 'pigeonhole'. However, the quasi-automated nature of recording remand decision-making should not be allowed to obscure the fact that a full and proper exercise of judicial discretion—by listening to the facts and drawing only legitimate inferences—is essential before any decision or record is made. No particular standard of proof is required on the part of the prosecutor.[12]

Reasons must be given for *granting* bail in the case of murder and certain other prescribed offences; whilst bail cannot be granted at all in the case of a charge of murder or attempted murder, rape or attempted rape, or manslaughter if the defendant already has a conviction for one of these offences.[13]

Repeat applications for bail

To counter the former phenomenon of a 'never-ending' number of applications for bail, there are statutory rules to prevent 'repeat applications', i.e. the same arguments being put forward by defendants or their legal representatives over

---

[12] Or for that matter evidence: although some evidence on oath is often given, especially where information is challenged, including evidence by the arresting officer.

[13] Or a conviction for the Scottish offence of culpable homicide.

and again at a series of fresh remand hearings. Under national law, courts are not obliged to listen to the same matters twice, although this statutory bar appears to have been applied in a somewhat relaxed manner since the Human Rights Act 1998. The bar does not, in any case, apply on a defendant's first two appearances.

Conditional bail
Bail can be granted subject to conditions, e.g. to live at a given address; report to the police, say, 'between 6 p.m. and 8 p.m. every Monday, Wednesday and Friday'; not to associate with the victim or witnesses (called a condition of 'non-association'); or to stay away from a defined geographical area. Reasons must be given for conditions.[14] A defendant can be arrested, with or without a warrant, for breach of a condition, but breach—as opposed to failure to surrender—is not an offence. Bail can then be revoked by the court where appropriate.

Sureties and securities
A frequently used pre-release bail condition is that the defendant must find a responsible individual who is prepared to vouch for his or her appearance at the end of the remand period—known as a 'surety'. The surety agrees to forfeit a sum of money to the court if the accused person absconds. The sum is set by the court and can be forfeited in whole or in part.[15] Quite distinct is a 'security'. Here, the defendant deposits money or some other valuable form of security with the court as a guarantee that he or she will return to court on the due date. Despite the existence of this provision, English bail arrangements do not, as matter of course, tend to involve deposits of money or valuables (in contrast, e.g. to the position in the USA where the requirement of a bail bond is commonplace).[16]

Bail information and bail support
Bail information schemes operated under the auspices of the National Probation Service (NPS), HM Prison Service (HMPS) or youth offending teams (YOTs) exist nationwide. These involve obtaining and verifying information about the accused person's circumstances that is relevant to the bail decision and providing this to the CPS and the defence. Possibilities for bail which were not investigated before an initial remand to custody are pursued during the first remand period,

---

[14] The police now have power to grant conditional bail once someone has been charged by them.

[15] Also known as a recognizance.

[16] The security provisions are, however, frequently used if the defendant lives or may travel abroad. Their under-use may stem from their somewhat cumbersome nature, for courts, of retaining and accounting for valuables deposited.

e.g. the existence of a fixed address (or sometimes a temporary address but well away from potential witnesses or local feeling), or of a surety, or whilst security is raised (above). The results are placed before the court at the next remand hearing. Many areas of the country operate bail support schemes to work with bailed defendants who might otherwise be at risk of offending if released into the community. Bail schemes may be linked into a range of referral schemes such as those designed to identify and assist people affected by drug misuse (*Chapter 7*).

Bail hostels

The NPS used to provide bail hostel or other accommodation for certain people who are on bail (and there were also 'combined hostels' catering for people on bail, a community sentence or post-custody supervision: see, generally, later chapters). Such premises are now used almost exclusively for high-risk offenders under probation supervision, either as part of a community sentence or who are on licence following release from prison.

CUSTODY TIME LIMITS

To encourage the expeditious processing of cases by police and prosecutors, there are limits on the length of time for which an accused person may be held in custody before a case starts (here in the sense that the hearing of the allegation against him or her begins by way of a trial in court). Either way cases tried by magistrates must be begun within 70 days or in some cases 56 days.[17] Where a case is sent to the Crown Court for trial, that process must be started within 70 days. A period of 112 days is then allowed between the date when magistrates send the defendant to the Crown Court and arraignment (*Chapter 4*). If a time limit expires, the defendant cannot be remanded in custody any longer for the offence in question. He or she can still be prosecuted, but must be released, usually on bail, pending further stages of the proceedings. Time limits can be extended by the court in an individual case for good cause. Various practices exist to prevent the former abuse whereby when a time limit ran out the accused would be re-arrested on some other holding charge.

---

[17] Depending on whether mode of trial (see later in the text) has been determined within the first 56 days, when the limit telescopes down to the shorter of the two periods.

ALLOCATION OF CASES (AKA 'MODE OF TRIAL')

Allocation is the modern label for mode of trial,[18] which is a key feature of the early stages of the criminal justice process in relation to all either way offences (as these are described in *Chapter 2*). The magistrates' court must decide whether—on the face of things—the case appears to be more suitable for trial by magistrates or trial at the Crown Court. In effect, it must predict the likely sentence if the accused person were to be convicted, i.e. whether or not it would fall within that court's maximum powers of punishment—at present of six months per offence or 12 months in aggregate (*Chapter 9*).[19] The defendant also has a free-standing right to claim trial by jury and an appropriate explanation is made by the court legal adviser as well as a warning about the possibility of the case being committed for sentence at the Crown Court if, notwithstanding allocation for trial in the magistrates' court it later transpires that a more severe sentence, one within the higher powers of the Crown Court, is appropriate (known as a 'caution').

The overall provisions are complex and beyond the scope of an introductory handbook of this kind. They were amended by the Criminal Justice Act 2003 so that the now involve not only a 'cross-cutting' procedures known as 'plea before venue' (introduced by earlier legislation)—whereby the accused can indicate, ahead of any decision as to the appropriate venue, his or her wish to plead guilty—but procedure whereby the magistrates' court can indicate to the accused what its likely sentence would be if he or she were to be convicted by that court (see generally on sentencing matters, *Chapter 9*).[20]

Listing

The word 'allocation' is sometimes used interchangeably with 'listing', albeit that the latter connotes something quite different. Listing involves the scheduling of cases at a particular court centre and as between courtrooms and occurs at both the Crown Court and magistrates' courts. This work is usually carried out by a listing officer whose role includes making optimum use of court resources, facilities and what is known sometimes called 'judge time'. As part of this skilled

---

[18] To complicate an already intricate picture, mode of trial can only be fully understood alongside a statutory 'plea before venue' procedure, which precedes it. Here, the defendant can intimate a plea of 'guilty' from the outset. This allows magistrates to by-pass mode of trial and move direct to the sentencing stage. Special 'hybrid' provisions apply to criminal damage.

[19] See the comments on changes to magistrates' sentencing powers in *Chapter 2*.

[20] These complexities are explained in some detail in *The Criminal Justice Act 2003: A Guide to the New Procedures and Sentencing* (2004), Gibson, B, Waterside Press.

task, he or she will also consider the needs of the parties and witnesses. Cases may even be transferred from one area to another if it transpires that local sensitivities are involved or there is some other sound reason. The practice in relation to juveniles whereby special arrangements are made to avoid the intimidating atmosphere of some courtrooms has also been noted in *Chapter 5*.

SENDING

'Sending' is the modern term for committal for trial, the process by which a case reaches the Crown Court, i.e. where magistrates send the case to the Crown Court following an allocation decision that it should be heard by that court. The Criminal Justice Act 2003 provisions as to allocation and sending are designed to ensure that either way cases are expedited from the outset and in conjunction with criminal directions and other preliminary hearings, new rules about disclosure (below) and other innovations to tackle delay are an important aspect of modern-day criminal justice. A holistic approach seeks to ensures not only that cases reach the correct court at the earliest state, inappropriate hearings when it comes to the sentencing stage, but also, e.g. 'cracked trials' are avoided, i.e. those which collapse at the last moment from a lack of evidence, a sudden change of plea to 'guilty', or failure to detect that a valid defence may exist to the charge.

DISCLOSURE

Disclosure is the description given to the provision of relevant information by one party to the other. A distinction must be drawn between disclosure by the prosecutor and that by the defence.

Disclosure by the prosecutor
Before a defendant is called upon to make any decision concerning mode of trial in respect of an either way offence, an accused has for many years been legally entitled to advance disclosure of the prosecution case. The prosecutor sets out the main features of the case, usually in the form of a written summary (it can, in appropriate cases, be disclosure of the entire evidence available). These original advance disclosure rules never applied to purely summary offences or indictable only ones—although, in response to human rights law (*Chapter 2*), prosecutors began to make disclosure in such cases if asked to. Similarly, the defence was originally under no obligation to 'disclose its hand' before trial (except for the

defence of 'alibi' in the Crown Court and cases involving allegations of serious fraud, the disclosure of official secrets or relating to the running of companies: all matters beyond the scope of this handbook). The 2003 Act altered the Criminal Procedure and Investigations Act 1996 which contained certain pre-trial disclosure provisions relating to both the prosecution and the defence.

Disclosure of unused prosecution material

Historically there were often complaints that the police or prosecutors withheld material from an accused person which may have aided his or her defence or undermined the prosecution, something that has featured in a number of miscarriage of justice cases. Another key change wrought by the 2003 Act was an amendment to the 1996 Act so as to create a fresh, single test concerning the disclosure of unused prosecution material (in effect that which is surplus to prosecution requirements).[21] The new test requires the prosecutor to disclose:

> . . . any prosecution material which has not previously been disclosed to the accused and which might reasonably be considered capable of undermining the case for the prosecution ... or of assisting the case for the accused.

Associated provisions place a continuing duty on the prosecutor to disclose unused material at all times until the accused is acquitted, convicted or the prosecutor decides not to continue the case. He or she must keep the situation under review and disclose relevant material which does emerge as soon as reasonably practicable or within given time limits. The accused can apply to the court for further disclosure of such material in specified circumstances.

Defence disclosure

The 2003 Act changes concerning the defence are significant and extend the defence information now available to prosecutors. That Act amended the 1996 Act so as to provide for what is, in effect, 'cross-service' of defence statements following an order of the court.[22] The court may make such an order of its own motion or on the application of any party to the proceedings. Under the pre-existing law, an accused person was required to set out—in general terms—the nature of his or her defence. The effect of the new provisions is to require him or her to provide a much more detailed statement. Certain existing requirements are replicated, including provisions requiring the accused to give details of any

---

[21] See Part 5 of the 2003 Act and the amended section 3 of the 1996 Act.
[22] See section 33 of the 2003 Act and the amended section 5 *et seq* of the 1996 Act.

alibi on which he or she seeks to rely (now with precise details of the alibi witnesses). In his or her 'defence statement' the accused must:

- set out the nature of his or her defence, including any particular defences on which he or she intends to rely;
- indicate the matters of fact on which he or she takes issue with the prosecution and in each case say why he or she does so; and
- indicate any point of law he or she wishes to take, including as to the admissibility of evidence or abuse of process, and any authority on which he or she intends to rely for that purpose.

The Lord Chancellor is given power to prescribe further details to be contained in defence statements and there are provisions for such statements to be updated if a situation changes—as well as for intended defence witnesses to be notified, including any expert witness who has been consulted (see, generally, *Chapter 12*). Magistrates or a jury may draw inferences from certain shortcomings in relation to disclosure by the accused when deciding whether he or she is guilty. However, he or she cannot be convicted solely on the basis of such inferences. Ministers are empowered to issue a code of practice for police interviews of any witnesses notified by accused where his or her details have been disclosed under these provisions.

Tactically and as a matter of common sense, defendants may need to disclose the substance of any defence in advance of the trial or risk adverse comment to the jury for not having come up with an explanation sooner. However, commentators who are concerned about civil liberties consistently point out the scope for abuse that is inherent where people are compelled to state their case.

OTHER PRELIMINARY MATTERS

Pre-trial procedures concentrate on clarifying and defining the issues in the case. Depending on a myriad of considerations, there may be several stages (usually involving the defendant's attendance at court) between the start of criminal proceedings and the time when he or she comes to enter a plea, i.e. to an allegation. These depend on various factors including the nature of the offence and tactical decisions made by the parties within what is essentially an adversarial system of justice. The modern CJS follows a pattern determined by rules of court and supplemented locally by agreements (or 'protocols') between courts and the other CJS agencies concerning, e.g. the expected maximum periods of time for completion of various tasks or stages. Certain cases before magistrates may be 'fast-tracked' to an early first hearing and the defendant given the opportunity to enter a guilty plea at this stage if appropriate (which in turn will attract a sentencing discount: *Chapter 9*). There may also be criminal directions hearings at which administrative matters are considered such as the grant of state funded legal representation (*Chapter 12*), the likely plea or a timetable for the case. A plea of guilty can be intimated at this early stage which, in the case of an either way offence, may obviate the need for the court to consider allocation (above).

In the Crown Court, judges hold preliminary hearings and give criminal directions concerning the course of a case and their expectations of the parties and of their legal representatives in preparing for trial. Legal arguments may also be indicated or rehearsed at this point and the need for any legal research identified. The whole purpose is to eliminate items which might delay or interrupt the proceedings once they reach a court hearing proper, with both justice and financial considerations in mind as matters of public interest. The procedure rules noted earlier in the chapter place considerable emphasis on the effective management of cases from the outset.

CHAPTER 9

Trial and Sentence

Central to the entire criminal process are two inter-related stages:

- the trial of an alleged offender, which must follow correct procedures and take place on the basis of legally admissible evidence; and
- if he or she is convicted, determination of the sentence to be imposed by the judge or magistrates, taking account of the facts of the case, the powers in relation to given kinds of offences, sentencing law and guidance.

This chapter looks at both these stages and a number of connected matters.

TRIAL

As noted in *Chapter 1*, it is in anticipation of a possible trial in court—at 'the hub' of the CJS—that all prior stages of the criminal justice process occur: gathering evidence, carrying out interviews, putting together a case file, the continuing review of the case file by the Crown prosecutor (*Chapter 7*) and checks to see that the witnesses will be available to give evidence. Similarly, within what remains a primarily adversarial system of justice (*Chapter 2*) there will be decisions for the lawyers of both parties about the tactics that they will employ. Some inroads into a wholly conflict-based system have occurred due to duties of disclosure and the work of the Criminal Procedure Rule Committee (CPRC) (*Chapter 8*).[1]

If there is no real defence, it may be better for the accused person to accept that position at the earliest possible stage in the legitimate expectation that credit will be given at the sentencing stage for a timely guilty plea (see later in the chapter). Conversely, the innocent person[2] who somehow finds himself or herself embroiled in the criminal process may find that his or her actions will lead to acquittal or may generate continuing suspicion and a miscarriage of justice—in which case justice in the courts or the work of the Criminal Cases Review Commission (CCRC) (*Chapter 10*) may ultimately prevail.[3]

---

[1] The full impact of these developments and how much they can impact on a legal culture in which conflict has often been the order of the day remain to be seen.

[2] The English CJS cannot really establish true innocence, rather whether or not the prosecution can establish its case, which is not quite the same thing.

[3] In 2008, a convicted offender 'praised' British justice after spending four years in prison, when it was discovered that a complete mistake had been made. He was quoted as saying that his one comfort during his incarceration was his undying belief that justice would eventually triumph.

Suspects and offenders

Before conviction there is a presumption of innocence (*Chapter 2*). Only if this changes by a conviction does a *suspect* change from being an *accused person* into an *offender*—someone convicted and due to be sentenced. Some media reports and government pronouncements prefer to use the term 'criminal',[4] whilst the traditional terminology for those sent to prison (in particular) is 'convict'. Other associated linguistic nuances revolve around the word 'prisoner', a term that can mean either a remand prisoner, convicted prisoner or sentenced prisoner, so that it is frequently necessary to use such descriptions with precision (see, further, in *Chapter 14*). As noted in *Chapter 7*, a trial will only go ahead if the Crown prosecutor, after reviewing his or her case file—as required by the Code for Crown Prosecutors—concludes that it should do so. This assumes that the accused does not plead guilty. Negotiations may occur with a view to a plea bargain or a preliminary indication of sentence, the former an agreement by the prosecutor to accept a plea of guilty to a lesser charge, the latter, in effect, a request to the court by the accused person's legal representative asking what, other things being equal, the sentence is likely be if the accused does plead guilty. This now takes place subject to provisions and constraints flowing from the Criminal Justice Act 2003.[5]

GUILTY PLEA

The procedure in all criminal courts on a plea of guilty follow a common pattern (and increasingly more generally due to the work of the Criminal Procedure Rules Committee (CPRC) mentioned in *Chapter 8*). The court moves directly to the sentencing stage (see, further, under *Sentence* later in the chapter). The facts of the case are outlined by the prosecutor and the defendant is invited to add any explanation or make representations—known as 'a plea in mitigation'. Mitigation may relate to the *offence* (i.e. where the offender claims that it is less serious than might appear on the face of things) or the *offender* (i.e. to his or her personal circumstances which he or she may claim indicate that a less severe or different kind of penalty should be imposed than might otherwise occur). Some offenders accept their fate and are sentenced at the 'going rate' or 'tariff' in

---

4   Various Home Secretaries, e.g. have emphasised that terrorists or people involved in organized crime are truly criminals. Some commentators have pointed to the implications in terms of potential abuse of much of the language of crime and punishment (such as 'thug', 'villain', 'toe-rag', 'ratboy', 'nasty piece of work' or 'ne'er-do-well')—that can be emotive, divisive and exclusionary in attitude—and that has hence been linked to criminological theories of labelling.

5   The provisions (which also interact with allocation and sending) are set out in *Criminal Justice Act 2003: A Guide to the New Procedures and Sentencing* (2004), Gibson B, Waterside Press.

accordance with sentencing guidelines (below) and any prior indication that may have been given by the judge or magistrates (above). Where mitigation is put forward this is usually relayed to the court on the defendant's behalf by his or her barrister or solicitor (*Chapter 12*) when it is common to describe the offender's involvement using some such device as 'My instructions are as follows...'. A list of any previous convictions is handed to the court by the prosecutor, together with other information concerning the offender's 'character and antecedents', usually meaning his or her social background and upbringing. There may then be a list of offences which the offender is asking the court to take into consideration (known as 'TICs') (see later under *Sentence*). With all the more serious matters there is likely to be a pre-sentence report (PSR) and the court may wish to consider making various ancillary orders (again see later in the chapter). Special provisions exist, e.g. in relation to harassment and football banning orders, which are designed to prevent hooliganism at football matches.

Equivocal plea

A criminal court cannot accept an 'equivocal plea' of guilty, i.e. one where the defendant admits the offence but then adds something which indicates a defence to the allegation or that the plea is being made purely for convenience—such as 'Yes, I did it, but I always intended to pay the money back', 'I never intended to cause any harm' or 'I just want to get it over with'. The case is then put back, normally to a new date, for the defendant to reconsider his or her position, take legal advice (or further such advice) and, if necessary, for a trial to be held later when the evidence can be called and fully considered and tested by cross-examination. Equivocal pleas are commonly identified at the mitigation stage and are not uncommon in magistrates' courts. With more serious matters they are nowadays likely to be discerned and 'weeded out' at a criminal directions or other preliminary hearing (see, generally, *Chapter 8*).

Written plea of guilty ('paper plea')

A special procedure exists in magistrates' courts (only) under which a written plea of guilty can be accepted by the court. This procedure has been refined and enhanced over the years since 1957 when it was first introduced. It can be invoked by a prosecutor in respect of certain summary offences. Cases dealt with under the procedure are known as 'paperwork cases' or 'paper pleas'.[6]

The defendant is served with a written statement of facts which contains an outline of the circumstances of the offence. If he or she then pleads guilty in writing, the statement of facts is read out in court together with any written mitigation and financial information put forward in writing by the defendant—a

---

[6] Alternatively as 'section 12 cases' (after section 12 Magistrates' Courts Act 1980, which sets out the procedure); or MCA cases (after the Magistrates' Courts Act 1957 which first introduced it).

special reply form being provided for that purpose. The court then sentences the defendant 'in absence'. An application for costs can be made in writing and notice can be served to cite relevant previous convictions.

The defendant does not have to plead guilty. This is made clear in an accompanying notice. There are also special procedures covering the situation where the defendant changes his or her mind, or turns up at court in person wishing to add to what he or she has set out in writing. There is also flexibility, in that the court can notify the defendant that the case will be dealt with at any time within a span of 28 days and a further procedure whereby the documentation served on the defendant can be used to prove the case if he or she fails to respond at all. Where the offence is a road traffic matter attracting endorsement of a driving licence, the defendant will also have to send to the court his or her driving licence for mandatory penalty points to be entered on it.

Increasingly, many lesser offences are now disposed of by way of the fixed penalty system under which a fixed penalty notice (or 'ticket') is issued by a police officer, community support officer, traffic warden or other authorised person. Various suggestions have been made for all low-level offences to become wholly administrative in nature, what are often styled 'non-convictions', but these have not been acted upon, pending which the full weight of criminal law and its procedure comes into play if the allegation is challenged, no matter how basic the offence or meagre the potential sentence on conviction.

NOT GUILTY PLEA

Again and broadly speaking, the procedure following a plea of 'not guilty' is the same whatever the offence or level of court. There are some exceptions to this, e.g. in relation to fraud trials and cases involving offences against children but most of what follows applies across-the-board. The presumption of innocence applies (now reinforced by Article 6 of the European Convention On Human Rights and Fundamental Freedoms) so that once such a plea is entered, the prosecutor must establish the allegation by evidence and to the required standard of proof, i.e. beyond reasonable doubt (all items which are noted in *Chapter 2*). Failing this, the accused must be acquitted.

Case for the prosecution
In the normal course of events, a criminal trial opens with the prosecutor outlining the case to the jury or magistrates. He or she will then call evidence to support the charge or indictment. Primarily this means the testimony of witnesses on a religious oath of their own choosing—or on affirmation. Other regular forms of evidence include written statements (which are admissible

provided certain formalities are complied with and the defence does not object to them); exhibits (such as weapons, drugs, stolen goods or forged documents); and any confession made by the accused person to the police in accordance with PACE (*Chapter 6*), or other admission, formal or informal.[7] There may also be forensic or other scientific evidence. Experts apart, evidence must generally be confined to fact rather than opinion. The court may determine that someone is an expert and thus allow opinion evidence to be given by him or her when it may also be faced with allowing contrary opinions to be asserted by experts for the opposing party.[8] Since 2003, it has been possible for certain evidence from remote locations to be given by video-link. The Criminal Justice Act 2003 deals with 'live links' in criminal proceedings, meaning from a place outside of and beyond the court premises. Since 2003, a court has power to authorise evidence via such a link where it believes this to be in the interests of the efficient or effective administration of justice.[9] The Act also regulates the way in 'evidentiary rulings' by judges can be challenged (*Chapter 12*) and extends the situations in which evidence can be received by video-recording. It modifies the law of criminal evidence more generally, including with regard to hearsay.[10]

At the end of the evidence of each witness for the prosecution, the defendant or his or her advocate can cross-examine, i.e. ask questions. The purpose is to challenge what has been said, cast a different light on the evidence that has been given, to discredit the witness and show that what he or she has said is unreliable or lacks credibility, or in the extreme that he or she is lying. The prosecutor may re-examine the witness to clear up any new matters arising from cross-examination. Witnesses are not normally allowed into the courtroom before they give evidence. An example of where they might be allowed in sooner is where an expert witness is given permission to observe the evidence of other people so that he or she can comment on it during his or her own later evidence and in the light of his or her expertise. Courts benefit from the existence of the Witness Service and Victim Support (*Chapter 14*). As noted in *Chapter 8*, certain rules of disclosure apply in relation to the calling of a witness and to the position of expert witnesses in particular.

---

[7] Controversy has been caused by 'cell confessions' to fellow prisoners, principally because there is a natural suspicion of vested interest on the part of the witness (e.g. in his or her early release).

[8] This process has fallen under scrutiny in relation evidence of child abuse in particular (but also more generally) following the case of a leading child expert, Sir Roy Meadows, subsequently disciplined and censured by his professional body for claims made about how injuries may have occurred and to the extent that such experts have become cautious about giving evidence at all.

[9] See section 51 of the 2003 Act. The Youth Justice and Criminal Evidence Act 1999 first allowed live links in limited situations, e.g. re young, disabled, vulnerable or intimidated witnesses.

[10] For further information, see *The Criminal Justice Act 2003: A Guide to the New Procedures and Sentencing* (2004), Gibson B, Waterside Press.

Refreshing memory

What a witness recalls about the facts of a case together with his or her general veracity is one of the most significant and uncertain variables in any trial, particularly given that cross-examination can place recollection under searching scrutiny. It is why the outcome of some cases cannot be predicted until it is seen whether the witnesses 'come up to proof' as it is sometimes described. Testimony tends to gain in power from directness and the accuracy of recollection of a witness—but he or she can be given permission to refresh his or her memory in certain circumstances. Police officers—who may attend many incidents in the course of their day-to-day duties—have always routinely been given permission to refer to their notebooks[11] although in the past this could only occur after the officer satisfied the court that the note was made reasonably close to the time of the events ('contemporaneously with') and from his or her own then recollection, not, e.g. copied over from a colleague's account. One advance in the 2003 Act was the creation of a new presumption in favour of a witness in criminal proceedings refreshing his or her memory from a document whilst giving evidence provided that:

- he or she indicates that the document represents his or her recollection at the time he or she made it; and
- his or her recollection was likely to be significantly better at the time the document was made (or verified).[12]

The fact that the witness has read the statement before giving his or her testimony does not affect this presumption. In view of the practical difficulties associated with refreshing memory in the witness box from an audio or video recording, the 2003 Act also makes provision for a witness to refresh his or her memory from a transcript of such a recording. These represent considerable changes, as does a good deal of what nowadays occurs in the courtroom.

Withdrawing the case from the jury

In the Crown Court, the judge may withdraw a case from the jury where he or she considers that there is no basis for the prosecution continuing. There is no immediate equivalent to this in the magistrates' court, but the situation is analogous to the procedure in relation to no case to answer (below)—save that a judge can withdraw the case at any time. The judge may also direct the jury to bring in a verdict of not guilty where, legally speaking, this is the correct course.

---

[11] Notebooks are increasingly being replaced by technological devices.
[12] See section 139. These provisions dispense with the common law rules and much cited rulings such as *R. v. Benjamin* (1913) 2 Cr App Rep 146 which concerned a police officer's notebook.

The 2003 Act makes provision for judge alone trials—which in some instances can rest on events that develop during a trial: see, further, *Chapter 12*.

No case to answer

Before a defendant is called upon to elect (i.e. decide) whether or not to give evidence there must be a *prima facie* case against him or her. There will be no case to answer where the prosecutor has failed to adduce any evidence whatsoever of an essential ingredient of the offence charged (e.g. no evidence that property the subject of an allegation of theft belonged to someone else); or if prosecution witnesses have been shown by defence cross-examination to be so unreliable that no reasonable court could convict on their evidence. The defence may make a submission of 'no case' at the end of the evidence for the prosecution, or the judge or magistrates can (indeed always should) consider whether there is a *prima facie* case in any event. If not, the case ends there and then. The defendant is discharged and is normally entitled to costs from public funds.[13] Otherwise, the trial continues. The defendant must then decide whether or not to give evidence and call witnesses, whether to the facts or, e.g. as to his or her character and reputation for honesty or non-violent nature.

Case for the defence

The procedure in terms of the defence case mirrors that for the prosecution case (above).[14] The defendant in a criminal trial is not obliged to give evidence albeit that it is possible since 1995 for inferences to be drawn if he or she remains silent either during the investigation or at the trial. Nonetheless, he or she may choose to say nothing at all. The court will then decide the case on the prosecution evidence alone (and any inferences which it may legitimately draw from the defendant's silence). It may be, e.g. that there is a *prima facie* case but that the evidence is weak and, even without any explanation from the defendant, would be incapable of satisfying the court beyond reasonable doubt. If the accused does give evidence then the procedure again mirrors that outlined in relation to the case for the prosecution. He or she normally gives his or her evidence first, followed by that of other defence witnesses if there are any. All will be liable to cross-examination by the prosecutor. Again this may be followed by re-examination of the witnesses by the defendant or his or her legal representative. As noted in *Chapter 8* there are now certain duties on the defence concerning

---

13 See later in the chapter under *Costs and witnesses' expenses.*

14 It should be stressed that nothing prevents an accused person representing himself or herself. Many do. It can sometimes prove to be unsatisfactory in terms of direct cross-examination of witnesses (especially in sensitive cases), in-built delay or the fact that an untutored person can 'shoot themselves in the foot'. But the right is well-recognised and courts often go to lengths to ensure even-handedness in such situations, even though there may be no real 'equality of arms'.

disclosure of his or her case and which can be seen as part of increasingly developed arrangements with regard to the management of cases in general.

Speeches and representations

As already indicated, the prosecutor will open his or her case with an outline of the allegations. The defendant or his or her representative is allowed a closing speech. This 'last word' in a criminal trial is regarded as a valuable right. But if the defendant puts forward legal argument at this stage, the prosecutor will be entitled to answer it, and also to counter any false or misleading impressions created by the accused person or his or her advocate, such as an incorrect or misguided summary of the evidence, or pejorative remarks about the victim. Sometimes there are speeches or representations within the course of a trial, or when there is a 'trial within' a trial as it is sometimes put, as where there is an issue over the admissibility of evidence or an outright dispute about whether a confession is admissible or should be ruled out as prejudicial because it was obtained in breach of the PACE Codes of Practice. In the Crown Court, such representations may take place in the absence of the jury so that it is not prejudiced by anything that it might otherwise hear. Similarly, there may be representations on law ('legal representations') during a trial.[15]

Onus on the defendant

Just occasionally the law reverses the normal onus of proof and the defendant must establish something such as the fact that he or she holds a particular licence, permission or authority, or that goods in his or her possession are not the proceeds of crime, matters which might be discernible from external appearances and which it would be impossible for the prosecutor to know the full truth of without putting the defendant to proof. In such cases the defendant is required to establish the relevant matter on a balance of probabilities (the standard of proof which ordinarily applies in civil, rather than criminal, cases).

Verdict

The jury or magistrates must reach their verdict, i.e. determine whether or not the accused person is guilty, based only on the facts and merits of the case. The process can be viewed as involving three steps, i.e. the court deciding:

- what facts it will accept from the evidence. This will involve decisions not simply about which evidence is true and which false, mistaken or

---

15 The much dramatised interjection, 'Objection your honour' is a USA device, but the sentiment, if not the method, is much the same in the UK—even if the advocates do not approach the bench in a huddle. One man who got this wrong was convicted of impersonating a solicitor.

unreliable, but also as to how much weight to give to individual pieces or strands of evidence and which to reject altogether;

- whether the facts found to exist add up to the offence in question; and
- whether, in all the circumstances and taking account of everything it has heard, that it is satisfied of guilt beyond reasonable doubt.

Alternative verdicts relating to other offences disclosed by the evidence may be returned in the Crown Court (and in limited situations in the magistrates' court). Thus, e.g. if someone is charged with murder the jury can bring in a verdict of manslaughter instead. The scope for alternative verdicts is a legal matter and rests on the nature of the indictment or charge and the evidence in a given case. Broadly speaking, such verdicts relate to lesser offences of a similar kind envisaged by the same events. All verdicts must be unanimous unless the judge accepts majority verdict in prescribed circumstances.

In the Crown Court, the judge will review the evidence and direct the jury on the law (*Chapter 12*). In the magistrates' court, this twin process is the responsibility of the magistrates who, technically speaking, 'direct themselves'. In practice any legal considerations are recognised to be the province and responsibility of the court legal adviser (*Chapters 3* and *12*).

Acquittal leads to the immediate discharge (and where applicable the release) of the accused person on the charge in question. Conviction leads to sentence. The position is then the same as when the accused enters a plea of 'guilty' (above) except that in the case of a trial the judge or magistrates will be at an advantage in that they will have heard more about the case than is contained in the summary that a prosecutor uses where there is a guilty plea. The defendant will also have lost any 'sentence discount' which might have flowed from a timely guilty plea (below).

SENTENCE

Notorious cases in particular—but also on an everyday basis in local newspapers and the media—sentencing is perhaps one of the most visible aspects of the CJS. It is what concerns ordinary citizens most (whether they fully understand its implications or not) and takes place against a background of high public interest, media comment and political jousting. A frequently heard complaint is that sentences are 'not long or harsh enough' and that judges are 'out of touch'. Viewed from a court perspective, sentences depend on the facts and merits of individual cases as these emerge in a particular court hearing, as to which many critics will have little knowledge or feel. Similarly, they probably do not have a full grasp of the aims and purposes of prison regimes (*Chapter 14*) or aspects of the generic community sentence (below). Few people other than those with a sound grasp of CJS matters do cultivate such an understanding. The nature and pace of modern-day developments has made it difficult even for such people and the situation may be exacerbated by the fact change is sometimes piecemeal or staggered as to its commencement dates. Most law-maker politicians are driven by a need to stay in or get into office, so that for them criminal justice policy becomes about who can 'talk toughest'. This has been the case particularly from the mid-1990s onwards, before which a more restrained ethos prevailed, almost in the nature of a convention that matters of justice were somewhat above the rough and tumble of politics.

Alongside questions as to what conduct, etc. should be prohibited as a crime (*Chapter 2*), that concerning what sentence should be passed on an offender is a key aspect of CJS policy-making, that takes place, since 2007, in the context of a Ministry of Justice (MOJ) with wide-ranging criminal justice functions (*Chapter 1*). Ultimately, that policy is formulated by Acts of Parliament, usually via Criminal Justice Acts (*Chapter 2*) as interpreted in due course by the courts in the light of advice from the Sentencing Guidelines Council (SGC)(below). Within the legal framework for sentencing, it is the task of the courts to reflect legitimate public concern as they see fit but to deal with each case on its individual facts and merits—again as guided by the SGC.

THE SENTENCING FRAMEWORK

Sentences and the varying extent to which they actually or notionally act as a form of 'restriction of liberty' fall into the following main categories:

- imprisonment (which may be immediate or suspended: below) or detention in a young offender institution (YOI);[16]
- the generic community sentence;
- fines;
- discharges (below);
- compensation (as a penalty in its own right or as an ancillary order); and
- ancillary orders as described later in the chapter.[17]

Discharge

These can be used where punishment is 'inexpedient'. An absolute discharge signifies a technical offence or extreme triviality. It puts matters at an end, and involves the offender in no further obligations or liability—other than that it ranks (as all sentences now do) as a conviction for the purposes of a criminal record. An offender may be conditionally discharged for up to three years. The

---

[16] There is provision for YOI to be replaced by imprisonment under the Criminal Justice Act 2003.

[17] A special range of sentences applies in relation to juveniles.

condition is that he or she does not commit another criminal offence in that time after which the discharge will lapse. If a fresh offence is committed during the period fixed by the court, the offender can be sentenced afresh for the offence in respect of which the conditional discharge was made. The offender then faces sentence for both matters. Conditional discharges rank as convictions.

Maximum sentences

The maximum sentence for an offence is laid down in legislation. Thus, e.g. the Crown Court can sentence within certain statutory limits:

- life imprisonment: see, further, the brief note later in this chapter;
- 14 years: house burglary, blackmail, handling stolen property;
- ten years: non-domestic burglary, obtaining by deception, criminal damage, indecent assault on a woman;
- seven years: theft, false accounting;
- five years: causing actual bodily harm; and
- two years: carrying an offensive weapon, aggravated vehicle taking.

The maximum term of imprisonment in the magistrates' court for an individual offence is six months; or 12 months in aggregate where consecutive sentences are passed for two or more offences.[18] It is common legislative practice for ancillary powers (see later) to be fixed by reference to whether or not an offence is 'imprisonable'[19] (e.g. the power to make an attendance centre order in respect of a young offender, issue a warrant, or include a particular requirement in a generic community sentence). Fines and compensation are not limited by statute in the Crown Court, but by reasonableness and the doctrine of proportionality (*Chapter 2*). Each has a ceiling of £5,000 per offence in the magistrates' court (subject, in the case of fines, to other ceilings set by five statutory fine levels).[20]

Aspects of the sentencing framework

The first comprehensive statutory sentencing framework was that in the Criminal Justice Act 1991.[21] This was replaced by that now in place under the Criminal Justice Act 2003.[22] Managing sentence-related aspects of the law-making and law

---

[18]   Increased to 12 months under the Criminal Justice Act 2003 (when in force).

[19]   i.e. the fact that an offence attracts imprisonment, even if not being imposed.

[20]   Currently (2008) Level 1: £100; Level 2: £200; Level 3: £1,000; Level 4: £2,500; Level 5: £5,000.

[21]   Based on the White Paper, *Crime Justice and Protecting the Public* (1990); Cm. 965 and concerned mainly with a 'just deserts' or 'commensurate' approach to sentencing.

[22]   The provisions of the CJA 2003 are set out in some detail in *The Criminal Justice Act 2003: A Guide to the New Procedures and Sentencing* (2004), Gibson B, Waterside Press. They stem from the White Paper, *Justice For All* (2002); Cm, 5563, based on recommendations in *Making Punishments Work: Report of a Review of the Sentencing Framework for England and Wales* (2001); Home Office

reform process is a key task of the MOJ. Guidance or guidelines created largely by the SGC are then overlaid on the legislative provisions. It would be impossible in a handbook of this type to describe the whole sentencing framework. More important here, is to describe what, in broad terms, it sets out to achieve. The framework in the Criminal Justice Act 2003 is contained principally in Part 12 of that Act which comprises nine chapters covering the general structure of the sentencing framework and specific aspects of it, ranging from life sentences and indeterminate sentences for public protection (ISPPs)[23] to long-term sentences of imprisonment (over four years) and short-term sentences of imprisonment (12 months to under four years) to what are termed 'sentences below 12 months'.[24] There is a separate tier of community-based options—now, since this change in 2003, known as the generic community sentence—from whose menu of requirements a court may select those that are most suitable for a given offender in a particular case.[25] The requirements are or concern:

- unpaid work to be carried out by the offender;
- his or her taking part in certain activities;
- similarly participation in programmes;
- a prohibition preventing him or her taking part in given activities;
- a curfew;
- exclusion from certain places;
- his or her place of residence;
- mental health treatment;
- drug rehabilitation;
- alcohol treatment;
- general supervision by a probation officer; and
- attendance at an attendance centre (up to age 25).[26]

Electronic monitoring (known as 'tagging') can be added to any of the 12 basic requirements and normally will be in relation certain ones such as a curfew. The

---

('The Halliday Report') that recommended that the sentencing framework should do more to support crime reduction and reparation whilst meeting the needs of punishment. There remains some difficulty in explaining the framework in full as a new scheme of sentences 'below 12 months' in the 2003 Act, comprising 'custody plus' and 'intermittent custody' has not been implemented (except for short-lived experiments and 'custody minus', i.e. the new-style suspended sentence). That scheme is explained in the work noted at the start of this footnote.

23 Certain amendments in the Criminal Justice and Immigration Bill seek to give force to what this sentence implies: a substantial period of custody followed by a long period of supervision.

24 As noted in an earlier footnote, this key aspect of the 2003 Act still awaits implementation.

25 The Criminal Justice and Immigration Bill (2008) would limit the power to make such sentences to offences which are imprisonable, as once applied to unpaid work (then community service).

26 Comparable requirements can be used in relation to post-custody supervision. Better use of such requirements at all stages is one way to tackle prison overcrowding. See, generally, *Chapter 14*.

2003 Act also deals afresh with deferment of sentence (see later in the chapter). A Drug Treatment and Testing Order (DTTO) was introduced by the Crime and Disorder Act 1998, so as to combine intensive offender supervision-cum-contact with drug treatment, regular drug-testing and review of progress by the courts. In 2003, the DTTO was replaced by the similar drug-related requirement within the generic community sentence, so that it is now possible to combine drug requirements with others such as unpaid work or a curfew. The 2003 Act also makes provision with regard, e.g. to firearms offences. Its extensive provisions about release from custody on parole, release licences, post-custody supervision, breach, enforcement and recall to prison are touched upon in *Chapters 13* and *14*.

At the time of the 2003 Act, its framework was promulgated as being clearer and more flexible than that in the 1991 Act. A further intention of Government was that courts would be equipped to provide every offender with a sentence 'that best meets the needs of his or her particular case', it being claimed that this way he or she would be more effectively managed.[27] The new arrangements occurred at the same time as a fundamental reconstruction of HM Prison Service (HMPS) and the Probation Service: *Chapters 13* and *14*. Despite the aspirations of these changes, some critics have been sceptical as a result of the various practical difficulties that have arisen in trying to meet them, a continual rise in the prisoner population leading to overcrowding and its attendant problems, such as the stifling effect that this has on prison regimes, programmes, courses and education. There have also been complaints more generally about lack of resources for generic community sentences which have an effect, not just on the availability of key requirements, but the capacity to enforce these and other orders, such as those in relation to drug requirements (above).

Imprisonment: a note

Except where it is mandatory, including for public protection purposes, imprisonment has always been seen as a sentence of last resort.[28] In relation to discretionary custodial sentences the Criminal Justice Act 2003 retained a 'so serious' threshold test for custody subject to certain modifications and a new emphasis on what a court must not do (below). Section 152(2) provides:

> The court must not pass a custodial sentence unless it is of the opinion that the offence, or the combination of the offence and one or more offences associated with it, was so serious that neither a fine alone nor a community sentence can be justified for the offence.

---

[27] One problem with this is what some practitioners call the risk of going too far 'up-tariff', i.e. given an inviting menu there is a temptation to construct complex or weighty sentences, leaving nowhere to go next time round but an even more punitive sentence. In broad terms all sentences should reflect the seriousness of the offence and a proportionate restriction of liberty.

[28] Prison regimes are described in *Chapter 14* as is the scheme for early release from imprisonment.

An offender can also be imprisoned if he or she refuses consent to a requirement of a community sentence which requires consent (few now do) or in analogous circumstances on breach of a community order or an order for a pre-sentence drug test. Other more severe provisions cover the situation where a sentence is needed for public protection with the result that the outcome may be a substantial sentence with a long period of supervision in the community afterwards. In all cases the question about the length of a sentence is separate and apart, but follows on, from that concerning whether a prison sentence should be used in the first place. With discretionary sentences, these 'must be for the shortest term ... that in the opinion of the court is commensurate with the seriousness of the offence, or the combination of the offence and one or more offences associated with it'.[29]

If discretionary imprisonment is used, the court must give its reasons for this. If the offender is not legally represented, state funded legal representation will be offered and a pre-sentence report (PSR) normally obtained and considered. Where there are several offences, separate terms of imprisonment can be made to run concurrently (simultaneously) or consecutively (one after another) and any earlier suspended sentence (below) can put into effect at the same time, when the latter term must normally be ordered to take effect consecutively.

Offenders below 21 years of age cannot currently be sent to prison but are sentenced to detention in a young offender institution (YOI).[30] Detention in a YOI cannot be suspended but always takes effect immediately.

Suspended sentence of imprisonment

Imprisonment may be suspended for between one and two years.[31] The court must first be satisfied that imprisonment is appropriate—and then go on to decide that, in the circumstances, it is correct to suspend its operation. Until 2003 there had to be 'exceptional circumstances' to justify suspension, but that requirement has now gone. If it suspends the sentence, the court must also consider imposing a fine and compensation. Reasons for imprisonment must be announced, even though the sentence is being suspended. If the offender then commits another offence within the operational period of the suspended sentence, the suspended sentence falls to be activated. Normally it will be activated, unless there is some very cogent reason for not doing so. The court can: take no action; alter the operational period (including, in effect, by re-starting it for a new two year period); or activate the sentence for a shorter term than that

---

[29] See section 153 Criminal Justice Act 2003 and related provisions.
[30] But this is scheduled to be replaced by imprisonment for people age 18 to 20 inclusive. There are other differences in the range of sentences available for this age group.
[31] The Criminal Justice and Immigration Bill (2008) disallows such sentences re summary offences.

originally imposed and suspended. An activated sentence will normally be ordered to run consecutively with any other sentence of imprisonment. Under the Criminal Justice Act 2003, conditions can be attached to a suspended sentence and breach of these can also lead to activation of the suspended sentence.[32]

Mandatory sentences and lifers: a note

Historically, the only mandatory sentence was the death penalty for murder, replaced since 1969 by a mandatory life sentence. In modern times, Parliament has passed various measures that have the effect of curtailing the discretion of the judiciary in relation to specific areas of sentencing: these include additional mandatory sentences of imprisonment such as those under the 'three strikes' law,[33] indefinite sentences for public protection from what, in effect, are dangerous, violent or sexual offenders, and minimum sentences for certain firearms offences. The dangerous offender provisions are mainly addressed to three distinct categories of offenders:

- people sentenced to life imprisonment (often called 'lifers');
- certain other long-term prisoners who receive ISPPs (above); and
- other, possibly lesser—though still dangerous violent and sexual— offenders for whom the 2003 Act creates extended sentences.

The extended part of such a sentence involves supervision in the community on release (often for a substantial period as set by the court), once an appropriate custodial term—known as a tariff and fixed by the judge (commensurate with the seriousness of the offence) has been served. Such sentences have attracted complaints from the judiciary that their hands are being increasingly tied by legislation, making true justice, fairness and consistency difficult or impossible. Situations in which judges have been obliged to pass certain sentences of this kind have led to tensions between the Government, Parliament and the judiciary and any future new constitution (*Chapter 15*) might be expected to touch on such matters. A similar standoff developed in relation to mandatory tariffs for offenders subject to life imprisonment or ISPPs, where, certainly at one stage and with a degree of irony, the Government sought to blame the judiciary for the escalating prison population (*Chapter 14*)—a slight that was later withdrawn. More generally, the convention is that ministers do not publicly criticise the judiciary in this way but rather have respect for its role. There are special

---

[32] The suspended sentence regime was altered (and may be further affected) by the 2003 Act.

[33] As it is known in the USA. In the UK, there is a 'two-strikes 'life-sentence for a second serious violent or sexual offence; and a minimum sentences of three years for a third offence of domestic burglary, or seven years for a third offence of supplying Class A drugs.

regimes within HM Prison Service (HMPS) for prisoners serving life sentences of whatever kind and a life sentence prisoner remains on licence after his or her eventual release for the rest of his or her natural life and can be recalled to prison at any time, e.g. if there is cause for concern about his or her behaviour.

The wide-ranging extent of sentencing considerations

As already intimated above, a wide range of inter-connected matters affect sentencing decisions. One practice that has developed is that of structured decision-making, which seeks to ensure that all relevant matters are taken into account and that irrelevant matters are discounted. This method involves the court in working through a series of stages or steps and also formulating reasons as it does so. Among key aspects of the framework that can only be mentioned here in barest outline[34] are such matters as:

- threshold tests for:
  - community sentences (known as the 'serious enough' test, i.e. serious enough for a community sentence rather than a fine or discharge); and
  - custodial sentences (known as the 'so serious' test, i.e. where the offence is so serious that neither a discharge, fine or community sentence can be justified for the particular offence in question);
- statutory purposes of sentencing (see further below); and
- an emphasis on:
  - drug-testing and rehabilitation, both before and as part of a sentence;
  - electronic monitoring in relation to a community order or when an offender is released from prison after or during a custodial sentence including on what is known as home detention curfew (HDC);
  - discounts (in effect) for a timely plea of guilty;[35]
  - the idea of reviewable sentences and far stricter enforcement;
  - totality and proportionality, i.e. if several sentences are being imposed on someone at the same time this should be looked at globally or 'in the round' and more generally all (non-mandatory) sentences should be in proportion (or at least not disproportionate) to the seriousness of the offence or offences committed by the offender;
  - disqualifications, especially those concerning working with children;
  - new approaches to the imposition and collection of financial penalties;
  - priority being given to compensation;[36] and
  - identifying and dealing appropriately with mental impairment.

---

[34] The framework is set out in *A Guide to the CJA 2003, etc.* noted in an earlier footnote.

[35] All now the subject of work and guidance by the SGC.

[36] See, also, now the reference to the Victim Surcharge Fund in *Chapter 15*.

Statutory purposes of sentencing

Historically, these have included items such as punishment, retribution, rehabilitation, protection of the public, crime prevention, marking public concern and deterrence.[37] In relation to youth justice the principal statutory purpose (which appears to include sentencing) is preventing offending. The CJA 2003 introduced statutory purposes of sentencing for adults that 'any court dealing with an [such an] offender . . . must have regard to' in arriving at its decision. These are listed in section 142(1) CJA 2003 as follows:

(a) the punishment of offenders;
(b) the reduction of crime (including through deterrence);
(c) the reform and rehabilitation of offenders;
(d) protecting the public; and
(e) reparation by offenders to people affected by their offences.

Section 143 CJA 2003 also sets out certain matters a sentencer must consider in determining the seriousness of an offence:

- the offender's culpability in committing the offence; and
- any harm caused by the offence, intended by it, or which 'might foreseeably' have been caused.

There are some situations in which a court is required by law to treat an offence as more serious than it would otherwise have done, e.g. if it is committed whilst on bail, involves racial or religious aggravation (also known as 'hate crime') or there are previous relevant convictions and thus, in practice (and other things being equal), the court should use a more severe penalty. Other categories have been added to this rule concerning hostility based on sexual orientation or disability (also sometimes called hate crimes) and offences linked to terrorism.

SOME OTHER KEY ASPECTS OF SENTENCING

Given the breadth of the subject matter, only a few selected items can be included here. Other items that are directly connected to sentencing, particularly

---

[37] Perhaps the most controversial of all. Practitioners soon come to recognize the complex relationship between available sentences and their effects on conduct or behaviour as well as the distinction between general deterrence (i.e. aimed at everyone, especially those who might be tempted to commit similar offences) and individual deterrence (i.e. of the offender in question). The 2003 Act includes 'deterrence' without making any such distinction and on the assumption that judges and magistrates will know when it will have some purpose in fact.

with reference to the way in which orders of the court are administered and the diversion of offenders towards less punitive measures appear in other parts of this handbook, see, especially, *Chapters 13, 14* and *15*.

Pre-sentence reports (PSRs)

If the likely (sometimes called 'predictive') sentence is a generic community sentence or custody, the case will normally be adjourned (i.e. put back for a number of weeks, usually three) for a PSR. The nature of the PSR is described in *Chapter 13*. In practice, PSRs or specific sentence reports (SSRs) (see also that chapter) are obtained in all the more serious cases—and with the possibility of reports from doctors and psychiatrists in addition.

Compensation and the victims' surcharge

By law, compensation to a victim of crime ('the aggrieved') must come before any punishment by way of a fine. This statutory rule was introduced to make sure that the victim of a crime receives recompense where the offender can afford this. Compensation should also be an automatic consideration in all other cases. It may be used in addition to any other method of dealing with the offender, or can stand alone as a sentence. Courts must give reasons for *not* awarding compensation where they could have done so. As part of the compensation process, matters concerning victims often nowadays encompass the use of a 'victim personal statement' (*Chapters 13* and *15*). Quite separately, the Criminal Cases Compensation Authority (CCCA) has a scale of payments that can be paid to victims of violent crime. There is also, since 2007, under the Domestic Violence, Crimes and Victims Act 2004, a victims' surcharge of £15 that is added to each fine. Rarely, victims receive compensation from the criminal courts if the offender is sent to prison and in many instances is thereby automatically deprived of the earning capacity necessary to fund such payments. Technically, an action can also be brought in the civil courts when similar questions are likely to prevail, i.e. will the offender have the money?[38] Some offenders make voluntary recompense ahead of being sentenced which they then ask the court to take into account when deciding upon the appropriate sentence. Such moves are also encouraged by restorative justice (see *Chapter 15*).

Costs and witnesses' expenses

Costs may be awarded against either party according to the outcome of a criminal case and events which occur during the proceedings. Where a

---

[38] An aspect that reached the public consciousness when the so-called 'Lotto Rapist', Ioworth Hoare, serving life imprisonment imposed 15 years earlier for attempted rape, won £7 million with a ticket bought whilst on day release from prison in 2004. His victims are pursuing Hoare in the courts, the House of Lords having ruled, innovatively, that their claims are admissible.

defendant is acquitted, or the case is withdrawn, abandoned or discontinued, he or she is normally entitled to costs from public funds. Costs can be ordered to be paid by the CPS or other prosecutor as appropriate. Conversely, a convicted defendant might expect to have to pay all or part of the costs of the prosecution, including those of any civilian witnesses who attended court to give evidence. Courts can also order legal representatives to pay costs where these have been wasted due to their actions, known colloquially as a 'wasted costs order'.

Other ancillary orders

Apart from costs and compensation (both above), other ancillary orders include: disqualification, e.g. from driving, endorsement of a driving licence with penalty points (that may lead to a 'totting up' disqualification if 12 points are accumulated, broadly speaking within three years), being a company director or keeping an animal. They also include confiscation, forfeiture or destruction of items, assets, offensive weapons, drugs, forged documents, implements used to commit or attempt to commit crime and the like, as well as restitution of stolen property or that obtained by deception. A restraining order can be made under the Protection From Harassment Act 1997, prohibiting specified conduct by the offender and breach of which is a criminal offence and the Criminal Justice and Public Order Act 1994 made such orders more widely available. From the end of the 1990s, there has also been the rise of the anti-social behaviour order that can have similar effects and precipitate subsequent criminal charges for failure to comply. The equally wide-ranging criminal anti-social behaviour order (or CRASBO) can be made as an ancillary order in criminal proceedings. This has similar ramifications to an ASBO in terms of the person against whom it is made being dealt with in the criminal courts if its terms are not kept to. Often, in the case of a foreign national, a sentence of imprisonment will be accompanied by a recommendation that the offender be deported to his or her home country at the end of his or her sentence. The decision is then one for the Home Secretary.[39]

Previous convictions

As indicated at the beginning of the chapter, it is the practice *after* conviction for the sentencing judge or magistrates to consider the offender's character and antecedents, including his or her previous convictions if any. These can be taken into account when assessing the seriousness of the present offence—as can failures to respond to previous sentences. Previous convictions were only rarely admissible *before* conviction, e.g. where a defendant attacked the character of a

---

[39] Failure to subsequently action such matters, or 'the foreign prisoner crisis' was one of the reasons behind the departure from office of Charles Clarke MP as Home Secretary in 2006.

prosecution witness his or her own character can be made known. But certain changes in this regard occurred in the Criminal Justice Act 2003 (see *Chapter 2*).

Offences taken into consideration (TICs)

The prosecutor may also produce a list of TICs. The non-statutory practice of a defendant asking for outstanding offences—for which he or she has not been prosecuted—to be taken into consideration developed as a way of encouraging offenders to 'make a clean breast' of things. Although not restricted in scope, applications are commonplace where the main prosecuted offences and the TICs are triable either way and similar in kind (i.e. 'a string of similar offences'). Endorsable motoring offences may become TICs if the principal offence carries a power to disqualify. The defendant is usually asked to sign the list in which the TICs are set out. In the event of a refusal by an offender to accept them, the prosecutor must decide whether to bring charges or let matters drop. It is common practice once someone has been convicted for police officers to try to 'clear up' any further outstanding offences that may have been committed by an offender where this has not already occurred. Similarly, even following a sentence of imprisonment in the hope that outstanding files can be closed.[40]

Deferment of sentence

Deferment is intended to deal with the situation where—because of what a court has learned about the offender—it considers that it is proper to postpone the sentencing decision so as to have regard to his or her conduct after conviction (including, where appropriate, the making by him of any reparation for his offence) or changes to his or her circumstances. The arrangements were revised and strengthened by the Criminal Justice Act 2003[41] by providing for reparative or similar activity to be undertaken during the period of deferment, and requiring the court to consider 'how well the offender complied'. Good progress on the part of the offender is thus likely to operate as a mitigating factor with regard to his or her eventual sentence. Sentence can be deferred only if the offender consents; and if he or she also undertakes to comply with any requirements laid down by the court—and only where the court considers that deferment is in the interests of justice. It cannot remand an offender when it defers sentencing; and sentencing cannot be deferred for more than six months.

Post-CJA 2003, the court can include requirements about an offender's residence. If he or she is to undertake requirements, it may appoint a supervisor to monitor compliance (a probation officer or anyone else the court sees fit).

---

[40] Also in relation to more serious 'cold cases' in the hope of solving them, when the offender is unlikely to escape the consequences simply because he or she is already in prison.

[41] See section 278 etc. amending the Powers of Criminal Courts (Sentencing) Act 2000.

Under the new provisions, the court can deal with the offender before the end of the period of deferment if satisfied that he or she has failed to comply with one or more requirements or if he or she commits another offence.

Discount (or 'credit') for a timely guilty plea

The principle of allowing a discount on the basis that an offender has saved time, expense, resources and not put a victim or witnesses through the ordeal of appearing in court is well-established and depending on its timing such a plea has normally attracted a sentence discount of 'up to about one third'. Reflecting existing law and practice built up over many years, the 2003 Act states that there should normally be a reduction in sentence in return for a timely plea of guilty. It provides that where an offender pleads guilty, the court must 'take into account' the stage in the proceedings when his or her intention to do so was indicated and the circumstances of that indication.[42] There is also a special rule in relation to required custodial sentences when the court is 'not prevented' from making a reduction to reflect a guilty plea provided that the sentence imposed is not less than 80 per cent of the required sentence.

No separate penalty

In magistrates' courts the practice of imposing no separate penalty (NSP) is regularly used. This device is employed when a defendant stands convicted of several offences but the totality of his or her offending behaviour can be dealt with by sentencing for the main offences only. This non-statutory approach might be used, e.g. where there is a catalogue of motoring or other minor offences, but where justice can be done by sentencing for just some of them.

Enforcement

Modern times have seen an emphasis on the enforcement of court orders; a concerted effort by courts, probation staff and other practitioners to make sure that action is taken concerning any default or breach—and by the police to make sure that recalcitrant offenders do not disappear and are returned to court. Financial orders, whether imposed in the Crown Court or magistrates' court, are enforced and collected by the magistrates' court. This is by way of a means inquiry, i.e. a court hearing to which the defaulter is summoned to give his or her explanation for non-payment, including by providing a financial statement. The main enforcement methods are: attachment of earnings orders (AEOs); distress warrants (i.e. sending in the bailiffs to seize possessions); money payment supervision orders (MPSOs); attachment of state benefits; and committal to prison for wilful refusal to pay but only after a full means enquiry

---

42   See section 144.

and subsequent review if committal to prison for non-payment is suspended on terms, e.g. £20 a week. The court can ensure disclosure of income or assets by making a financial circumstances order. Committals are by reference to a scale matching maximum periods of imprisonment to amounts unpaid. There are some 20,000 committals a year for fine default, usually for quite short periods. A defaulter can buy himself or herself out of prison by settling the amount due. Wider pursuit of the proceeds of crime is mentioned in *Chapter 2*.

With generic community sentences, there is either punishment for breach of an order or a court can sometimes revoke the order and sentence afresh, e.g. by way of a differently constituted generic community sentence or imprisonment. Much will depend on the extent of compliance and the length of time for which the order has already run, as well as the level of performance by and attitude to the order of the offender. Again, this has been tightened-up considerably.[43]

MENTAL IMPAIRMENT

Mental impairment can affect a criminal case at various points, including diversion from the criminal justice process altogether into hospital or other facilities. The accused may be mentally unfit to plead as certified by two doctors. There is a defence of insanity although this is not commonly encountered in the present day and age: at a time of capital punishment it was a way of avoiding execution. There is also a defence of diminished responsibility that reduces what would have been a murder conviction to one of manslaughter, thereby giving the judge a discretion concerning sentence (as opposed to a mandatory life sentence). Where the accused is shown to be mentally impaired in what would have been a life sentence case, this will usually result in him or her being ordered to be detained at Her Majesty's pleasure without limit of time.

In other cases, the Mental Health Act 1983 allows courts to dispose of cases in a variety of ways when problems arise from the defendant's mental state. This includes power to make hospital orders or guardianship orders (the latter usually supervised in the community by the local authority). Also, conditions of treatment for a person's mental state can be a requirement of a generic community orders as already noted above. If an offender is sent to hospital, a judge of the Crown Court (but not magistrates) can make an order preventing his or her discharge solely at the behest of the hospital authorities. This is known as an order restricting discharge. Further examination of these important

---

[43]   In contrast to the greater leeway that may have been allowed to offenders in the past. However, some of that was no doubt a recognition that a level of tolerance might eventually succeed with certain offenders who are often people with chaotic lifestyles.

but specialist areas are beyond the scope of this handbook but some further information does appear in *Chapter 13*.

BINDING OVER TO KEEP THE PEACE: A NOTE

This ancient jurisdiction to bind over citizens can be used to mark behaviour which might lead to a breach of the peace—as a form of 'preventive justice'. It stems from the Justices of the Peace Act 1361. Bind overs were to some extent curtailed by human rights considerations and have since been largely superseded in practice by the anti-social behaviour order (ASBO) (*Chapter 2*).

SENTENCING GUIDELINES COUNCIL (SGC)

Sentencing guidelines have a long and reputable history. Hence, e.g. Court of Appeal guidelines stemming from certain key rulings by that court when dealing with an appeal against sentence (*Chapter 10*) have long been termed 'guideline cases'. Other mechanisms have included guidelines created by the Magistrates' Association (*Chapter 12*) or local benches of magistrates. These are now being superseded by or operating in tandem with the work of the Sentencing Guidelines Council (SGC). The SGC is headed by the Lord Chief Justice and promulgates advice and guidance to all those who pass sentences. It has seven other judicial members and four non-judicial members to reflect the views of people regularly dealing with criminal cases. Under the Criminal Justice Act 2003, by which the SGC was established, other members are drawn from the ranks, e.g. of the police, prosecutors, defence lawyers and people concerned with 'the promotion of the welfare of victims of crime'. Amongst those 'eligible by experience' is the Director of Public Prosecutions (DPP) (see, generally, *Chapter 7*). The Lord Chancellor must consult with the SGC at one arms-length, but can appoint an experienced observer who may attend, and speak at, meetings of the SGC. The former can also make proposals. The SGC must report annually to Ministers. It is supported by a secretariat that acts as a liaison point for interested parties, administers consultations, and provides information. Crucially, once a sentencing guideline is definitive, then, under section 172 of the 2003 Act, all courts must follow it, or, if it departs from the guideline, explain why it is not being adhered to in an individual case.

The Sentencing Advisory Panel (SAP)
The SGC is supported by a Sentencing Advisory Panel (SAP) (originally set up under the Crime and Disorder Act 1998 and thus pre-dating the SGC by some

five years). The SAP is no longer confined, as it once was, to suggesting 'approaches' to particular types of offences. It is appointed by the Lord Chancellor (after consultation with the Lord Chief Justice) who also appoints its chair. It is responsible for research into sentencing and for producing reports and information. The outcome of its findings and deliberations are passed to the SCG for consideration together with data and other relevant materials. The SAP may make proposals to the SGC which the SGC must then consider. In the opposite direction, the SGC must notify the SAP of any proposed or revised guidelines and the SAP must consult with any further people stipulated by the SGC (except in cases of urgency) and then respond to the SGC.

Guidelines

A key aspect of the provisions are those whereby the SGC may from time to time consider whether to frame sentencing guidelines and under which the Lord Chancellor[44] may propose to the SGC that this ought to occur (or that existing guidelines should be revised) in respect of:

- offences or offenders of a particular category; or
- a particular matter affecting sentencing.

The SGC must then consider such proposals (plus any from the SAP) and, in effect, decide whether or not to act upon them. This represents a critical buffer in terms of the independence of the judiciary (*Chapter 2*). There are the following statutory criteria when considering the issue of sentencing guidelines:

- the need to promote consistency in sentencing;
- the sentences imposed by courts in England and Wales;
- the cost of different sentences and their relative effectiveness in preventing offending;
- the need to promote public confidence in the criminal justice system; and
- the views communicated to the SGC by the SAP.

The SGC can act of its own initiative to create guidelines and there are various provisions aimed at keeping SGC guidelines current and up-to-date. As intimated above, the SGC must consider whether to frame guidelines if it

---

[44] Post-MOJ. Formerly this fell to the home secretary, quite correctly in terms of the then legislative function concerning criminal offences, but somewhat questionably in overall constitutional terms. The pre-2003 Act proposals included one suggestion that Parliament should have a role in the framing of sentencing guidelines or that a (then) home office official should sit as a member of the SGC. Again, an entrenched constitution or fundamental law (*Chapter 6*) might be expected to cover such matters.

receives a guidelines proposal from the SAP (as it must where this stems from the Lord Chancellor: above). Guidelines must be kept under review and the SGC must revise them if appropriate (section 170(5)); there is a statutory process of drafts, consultation and eventual publication (section 170(8), (9)). As already indicated above, courts must follow the definitive guidelines of the SGC or explain themselves alongside the new statutory reasoning process already referred to earlier in this chapter.

It has published a range of guidelines, advice or proposals, including on such matters as: assault, Bail Act 1976 offences, domestic violence, 'discounts' for guilty pleas, robbery, sexual offences, manslaughter and causing death by dangerous driving. It has also referred certain matters such as child pornography to the Court of Appeal.[45]

OTHER INFLUENCES ON SENTENCING

The Lord Chancellor has a statutory duty to publish information about sentencing. Section 175 Criminal Justice Act 2003 extended a key provision: that in section 95 Criminal Justice Act 1991, under which he or she is under a duty to publish information to people engaged in the administration of justice concerning the costs of different types of sentence and a range of discrimination issues extending to such matters as race, religion, gender or hate crime. Thus, various people concerned with the administration of justice now regularly receive information from the MOJ (formerly from the Home Office) so that they can be aware of 'the relative effectiveness of different sentences in ... preventing re-offending and ... promoting public confidence in the criminal justice system'.

A proposed Sentencing Commission

An independent Sentencing Commission Working Group (SCWG) is seeking views on how a structured sentencing framework could be adapted for England and Wales, drawing references from experiences in the USA.[46] The general aim is to develop a set of proposals to improve the operation of the CJS in relation to sentencing. In its consultation paper, the SCWG notes that:

> Recent years have seen a rapidly rising prison population ... leading to extensive use of police cells, the use of court cells and the introduction of the early release scheme [known as] 'end of custody licence' which reduced demand for prison places by about 1300 places. Since then the population has continued to grow and [has

---

[45] Full details appear at www.sentencing-guidelines.gov.uk

[46] See Sentencing Commission Working Group, A Consultation Paper: A Structured Sentencing Framework and Sentencing Commission (2008) available at www.judiciary.gov.uk

reached] the edge of capacity despite the new spaces brought on stream by the current building programme. There is therefore a continuing inconsistency between the demand for and supply of correctional capacity, both for probation and imprisonment ...

The paper also contains a wealth of information, data and views on the state of sentencing in England and Wales and the outcome of its work is likely to be highly influential in shaping any revised sentencing framework.

CHAPTER 10

Appeal and Review

It is fundamental in a democratic society that channels exist by which the decisions of courts and other public authorities can be challenged, reviewed and, if shown to be wrong, corrected. As noted in *Chapter 5* when looking at the structure of the courts, various domestic channels of appeal exist for people convicted and sentenced by the Crown Court or a magistrates' court, whether against conviction, sentence or both. Ultimately there are various ways of testing the law and its correct application, whether in relation to offences, procedure, sentencing or the administration of sentences—all of which now takes place in a human rights context. The creation of the new Supreme Court from 2009 has also been noted and everything said in this chapter must be read against that backdrop.

Within the court hierarchy, appeals may concern the facts of a case (often styled 'the merits'), the law or both (sometimes described as 'mixed fact and law' signifying that the point at issue is affected by both). UK domestic courts apply English law in the light of the European Convention On Human Rights and Fundamental Freedoms (*Chapters 2* and *5*) to which appropriate appeals can also be made (see later in the chapter). Additionally, miscarriages of justice can be corrected by the Court of Appeal following a reference to it of a case by the Criminal Cases Review Commission (CCRC) which is charged with investigating such matters at the behest of the person who has been convicted.

APPEALING TO THE COURT OF APPEAL

Anyone convicted and sentenced by the Crown Court can appeal to the Court of Appeal against conviction, sentence or both. This includes the situation where sentence is imposed in the Crown Court following committal for sentence by magistrates and since the Criminal Justice Act 2003, without the need for the former minimum threshold of at least a six month sentence of imprisonment.[1] The Court of Appeal (Criminal Division) is situated in the Royal Courts of

---

[1] See section 319. The 2003 Act does away with committals for sentence, when in force.

Justice in London (situated in London in, and hence known as, 'The Strand'). Courts comprise the Lord Chief Justice and Lords Justices of Appeal assisted by High Court judges.[2] A further appeal may be made to the House of Lords when it has been certified that a point of law of general public importance is involved and the Court of Appeal or the House of Lords grants leave to appeal. A prisoner can be released on bail following his or her application to the Court of Appeal but this is unusual and, generally speaking, will continue to serve his or her sentence as a convicted prisoner and subject to the regime for such prisoners (*Chapter 14*). Certain commentators have described as Kafkaesque the situation whereby a prisoner who maintains his or her innocence after conviction will be deemed to be in denial for the purposes of release decisions and may be barred by his or her protestations from taking part in offending behaviour or other courses as a prelude to gaining his or her freedom.[3]

Appeal against conviction

A defendant may appeal against his or her conviction as of right on any question of law (e.g. whether the judge properly directed the jury by correctly outlining the ingredients of the offence). In cases which involve questions of fact (e.g. whether the jury should have convicted on the evidence in the case) the offender may only appeal if he or she obtains a certificate from the trial judge that the case is fit for appeal or, more usually, leave from the Court of Appeal. Originally, the governing statute, the Criminal Appeal Act 1968, provided that:

- a conviction should be set aside on the grounds that in all the circumstances of the case it was unsafe or unsatisfactory; or
- the judgment of the court of trial should be set aside on the grounds of a wrong decision on any question of law; or on the basis that there was a material irregularity in the course of the trial.

Somewhat tortuously, the court could also dismiss an appeal when, although there had been a wrong decision on a point of law or irregularity in the trial, it considered that no miscarriage of justice had actually occurred. Following the report of the Royal Commission on Criminal Justice in 1993 and subsequent amendments to the 1968 Act contained in the Criminal Appeal Act 1995, the law

---

[2] For a note of each of these judicial personnel, see *Chapter 12*.

[3] See, e.g. *The Longest Injustice: The Strange Story of Alex Alexandrowicz* (1999), Alexandrowicz A and Wilson D, Waterside Press. HM Prison Service would probably claim that it could not function if special arrangements had to be made for everyone convicted by the courts claiming to be innocent and that conferring some special status would simply encourage tactical appeals.

was simplified so that there is now a single requirement, i.e. that the court shall allow an appeal against conviction if it thinks that the conviction is unsafe.[4]

Appeal against sentence

Appeals against sentence to the Court of Appeal always require the leave of the Court of Appeal. The Court may quash a sentence imposed by the Crown Court and in its place substitute any sentence which that court could have imposed. It must exercise its powers so that, taking the case as a whole, the applicant is not more severely dealt with on appeal than by the Crown Court.

Application for leave to appeal

In order to obtain leave from the Court of Appeal, the appellant must within 28 days of conviction or sentence file an application for leave and notice of the grounds of appeal. The application is considered by a single judge on the basis of a written application for leave and any supporting material sent with the application. If the single judge refuses the application, the appellant may apply to the full court against that decision. In order to discourage appellants who have no chance of success, the single judge or the full court may direct that time spent in custody pending the appeal hearing shall not count towards the sentence. However, this power is not often exercised and may now, in any event, have human rights implications.

Prosecution references to the Court of Appeal[5]

The Attorney General (see, generally, *Chapter 12*) may refer a case to the Court of Appeal in order to seek a ruling on a point of law which has been material in a case where a person is tried on indictment. The Court of Appeal has power to refer the point to the House of Lords if necessary. The ruling will constitute a binding precedent (*Chapters 2* and *4*), but any acquittal in the original case is not affected. Also, where he or she considers that an over-lenient (frequently described as an 'unduly lenient') sentence has been passed by the Crown Court in certain circumstances. The power is restricted to the most serious offences. It applies to all those which are indictable only and to a number of offences which are triable either way (both as explained in *Chapter 2*) and, in relation to the latter, which are specified by order as being subject to the power to refer. The Criminal Justice Act 1988 (Review of Sentencing) Order 2006 extended the

---

[4] There have been fresh suggestions that the Court of Appeal should nonetheless be required to uphold a conviction where it is satisfied that there has been no injustice.

[5] Contrast references by the Criminal Cases Review Commission (CCRC): see later in the chapter.

power to a number of offences including making threats to kill, cruelty to a child, certain serious and complex frauds, certain sexual offences, certain offences in relation to the illegal importation of controlled drugs or indecent material, the production, supply or possession with intent to supply of controlled drugs or the cultivation of cannabis, and to racially or religiously aggravated forms of assault, criminal damage, public order offences and aggravated forms of harassment. It also applies to attempting to commit or inciting the commission of all of these offences. It is also possible to refer the minimum term (or 'tariff') fixed before a prisoner convicted of murder and serving a life sentence can be considered for release (*Chapter 9*).

This concept was introduced by the Criminal Justice Act 1988[6] which provides that the sentence must 'fall outside the range of sentences which the judge, applying his or her mind to all the relevant factors, could reasonably consider appropriate'. The definition of 'reasonable factors' has been fleshed out over the years, in modern times controversially in relation to very serious offences due to the interaction of those provisions of the Criminal Justice Act 2003 under which a sentencing judge is required to take into account the stage at which a defendant pleads guilty and the circumstances in which an intention to plead guilty is indicated, i.e. those concerning discount for a guilty plea (*Chapter 9*). Requests to consider referring a sentence may stem, e.g. from the prosecuting authority, the victim or victim's family, Members of Parliament, pressure groups or members of the public. The law officers consider all requests for a sentence to be referred in this way. There is a strict time limit of 28 days from the date of sentence for the Attorney General to apply to the Court of Appeal to allow for the necessary court papers to be obtained and the legal situation to be considered where appropriate.[7]

Prosecution appeals against judges' rulings and evidentiary appeals

The Criminal Justice Act 2003 introduced a general right of appeal by a prosecutor in relation to certain decisions or evidentiary rulings by the judge in the course of criminal proceedings together with provisions for such appeals to become expedited appeals so that the trial itself is not disrupted or held up unduly. Although the prosecutor has these rights, they do not extend to a ruling that the jury be discharged or where an appeal can be made to the Court of Appeal under any other enactment, e.g. from a ruling at a preparatory hearing

---

6   See section 36 of that Act. As noted the right is cast on the Attorney General (*Chapter 12*).
7   There is no power to extend this.

about the admissibility of evidence or on a point of law. Leave to appeal must be obtained from the trial judge or the Court of Appeal.[8]

The 2003 Act forbids publication of reports of appeals occurring under the various provisions relating to decisions or rulings of the judge in the proceedings. The restriction ends with the conclusion of the relevant trial. Neither does it apply to the usual purely formal details, including the court venue, the nature of the offences, or the names of the accused person, witnesses and legal representatives. The Court of Appeal or the House of Lords can order a reporting restriction to be lifted, either in its entirety or to a specified extent. If one or more defendants objects to this, such an order can only be made if it would be in the interests of justice.[9]

Procedure on appeal

The hearing of the appeal is by a court of three judges. They will have received a note on the case prepared by a barrister employed by the Court of Appeal, which sets out a summary of the facts and arguments. Counsel on behalf of the appellant and respondent address the court and the decision is by a majority.

Rulings of the Court of Appeal and *Practice Directions*

Rulings of the Court of Appeal are regularly reported in the law reports and form part of the doctrine of precedent (*Chapters 2* and *4*). Closely allied to appeal rulings but not stemming from an individual case are *Practice Directions*. These are of a more general nature and usually set out broad advice on a given aspect of law or procedure. More often than not these are promulgated by the Lord Chief Justice. To an extent, procedural guidance is being superseded by the work of the Criminal Procedure Rules Committee (CPRC) noted in *Chapter 8*.

APPEALS TO THE CROWN COURT OR HIGH COURT

There are different avenues of appeal from magistrates' courts according to whether the subject matter involves a question of fact or sentence (when the appeal is to the Crown Court) or of law or the proper exercise of judicial discretion (when the appeal or application is to the High Court).

---

[8] These are listed in *The Criminal Justice Act 2003: A Guide to the New Procedures and Sentencing* (2004), Gibson B, Waterside Press.

[9] See section 71 of the 2003 Act. Section 72 creates various related offences.

Appeal from magistrates to the Crown Court

Anyone convicted of a criminal offence by magistrates can appeal to the Crown Court against conviction, sentence, or both. A prosecutor cannot appeal against an acquittal but can appeal by way of case stated where the magistrates have erred in law or formed an unreasonable conclusion. The convicted person must give notice of appeal within 21 days of being sentenced. This can be extended by the Crown Court (known as 'leave to appeal out of time'). The notice must give details of the conviction, sentence and set out the general grounds for appealing.

- *Appeal against conviction*
  This is heard by a judge sitting with two magistrates. There is no jury. The case is heard afresh. The Crown Court either upholds the conviction or substitutes an acquittal. If it convicts the accused it proceeds to sentence. The sentence must be within the maximum powers of the magistrates' court (*Chapter 9*), but, within that ceiling, the appellant always risks a more severe sentence at the discretion of the Crown Court.

- *Appeal against sentence* An appeal against sentence is heard by a judge sitting alone. The court is addressed by the appellant or his or her legal representative. The Crown Court judge can confirm the decision or substitute its own sentence, either more or less severe than that originally imposed by the magistrates but limited to magistrates' maximum powers of punishment (*Chapter 9*). Again, there is a risk of a more severe sentence.

Appeals from magistrates to the High Court

Appeals on points of law go to the Queen's Bench Division of the High Court of Justice (QBD)—where they are heard by a Divisional Court of the QBD. The court is presided over by the Lord Chief Justice, who by convention often sits in the court in person. Appeals may involve points of law of general importance, the outcome of which will have wide scale implications, but such appeals also extend to more mundane or narrow technicalities. Usually, three High Court judges will sit to hear such appeals—which are open to both the defendant and the prosecutor. Rulings (or 'judgements') of the Divisional Court constitute legally binding precedents (subject to any human rights considerations in relation to cases decided before the Human Rights Act 1998: *Chapter 4*). There are three methods of challenging a decision:

- *Case stated* Here the magistrates (or Crown Court where applicable: below) are required to state a case for the opinion of the High Court, i.e. to set out

in writing what facts they found to exist from the evidence in the case—
and then to say what law or legal principles they applied to those facts.
The Divisional Court will either uphold the magistrates' decision or make
some alternative order, e.g. to quash the conviction; or to order the
magistrates to rehear the case and apply the correct law and procedures.
The process starts with an application by *either* party for the magistrates to
state a case for the opinion of the High Court—which must be made within
21 days of the decision of the magistrates' court. Magistrates can refuse a
'frivolous' application, or ask the applicant to identify the point of law at
issue.

- *Judicial review* Anyone aggrieved by a decision of magistrates[10] may ask the
High Court to review the case in order to see whether, e.g. the magistrates'
court acted judicially, fairly and followed correct procedures. If not, the
remedy is one or more of the prerogative orders: *certiorari* to quash the
decision; *mandamus* to compel the magistrates to act properly (e.g. by re-
hearing the case in a proper manner); or *prohibition* to prevent magistrates
acting in error. Review must normally be pursued within six months.

- *Application for a declaration* Applications for declarations are unusual (due
to the existence of the standard remedies outlined so far). They are
applications to the Divisional Court by either party for that court to declare
the law on a particular point. Declarations are binding on public
authorities (e.g. magistrates' courts, the police, the Crown Prosecution
Service and Criminal Defence Service). There is no mechanism to ensure
compliance with a declaration but public authorities in particular will
usually follow their substance whenever possible.

Appeals from the Crown Court by way of case stated: a note

Where the Crown Court is sitting to hear appeals from magistrates' courts
(*Chapter 10*), its decisions cannot be challenged in the Court of Appeal.
However, the appellant has the right to apply for a case to be stated by the
Crown Court for determination of a point of law by the High Court. Such
appeals are heard by a Divisional Court of the Queen's Bench Division: above.

Rectification of decisions

The underlying principle is that once a decision has been formerly announced by
a court then the court cannot go back on that decision and change it, known as

---

[10]   This can extend beyond the prosecution and defence to other people affected by the decision,
who have a legitimate interest in the outcome: known as the doctrine of *locus standi*.

the doctrine of *functus officio*. However, magistrates' courts have a statutory power to alter their own sentences or orders or to correct their own mistakes in certain limited circumstances. These provisions were introduced so that a court can ensure that its original sentence decision is complete and appropriate and based on the facts as they appeared to be at the time. Section 142 Magistrates' Courts Act 1980 (as amended) conferred power to amend a sentence following a mistake, unlawful penalty, omission or where there are other compelling reasons for this. Crown Court judges have traditionally altered their decisions where they realize in good time that an error has occurred. Use of these powers can often avoid unnecessary appeals and save time and expense.

Statutory declaration

Not exactly a right of appeal as such, but analogous in effect (if only, possibly, temporarily) is the right of a defendant to make a solemn declaration that he or she never knew of the proceedings against him or her. The effect is that proceedings will be restarted relying upon the original court process.

CRIMINAL CASES REVIEW COMMISSION

Until the mid-1990s, it was a function of the Home Secretary (acting under the Royal Prerogative) to consider complaints of wrongful conviction and to refer these to the Court of Appeal if he[11] considered this appropriate and if all the normal rights of appeal had been exhausted. This was normally done only where there was new evidence or other consideration of considerable substance that was not before the original trial court. Seemingly, there was a prevailing sense of the 'infallibility' of British justice, so that it often took an arduous campaign and a strong case before a conviction was dislodged. Often there was little public visibility concerning this process. Following the Royal Commission on Criminal Justice of 1993 and its examination of various high profile alleged miscarriages of justice this arrangement was superseded by the Criminal Cases Review Authority, later the Criminal Cases Review Commission (CCRC), which was given authority to review and refer cases to the Court of Appeal.

Role, nature and responsibilities of the CCRC

The CCRC is an independent public body whose origins are to be found in the Criminal Appeal Act 1995. It was set up to review possible miscarriages of

---

[11] Up until 2007 and the appointment of Jacqui Smith MP, all Home Secretaries were men.

justice that formerly fell to the Home Office and Northern Ireland Office to consider. It normally has some 13 members who are appointed by the Queen on the recommendation of the Prime Minister. One of these is designated as its chair. It also has a chief executive and around 90 staff. It can now consider cases heard in magistrates' courts or the Crown Court, its principal purpose being to review suspected 'miscarriages of justice' and to refer a conviction, verdict, finding or sentence to the Court of Appeal (or other appropriate court) if it considers that there is a real possibility that it would not be upheld. It does 'not consider innocence or guilt, but whether there is new evidence or argument that may cast doubt on the safety of an original decision'. Except on rare occasions the case must already have travelled via the normal channels of appeal (above). It has no power to overturn convictions or sentences itself.

The CCRC also investigates and reports on any matter referred to it by the Court of Appeal itself and assists the Lord Chancellor in relation to the prerogative of mercy. The CCRC publishes an annual report.[12]

Since the CCRC began its work it has received over 5,000 applications of which approaching three-quarters have been completed, the remainder being cases in progress or new applications awaiting attention. The CCRC provides an applicant with a full explanation of its decision to refer or not to refer the matter to the Court of Appeal which is known as a 'Statement of Reasons'. The CCRC has wide-ranging investigative powers and can obtain and preserve documentation held by any public body. It can also appoint an investigating officer from another public body to carry out inquiries on its behalf.

Independence and sponsorship

The CCRC's statutory role and responsibilities are set out in the 1995 Act as to:

- review suspected miscarriages of justice and referring a conviction, verdict or finding or sentence to an appropriate court of appeal where it is felt that there is a 'real possibility' that it would not be upheld;
- investigate and report to the Court of Appeal on any matter referred to the Commission;
- consider and report to the Secretary of State on any conviction referred to the Commission for consideration of the exercise of Her Majesty's prerogative of mercy.

---

[12] See www.ccrc.gov.uk

Although wholly independent of Government, the CCRC has agreed wider objectives with its sponsor department, (since 2007) the Ministry of Justice, i.e. to:

- ensure that all cases are dealt with effectively and expeditiously;
- deliver services in ways appropriate to stakeholder needs;
- promote public understanding of the CCRC's role; and
- enhance public confidence in the CJS.

THE EUROPEAN COURT OF HUMAN RIGHTS

As already outlined in *Chapters 2* and *4*, the correct application of human rights law or the administration of domestic law within a human rights context can be tested either within the national appellate system (as described in this chapter) or by means of a free-standing right of appeal to the European Court of Human Rights in Strasbourg. If a provision of English law is incompatible with the European Convention, then a declaration of incompatibility (which in practice should normally only be made by or on appeal to the higher courts) will oblige ministers of state to reconsider the matter with a view to fast-track amending legislation. However, it remains the right of every citizen involved in proceedings before courts of law in the UK to appeal to the European Court of Human Rights (either at an earlier or later stage).

Human rights law is a specialist topic but one that all courts in the UK must observe on a day-to-day basis and in relation to every case coming before them. Ultimately it is a different kind of law, some key aspects of which are described in *Chapter 2*. It takes place and develops its own jurisprudence in an international context and in a way that may sometimes seem alien to English judges and magistrates, not least because it is regarded as a 'living instrument' capable of adapting to events and society as it progresses and without the necessity of new legislation. But there can be no denying that its impact within the UK has been considerable and that domestic appeal and review systems have all adapted to its requirements and dictates.[13]

---

[13] Some further information can be found in *Human Rights and the Courts: Bringing Justice Home* (1999), Ashcroft P *et al*, Waterside Press. This work was used for training purposes across England and Wales at the time of the implementation of the Human Rights Act 1998.

CHAPTER 11

Before Court

As explained in earlier chapters, there are networks of law enforcement agencies and prosecutors working across the CJS. Most investigations are carried out by police officers from one of the ordinary ('civil') police forces or by investigators from other public authorities given powers in relation to specific types of crime, such as health and safety matters, tax evasion, smuggling or immigration offences. There are also 'non-geographic' police forces including those from the Ministry of Defence (MOD) and British Transport Police (BTP). A Border Agency (see the note at the end of this chapter) is responsible for various matters connected to entry to and exit from the UK by UK citizens or foreigners.

Also as already noted, the Crown Prosecution Service (CPS) has an advisory and a prosecution function that, since 2003, extends to decisions concerning the appropriate charge (if any) in relation to arrests by police officers (in all but the most minor or urgent situations). The police and CPS are increasingly located alongside one another in Criminal Justice Units (CJUs)(*Chapter 3*)[1] or Trial Units (*Chapter 8*) in an effort to maximise efficiency, eliminate waste, improve inter-agency relationships and provide timely and ongoing communications.

THE POLICE AND POLICE WORK

There are 43 police forces in England and Wales each covering a county or group of counties, except in London where there is one force for the City of London and the Metropolitan Police Service (MPS) covers the rest of the capital.[2] A classic and enduring statement of the main aims of policing is that which was contained in the White Paper *Police Reform* (1993), i.e. to:

- fight and prevent crime;
- uphold the law;
- bring to justice people who break the law;
- protect, help and reassure the community; and
- provide good value for money.

---

[1] Based at a police station or in 'neutral' accommodation.
[2] Despite occasional moves to amalgamate the two forces. Efforts by the Home Secretary from 2005 onwards to reduce the number of police forces foundered due to a lack of local momentum.

The modern policing context

The Crime and Disorder Act 1998 placed obligations jointly on the police, local authorities and other agencies to co-operate in the development and implementation of a strategy for tackling crime in their area. This is discharged through local Crime and Disorder Reduction Partnerships (CDRPs) as part of a nationwide Crime Reduction Programme (CRP). This was kick-started in 1999 as a £250 million project and evidence-led approach to law and order. It comprises a range of diverse initiatives which support projects operated by local agencies, which are monitored regionally by government. A Safer Communities Initiative (CSI) addresses crime and disorder in individual communities by concentrating on repeat offenders and so-called crime 'hot spots'. In some areas this is paralleled by community justice initiatives (*Chapter 13*). In conjunction with local authorities, the police also confront anti-social behaviour (ASB) (*Chapter 2*) and can issue fixed penalty notices either for ASB or a range of lesser offences. The Police Reform Act 2002 introduced interim ASBOs and extended the geographical area to which an order can apply.[3]

Since the 2002 Act, all police work now takes place against the backdrop of a National Policing Plan, a National Policing Board and the work of the National Police Improvement Agency (NPIA) (below). Law and order, internal (or homeland) security, public safety and border controls all fall firmly within the revised remit of the Home Office rather than the Ministry of Justice (MOJ) (*Chapter 1*). The police are accountable to Parliament through a tripartite structure: the local chief constable, local police authority and Home Secretary. The chief constable (or 'commissioner' for the Metropolitan and City of London Police) is responsible for every aspect of the conduct of his or her force. He or she has power to appoint, promote and discipline officers below the rank of assistant chief constable—and has a duty to enforce the law and bring offenders to justice.

Local policing arrangements

Despite various trends towards nationwide provision of police services, at an everyday, operational level policing remains predominantly locally-based, even though, since 2002, the Home Secretary has considerable powers of intervention where a force fails to perform satisfactorily. Each police force is divided into districts or divisions, known as Basic Command Units (BCUs) which are normally led by a police superintendent. They will usually house a Criminal Investigations Department (CID), drugs squad and a communications room. Districts or divisions are in turn split into sub-divisions, based on local police

---

[3] Also under the Police Reform Act 2002, the British Transport Police and registered social landlords can apply for ASBOs, county courts can make them, and an order can be imposed on conviction by a criminal court for any offence where there is evidence of persistent anti-social behaviour, the criminal anti-social behaviour order (or CRASBO): see, generally, *Chapter 2*.

stations. Designated police stations at whatever level have facilities for charging people and cells for holding those who are kept in police detention pursuant to the Police and Criminal Evidence Act 1984 (PACE) as described in *Chapter 6*.

Nationwide provision

Across the years, individual police forces came to be supported by various nationwide or regional services that developed into a National Crime Squad (NCS)[4] and National Criminal Intelligence Service (NCIS), functions that have been subsumed since 2005 within the Serious Organized Crime Agency (SOCA) (below). A range of centralised databases or specialist or tactical squads and support units exist which can be called upon as and when required by local police and there are also standing arrangements and bodies such as the Forensic Science Service (FSS), now privatised as a government company.[5] FSS scientific support to detectives includes work in the laboratory in relation to exhibits and suspicious deaths, DNA testing in conjunction with a National DNA-database, and police awareness training. The National DNA-database contains some four million offender profiles. DNA samples are now taken and stored following simple arrest for a recordable offence. Police forces also supply mutual aid to one another on a broad front, e.g. when policing protests, demonstrations or major events. In modern times policing has had a global dimension (as has crime and especially organized crime) with close links to such organizations as the UK Border Agency, Interpol, Europol and the USA's Federal Bureau of Investigation (FBI), including through the UK's police-based Child Exploitation and Online Protection Agency (below) to track down paedophiles on the internet and the Joint Terrorism Analysis Centre (JTAC). There is also an element of coordination at national level through relevant Cabinet committees. Policing nowadays has an international and sometimes global dimension—as does the nature of crime itself increasingly—including, e.g. through Europol and Interpol, extradition treaties, agreements and cross-border arrest warrants.[6]

Police personnel

Nationwide there are over 140,000 regular police officers. Since 2002, some 25,000 police community support officers (PCSOs) have been appointed, initially 'on the streets' in London and, gradually, PCSOs have been 'rolled out' nationwide. Police forces also employ administrative or 'non-policing' staff, mostly behind-the-scenes. Quite distinct are special constables, ordinary citizens

---

[4] Unlike the American FBI, the NCS—established in 1992 to target criminal gangs—was an operational mechanism rather than an independently functioning nationwide agency.

[5] Known as a GovCo. For further information about the FSS and other police-related services noted in this chapter, see *The New Home Office*.

[6] Though certain countries, including notoriously Northern Cyprus (but no longer the one-time favourite 'safe haven', Spain) lie beyond the reach of UK law enforcement.

who wear police uniforms and, in their spare time, assist the regular police officers as a form of voluntary service. Special constables, CSOs and backroom staff relieve such officers from routine tasks for operational duties. In a new departure, the Police Reform Act 2002 allowed chief constables to authorise individuals such as civilian investigation, detention and escort officers to exercise specified police powers, including, e.g. experts in fields of science, technology or the internet so that they can directly assist with an investigation.

Partnerships
CDRPs apart (see above), police forces work in partnership with a range of other agencies, including Multi-agency Protection Panel Arrangements (MAPPAs) and the CPS on case preparation and with regard to decisions about charging a suspect as described in *Chapter 7*. Apart from the Forensic Science Service (above), they may also work during an investigation with other professional experts as well as their own scenes of crime officers (SOCOs). Other key support organizations that have existed or are now part of SOCA include the Police Information Technology Organization (PITO), the National Identification Service (NIS) and the Criminal Records Bureau (CRB) which is operated jointly by the Home Office and a private contractor. Increasingly, there are also arrangements with the private sector to obtain intelligence and other policing leads, e.g. from insurance companies or oyster cards as used by London Transport. Ultimately, the National Identification Service (NIS) can be expected to play a leading role in this regard, as will identity cards, causing significant public concern about the uses to which these might be put. A number of existing duties placed, e.g. on lawyers, bankers and accountants mean that a considerable amount of other formerly 'private' data is now available to the authorities: although such contributors to law enforcement might not regard themselves as partners.

Low visibility police activities
Beyond the confines of visible policing there are arrangements for undercover police work (sometimes called 'covert policing') and the handling of related 'human intelligence sources', including informants and 'supergrasses'.[7] This may also be linked to witness protection schemes. Local forces may retain their own special branch and the police also work in conjunction with the security services MI5 and MI6 across a broad range of policing matters, many of which may have political or other sensitivities that fall to be taken into account.[8]

---

[7] See *Covert Human Intelligence Sources: The 'Unlovely' Face of Police Work* (2008), Billingsley, R, Waterside Press. For other instructive information, see *Police Leadership in the 21st Century: Philosophy, Doctrine and Developments* (2003), Adlam R and Villiers P (Eds), Waterside Press.

[8] Long renamed the Security Services and Special Intelligence Services, but still widely known as MI5 and MI6, respectively. Each has own web-site in its historic name and regularly advertises for staff using these descriptions. The opening-up of files under the Freedom of Information Act

Some other modern-day developments

At an every day practical level in relation to serious crime, a main function of the police is to act as a public protection agency so that citizens can go about their daily business in the knowledge that safeguards are in place to protect them from a range of threats, including:

- people involved in violent gangs;
- people involved in the underworld, organized crime or 'drugs world';
- those who carry or use weapons such as guns or knives;
- people affected by anger, rage or serious forms of mental impairment;
- the occasional serial killer;[9]
- sexual predators, especially serial rapists and paedophiles (hence, e.g. the huge resources and effort devoted to Operation Ore in an attempt to identify paedophile networks operating via the internet);
- terrorists and people involved in other forms of extremism or direct action who may be driven by a quasi-political or religious imperative;
- fraudsters and other dishonest offenders, especially those who nowadays operate on a large scale (including remotely over the internet) or who rely on the use of intimidation, bullying, coercion or fear;
- similarly those who concentrate on offences that have been styled 'identity theft' or 'cyber-crime' often on a global or international basis; and
- people who place their potential victims or their property at risk of harm in a variety of other and different ways.

Many of the modern-day developments in policing concentrate on the use of specialist task forces such as those that exist within local police forces to deal with, e.g. local drug or alcohol problems, shoplifting, football related violence and the policing of sports grounds,[10] demonstrations and marches, weapons and road traffic matters. Each force also has links to the Forensic Science Service (FSS) and scenes of crime officers (SOCOs) and makes optimum use of science and technology, e.g. in relation to:

- advanced communications systems and problem-solving policing in conjunction with Scanning Analysis Response Assessment (SARA);
- advanced forms of data sharing with government departments and other agencies, services, units or links to the private sector;

2000 disclosed the strange dichotomy of how much (and at least in the past) the police have been involved in buttressing what can only be described as the political priorities of the Government in power, or alternatively keeping watch on its activities or members. Anyone can now ask to see their security file and the security services, in turn, have become more open and broad based.

9   For the extent of this threat and the kind of people who are most at risk of becoming victims, see *Serial Killers: Hunting Britons and their Victims* (2007), Wilson, D, Waterside Press.

10   Although in practice the latter, in many instances, involves private sector security.

- enhanced forms of surveillance using modern day control rooms;
- internet-based investigations, including the retrieval of electronic data, e.g. from hard discs and electronic chips (including 'deleted' data);
- new and remote ways of monitoring people, traffic, animals or items, including by means of heat imaging equipment and global satellite positioning technology, especially in relation to the use of mobile telephones at a given place and time;
- the use of CCTV(including that provided by the private sector), extending now, e.g. to experiments with intelligent CCTV (talking cameras);
- the use of video recording, including developments in relation to 'real time video analysis, cameras fitted to police vehicles and inside police officers' helmets and the application of various forms of video footage to investigations, court proceedings and evidence;
- DNA-testing or 'genetic fingerprinting';
- a range of advances and initiatives in relation to drug-testing;
- facial recognition technology, often in conjunction with an electronic 'rogues gallery' of offenders and suspects;
- developments in biometrics, iris recognition and towards identity cards;
- secondary uses of speed cameras or congestion charging equipment and data (currently limited to terrorism);
- a range of developments in relation to road traffic, including instant access to databases and stinger devices to bring a vehicle to a halt; and
- modern-day forms of non-lethal force (where any such force is necessary) as well as access to specialist, rapid response firearms units.[11]

However, it would be wrong to assume that all crime has moved in the direction that the above methods are intended to counter. A great deal of crime continues to occur, as it has always done, at the lower end of the spectrum and may involve people of limited means, abilities, education and employment prospects. It is with regard to such offenders that more fundamental and structural approaches are needed and sometimes provided, such as regeneration schemes, those in relation to social exclusion (now a high priority for Government),[12] the widening of opportunities and access to public services. Well into 2008, official pronouncements were identifying drugs and alcohol as still being the two most pressing underlying connectors to crime at all levels.

Police membership organizations

Various membership bodies exist for police officers, who are not allowed to join a trade union or strike.[13] All ranks have their own staff organizations including

---

[11] Each of these a subject in itself. A useful starting point is the companion volume to this work, *The New Home Office: An Introduction* (2007), Gibson B, Waterside Press.

[12] There is a Social Exclusion Unit (SEU) within the Cabinet Office and associated committees.

[13] In 2008 they marched through central London in open protest at a constrained pay rise.

the Police Federation for rank and file officers, which is the representative body for all officers below superintendent. The federation was established in 1919 to provide the police with a ready and lawful means of bringing their concerns to notice. Officers of the rank of superintendent can belong to a Superintendents' Association and beyond this is the highly influential Association of Chief Police Officers (ACPO) which exists 'to promote leadership excellence by the chief officers of the police service, to assist in setting the policing agenda by providing professional opinion on key issues identified by the Government, appropriate organizations and individuals and to be the corporate voice of the service'. There is also Black Police Association.

Maintaining the Queen's peace

The police have a duty to maintain law and order, to protect people and property, to prevent crime (in conjunction with local authorities and communities) and, when crime occurs, to try to detect offenders and prepare case papers with a view to prosecution (*Chapter 6*). They control road traffic and advise local authorities on traffic matters. They also carry out certain duties, such as immigration enquiries, for the government or its Borders Agency (below). By tradition they assist anyone who needs help and deal with a range of emergencies, often in conjunction with other agencies and public authorities. Much of this work (aspects of which are described below) is carried out by patrol officers. They are deployed on foot or in vehicle patrols and organized on the basis of beats. Ordinary beat officers normally work a shift or relief. More specialised work is undertaken by operational officers.

The maintenance of the Queen's peace ranges from the day-to-day policing of the streets to the control of crowds and demonstrators to policing public order situations and responses to terrorist attacks. Patrol officers are supported by special patrol groups or task forces, seconded officers specially trained and equipped and put on standby to react to any incident or potential disorder. Forces also have Police Support Units (PSUs), which are made up of ordinary officers who carry out normal policing duties but who are given special training in the use of shields and riot techniques. PSUs will aid other police forces in emergencies. The MPS also has District Support Units, mobile instant response units which patrol the streets in vans. Ever since the urban riots in the early 1980s, the police have been given more powers and equipment to deal with disorders, and more resources have been devoted to public order training. This has increased significantly in the wake of September 11.

Whilst a police officer may rarely discover 'invisible' (i.e. off-street) crimes such as burglary, it is argued by many people that their presence on the streets may reduce the number of 'visible' crimes and the fear of crime. In addition to these officers, every force employs crime prevention officers in their own right. These officers carry out security surveys of domestic or commercial premises, advise on security and distribute crime prevention publicity. In conjunction with Neighbourhood Watch and similar schemes they work to prevent crime.[14]

Many police forces work alongside other agencies in analysing and tackling problems such as run-down housing and domestic violence. Police officers are also involved in youth offending teams (YOTs) (*Chapter 5*), prisons, hospitals and other institutions. Some officers give up part of their spare time to work with young people and to encourage them towards constructive use of their time.

Helping victims

The police play a crucial role in supporting and advising victims of crime through a range of operational and liaison activities and by their involvement in taking witness statements and 'victim personal statements' (see, in particular, *Chapters 9, 13* and *15*). For many years this aspect of police work was criticised but there are now much more developed schemes of victim liaison and updating.

Special provisions for sex offenders

Adding to myriad existing police duties, the Sex Offenders Act 1997 imposed a requirement on offenders convicted or cautioned for specific sex offences to notify the police of their name and address and any subsequent changes thereto. Later, the Crime and Disorder Act 1998 introduced 'sex offender orders' and the Police Reform Act 2002 introduced greater flexibility concerning how applications for such orders could be made as well as allowing them to run UK-wide and providing for interim orders to cover urgent situations. A replacement 'sexual offences prevention order' under the Sexual Offences Act 2003, a civil construct (but a variant of which can also be made if someone is convicted of a sexually-related offence), is a pre-emptive measure—in broad concept not unlike the anti-social behaviour order (ASBO) (or, as appropriate, the CRASBO))(*Chapter 2*))—breach of which is an offence or basis for enforcement. It can also be made with regard to people convicted of violent (non-sexual) offences provided that the court is satisfied that the order is necessary to protect the public from serious harm from the offender. Such matters are now vital to the work of Multi-agency Public Protection Arrangements (MAPPAs) (*Chapter 6*).

THE SERIOUS ORGANIZED CRIME AGENCY (SOCA)

SOCA was launched in 2006 under the Serious Organised Crime and Police Act 2005.[15] Its aim is 'to reduce the harm caused to the UK by serious organized

---

[14]   Such initiatives include, e.g., Boat Watch, Business Watch, Cab Watch, Campus Watch, Caravan Watch, Child Watch, Farm Watch, Hospital Watch, Pub Watch, School Watch and Shop Watch.

crime'; estimated at over £20 billion a year. SOCA brought together the former National Crime Squad (NCS), National Criminal Intelligence Service (NCIS) and their associated databases and those parts of HM Revenue and Customs that dealt with drug-trafficking and criminal finance and of the then UK Immigration Service (all now integrated with the Border Agency: below) that dealt with organized immigration crime (including, e.g. 'people trafficking').

A key SOCA responsibility is dealing with financial information in relation to the suspected proceeds of crime and money laundering; a function that it took over from the former and short-lived Assets Recovery Agency formed under the Proceeds of Crime Act 2002. Increasingly, sophisticated ways of tracing transactions have led to the seizure of property and funds.[16]

SOCA is an executive non-departmental public body (NDPB) sponsored by, but operationally independent from, the Home Office. It is led by a board with a majority of non-executive members. The board is responsible for ensuring that SOCA discharges its statutory responsibilities and meets strategic priorities set by the home secretary. The director general of SOCA is responsible for all that SOCA does operationally and administratively, as well as for day-to-day management, including expenditure. Under the 2005 Act, SOCA must publish an annual plan before the start of each financial year and an annual report as soon as possible after the end of each financial year.[17]

SOCA Online is a secure system designed for use by those people and entities who must, under the Proceeds of Crime Act 2002 and the Terrorism Act 2000, submit 'Suspicious Activity Reports (SARs)' to SOCA. These target such criminal proceeds via, e.g. banks, lawyers, accountants and businesses who may, e.g. encounter money laundering when dealings with clients or customers. This has been enhanced by provisions that allow any police officer to seize cash above a statutory amount[18] in the absence of a satisfactory explanation for carrying it; and associated Crown Prosecution Service (CPS) procedures. SOCA would also appear to have superseded Special Branch except in the context that such 'branches' still sometimes exist locally.

CHILD EXPLOITATION AND ONLINE PROTECTION

The Child Exploitation and Online Protection Centre (CEOP) operates across the UK and maximises international links to tackle child sex abuse wherever and whenever it happens. Part of CEOP's strategy for achieving this is by providing

---

[15] Also known as SOCAP.

[16] Although these procedures have sometime been delayed by complexity and legal challenges.

[17] Plans can be viewed at www.soca.gov.uk

[18] Initially £10,000 or more; but subsequently £5,000 or more; under section 294 of the 2002 Act and subject to police codes of procedure. It is now unusual for businesses to accept cash above £1,000.

internet safety advice for parents and carers and delivering a virtual police station for reporting abuse on the internet. CEOP grew out of a number of earlier initiatives including Operation Ore that from 2002 onwards targeted some 7,000 people suspected of downloading child pornography from the internet.

The CEOP Centre is affiliated to SOCA (above) and its main powers are derived from the Serious Organised Crime and Police Act 2005. It is based in Pimlico, London with developing outreach channels to all areas of both domestic and international policing. Within SOCA (above), there are also separate arrangements covering operations, intelligence, education and victim identification. SOCA is a member of the Virtual Global Taskforce (VGT).[19]

THE NATIONAL POLICING IMPROVEMENT AGENCY

The National Policing Improvement Agency (NPIA) supports police forces to improve the way in which they work. It is police owned and led and replaced or incorporated former national policing organizations such as the Police Information Technology Organization (PITO) and CENTREX,[20] as well as certain functions that were formerly carried out by the Home Office and Association of Chief Police Officers (ACPO) (below). Its origins lay in Home Office responses to suggestions by ACPO that an agency should be established to support the implementation of national standards. The Government committed itself to the NPIA under a five-year strategic plan, first published in July 2004 and updated on a rolling basis.[21] According to the Home Office, the NPIA 'will:

- look ahead to identify and plan for the future challenges to face policing;
- define the police service's capacity to implement change and inform the priority and sequence of change programmes;
- find and develop evidence-based policing good practice that works and support the service to ensure good practice is applied;
- play a lead role in ensuring that an agreed programme of key reforms takes place;
- co-ordinate the future development, purchase and deployment of nationally-compatible systems and infrastructure, particularly information and communications technology;
- design, develop, deploy and quality assure nationally-compatible learning programmes;

---

[19] Further details are available at www.ceop.gov.uk and www.virtualglobaltaskforce.com

[20] Based at what is still generally referred to as the Police Training College at Bramshill, Hampshire, UK and now also operating from other UK locations.

[21] See. also, the police reform White Paper, *Building Communities, Beating Crime: A Better Police Service for the 21st Century* (2004) Cm 6360.

- help the police service to recruit, train and develop its people and improve leadership at all levels;
- ensure the workforce, processes, procurement and systems that support policing are as efficient and effective as possible;
- use research and analysis and specialist systems and advice to improve policing and provide a better service to the public;
- ensure that police forces and police authorities are involved in every aspect of the agency's work.'

As its name implies, a main focus of the work of the NPIA is improving policing in England and Wales. This it is intended to do via a fair and equitable service to diverse communities and police staff. Its functions include enhanced coordination of major national projects previously managed by separate organizations; the rationalisation of policing agencies; and removal of duplication and waste—all matters that have tended to characterise nationwide policing functions in the past. Science and technology (above) will be at the fore.

POLICE AUTHORITIES

Each police force operates under the auspices of a police authority. An autonomous Association of Police Authorities (APA) (which works in partnership with the Local Government Association) has existed since 1997. Chief constables are appointed by and make reports to their police authority, which fixes the maximum strength of the force, subject to approval by central government, and provides buildings and equipment. They can advise a chief constable, e.g. on law enforcement, priorities and the allocation and deployment of police resources. The Police and Magistrates' Courts Act 1994 made police authorities free-standing bodies, reduced their size and introduced independent members (in addition to local councillors and magistrates). Further changes occurred with the Police Reform Act 2002 (see next section).

POLICE REFORM IN GENERAL

The Police Reform Act 2002 introduced what the Home Office described as part of an 'ambitious police policy' which will:

. . . support the police service in tackling crime and anti-social behaviour. It contains measures to ensure that the most effective policing methods are used by all police forces, and so tackles the variations in performance between forces. The Act will make anti-social behaviour orders more flexible and widely available. It will enable trained civilians to exercise some police powers, freeing a growing number of police officers from unnecessary duties and providing a presence in local communities. And it will enable the police to work closely with other agencies like neighbourhood and street wardens. (News and Press Release, 25 July 2002)

Among other measures, the Act provides for the following:

- a National Policing Plan, setting out the Government's priorities for policing, their delivery and indicators for performance measures;[22]
- powers enabling the Home Secretary to issues codes of practice to chief officers and make regulations governing the use of police equipment or requiring forces to adopt particular procedures or practices;
- the strengthening of the powers of police authorities to remove chief officers in the interests of efficiency and effectiveness;
- arrangements so that, in exceptional circumstances and where a police force is manifestly failing in its duty to protect and serve the public, the Home Secretary can intervene. Former powers that required a police authority to take remedial action were also reinforced;
- extra powers in relation to HM Inspectorate of Constabulary (below);
- the formation of an Independent Police Complaints Commission (below);
- powers enabling chief constables to confer appropriate police powers on civilian investigation, detention and escort officers (above);
- streamlined procedures for anti-social behaviour orders (ASBOs) (above);
- measures to improve the effectiveness of sex offender orders (above); and
- provision for community support officers (see earlier in the chapter).

HM INSPECTORATE OF CONSTABULARY (HMIC)

For around 150 years, HMICs have been charged with examining and improving the efficiency of the police service, the first HMIC being appointed under the County and Borough Police Act 1856. In modern times, they are appointed by the Crown on the recommendation of the Home Secretary and report to HM Chief Inspector of Constabulary (HMCIC), who is also the home secretary's principal professional policing adviser. The HMCIC is independent of the Home Office and the police service. His or her functions include certifying police forces as efficient and thus qualified to receive a police grant. The inspectorate's role has been progressively developed over the past 30 years to be more open and transparent and to include not only the inspection of individual forces but also analysis, assessment and promoting Best Practice.

---

[22] This can be accessed at www. police.homeoffice.gov.uk/national-policing-plan.

Under the Police reform Act 2002, an adverse report by HM Inspectorate of Constabulary (below) can trigger intervention by the Home Secretary, who may require the police authority and the chief constable to produce an action plan to address failings within 12 weeks. The Home Secretary has the right to comment on the action plan, and such comments are considered by the police authority before they implement their plan. HMIC adopts a risk-assessment approach to prioritising work, based on core objectives of: driving up police performance; providing assurance to stakeholders; making an input to Home Office policy-making; contributing to improvements to the CJS; and providing advice and support to chief constables and police authorities. The inspectorate can also carry out thematic inspections on particular aspects of policing. Reports are normally published together with a business plan setting out priorities and targets.[23]

COMPLAINTS AGAINST THE POLICE

A complaint about the police may be informally resolved between the police and complainant or formally investigated by the police. It can be considered for informal resolution if it would not justify criminal proceedings. If the complainant agrees to informal resolution, a senior officer will investigate and mediate between the complainant and the officer subject to the complaint. If mediation fails, another officer is appointed to deal with the complaint formally.

Historically, the Police Complaints Authority (PCA) was the independent body that oversaw complaints against serving police officers in England and Wales.[24] Additionally, voluntary (or 'non-complaint') referrals to the PCA were made by the police themselves and certain complaints or events had to be so referred, e.g. where death or serious injury occurred in police custody or stemmed from firearms being used by the police or 'hot pursuit' in police vehicles. There were also certain discretionary report areas.

In order to give greater reassurance that complaints against the police are investigated openly, fairly and impartially an Independent Police Complaints Commission (IPCC) was established in 2004 under the Police Reform Act 2002 to investigate and oversee serious complaints against the police. One aim was to encourage greater openness and transparency in complaints procedures, leading to increased confidence 'in the robustness of the complaints system'.

Some people sue the police in the civil courts for damages as an alternative to using the PCA procedure.

---

[23] See http://inspectorates.homeoffice.gov.uk/hmic/

[24] There has been a general downward trend in complaints, but the figures show that a disproportionate number of complainants are unemployed, black (11 per cent), or of Asian origin (4.5 per cent) (compared to 1.8 per cent and 3 per cent of the population as a whole, respectively). More information is available at the PCA web-site www.pca.gov.uk

SOME OTHER AGENTS OF LAW ENFORCEMENT

Among other law enforcement agencies with an investigation or prosecution function are:

- 'non-geographic' forces, e.g. the British Transport Police (BTP), Ministry of Defence Police and UK Atomic Energy Constabulary (UKAEC);
- the Serious Fraud Office (SFO) (*Chapter 7*);
- the customs part of Revenue and Customs which is responsible for ports, airports (below), drug trafficking, rivers and tunnels and such items as the seizure of drug-related cash and evasion of Value Added Tax (VAT);
- the Health and Safety Executive which deals not only with everyday prosecutions of employers for day-to-day failures to comply with safety legislation but also with serious cases, e.g. where an accident or even a fatality has occurred or where the defect complained of may require a change of manufacturing practices generally;
- TV Licensing (TVL) which prosecutes people for having no TV licence and other broadcasting offences; and
- local authorities (as described in this and various other chapters).

Among voluntary sector organizations, the following have been given statutory powers to prosecute within their field of operations, i.e. the:

- National Society for the Prevention of Cruelty to Children (NSPCC); and
- Royal Society for the Protection of Animals (RSPCA).

POLICING UK BORDERS: A NOTE

Policing the UK's borders has become a priority in a world in which terrorism and the threat from large scale, global organized crime are everyday concerns. In 2007, the Home Office announced a unified Border Agency (or 'Border Force') which was eventually launched by the Home Secretary at Gatwick Airport in 2008. The idea was that staff would wear distinctive uniforms and to 'strengthen the powers and surveillance capabilities of those working to stop terrorists and other would-be illegal entrants coming to the UK'. The force integrates or connects up the work of the former Borders and Immigration Agency with that part of Revenue and Customs dealing with ports and airports, and UK Visas, the agency that considers applications from people who wish to enter the UK, e.g. to study or conduct international trade. At around the same time, the Home Office became more sensitive to issues such as the non-deportation of foreign prisoners at the end of their sentences ('the foreign prisoner crisis') and the Home

Secretary's inherent powers to remove undesirable aliens from the UK (see, further, below)

The Identity and Passport Service (IPS)

Passports are a central instrument of international travel and also identity fraud, to which increasingly sophisticated mechanisms are being applied worldwide as more and more people become increasingly and globally mobile. The IPS was established as an executive agency of the Home Office in 2006 so as to build on the foundations of the UK Passport Service (UKPS) to provide passport services. In conjunction with an embryonic National Identity Scheme (NIS) it now looks to the development of biometric passports and identity cards for British citizens and Irish nationals who are resident in the UK as a way to ensuring effective border controls. Associated developments included the introduction of moves towards face-to-face interviews for all applicants for new passports.[25] On a wider front, identity fraud—passing oneself off as someone else for criminal purposes—has become one of the fastest growing types of crime, especially by means of the internet. Nonetheless and despite the long time existence of identity cards in many parts of the world, general attitudes in the UK towards them remain negative and controversial, or at best equivocal. Concerns that they will be misused by the authorities or become the source of an instant collection of personal data (which might be misused in less benign times) have been countered by claims that identity cards are essential for policing in the modern era and that the innocent have nothing to fear.[26]

Inherent powers of the Home Secretary

The Home Secretary has certain inherent powers to deport or exclude undesirable aliens, people who are 'not conducive to the public good'.[27] These have been used to exclude aliens in war-time or in modern times people involved in organized crime, professional hit-men, members of the Mafia, Chinese Triads, Jamaican Yardies, suspected al-Qaida terrorists and so-called 'preachers of hate'. Though often largely dormant, the power has been revived to counter the global or international nature of certain threats to law and order.

---

[25] For further information, see: www.ips.gov.uk

[26] Which is particularly open to question, given the extent to which miscarriages of justice, breaches of human rights and instances of misconduct in public office tend to occur, to which government sometimes seems to be quite 'blind' in terms of its interpretation of events or involvement.

[27] Seemingly under the royal prerogative rather than at Common Law.

CHAPTER 12

In Court

Most readers will be familiar with the setting in a courtroom from dramatic or educational presentations. The scene differs little across England and Wales, or, indeed, the world. Usually, there is a raised bench (or dais) on which the judge or magistrates sit with their officials beneath. Facing them will be desks and seating for legal representatives and, usually to one side, a witness stand to which people are called by an usher to give their testimony when their turn arrives. There will also be a dock where the accused person stands, possibly secure and protected by reinforced glass (although many courtrooms now have no physical dock), especially magistrates' courts, even if the expression 'in the dock' may still be used in a metaphorical sense. Outside the courtroom will be a waiting area (or 'foyer') and nowadays in most places smaller consulting rooms and separate waiting areas for prosecution witnesses and defence witnesses.

JUDGES

Every criminal court above the magistrates' court relies on professional lawyer-judges drawn principally from leading practitioners at the Bar—although, increasingly, judges are appointed from the ranks of solicitors or, occasionally, academic lawyers. District judges sit in magistrates' courts.

The Judges' Council
The council was originally set up under the Judicature Act 1873 when it was chaired by the Lord Chancellor. All the judges of the ('old') Supreme Court (*Chapter 5*) were members. It continued until 1981. Lord Lane, Lord Chief Justice, set up a new Judges' Council in 1988. This was chaired by the LCJ, had a smaller membership of the more senior judges and, in 2002, adopted a written constitution. It has since widened its membership to include representatives from all areas of the judiciary. In 2006 it was further revised following the Constitutional Reform Act 2005 which, along with The Concordat, vested in the LCJ considerable responsibilities in respect of the judiciary and the general business of the courts of England and Wales. The Lord Chief Justice exercises these responsibilities through the Judges' Council and a Judicial Executive Board.

Constitutional change
Central to changes in the 2005 Act, the head of the judiciary is now the Lord Chief Justice rather than, as previously, the Lord Chancellor. Judges are still

appointed by the sovereign on the recommendation of the Lord Chancellor but in response to the recommendations of a Judicial Appointments Commission (JAC) to whom applications can be made by anyone qualified for the role. Most senior appointments, those to the Supreme Court in future (and House of Lords until then) or Court of Appeal are routed via the Prime Minister (assuming that this practice continues). As indicated in *Chapters 5* and *10*, Supreme Court Justices will be appointed in readiness for that court, initially the existing Law Lords.

Other new mechanisms to protect the independence of the judiciary include a statutory duty on the part of the Lord Chancellor in this regard, the creation of a Judicial Office (JO) to support the work of the LCJ and other senior members of the judiciary, a Judicial Communications Office (JCO) to provide internal and external communication links for and to the judiciary and an Office for Judicial Complaints (OJC) that is intended to make the process of complaining about the behaviour of a judge or magistrate (rather than the outcome of a case: which can always be appealed in the normal way: *Chapter 10*) more visible and transparent.

Law Lords

As noted in *Chapter 5*, judges of the House of Lords are known as Lords of Appeal in Ordinary or 'Law Lords' and on appointment become life peers. By convention they do not participate in the general business of the House except where there is a direct legal or judicial context such as debates on criminal justice bills or measures affecting the powers, jurisdiction or administrative arrangements for the courts or services on which the courts depend for the proper and effective administration of justice. With the transition to a Supreme Court this constitutional anomaly will evaporate in any event. The Law Lords usually number between nine and eleven and never more than 12. They sit as an Appellate Committee of the House in an ante-room (not in the chamber of the House) to hear appeals from the Court of Appeal (Criminal Division) and the Queen's Bench Division of the High Court of Justice (and non-criminal courts). A senior Law Lord chairs the committee. The rule is that Law Lords are either former holders of high judicial office or former practising barristers of at least 15 years' standing. They are appointed to a 'judicial committee' of the House.

Lords Justices of Appeal

Each of the 30 or so judges of the Court of Appeal is known as a 'Lord Justice'. Lords Justices (often shortened in writing to LJ) are promoted from among High Court Judges (some of whom may also deputise as Court of Appeal judges from time-to-time). They sit regularly in the Civil Division of the Court of Appeal and some also in the Criminal Division. High Court judges may deputise for Lords Justices, including as part of being 'tested out' for higher office.

High Court judges

There are around 100 High Court judges who, as well as sitting in the High Court to hear cases in its various divisions, may also sit in the Crown Court. At Crown

Court centres where a High Court judge sits, cases are assigned between different types of judges on the principle that the High Court judge should usually try the more serious or difficult allegations (sometimes called 'first tier' cases). A High Court judge will often serve as the presiding judge for a court centre or circuit. These functions apart, the main significance for the criminal process is that High Court judges sit to hear appeals by way of case stated and applications for judicial review or declarations in the Queens Bench Division (*Chapter 10*). As noted earlier in this chapter, they may also serve in the Court of Appeal (Criminal Division) from time to time. High Court judges tend to be selected from amongst senior barristers, Queen's Counsel (QCs) or solicitors, who are also eligible for appointment.

Circuit judges, recorders and assistant recorders

Circuit judges, recorders and assistant recorders (the last two being part-time circuit judges: below) sit in the Crown Court. Any reasonably senior barrister or solicitor can apply to be interviewed and assessed by the JAC. Circuit judges, tend to be drawn from the middle ranks of senior barristers. However, solicitors are also eligible for the circuit bench if they have served for a period as a recorder although they number less than a fifth of the 500 or more regular circuit judges. A recorder is a practising barrister or solicitor who sits as a part-time circuit judge. There are some 900 recorders who sit for around 20 days a year in the Crown Court whilst continuing with their normal legal practice or other occupation for the rest of the year. There are approaching 400 assistant recorders. Each centre has a 'resident judge' who acts as a link between that centre, its administration, and other courts, judges and agencies. Circuit judges are styled and addresses as 'Your/His/Her Honour'. The role of the trial judge and the different functions of the judge and jury are noted in *Chapter 9*.

THE JURY

The jury is the incarnation of the right of a citizen to be tried by his or her peers (presumed to stem from Magna Carta in 1215[1]). Jurors are chosen at random from the electoral roll. A much heralded aspect of the Criminal Justice Act 2003 was the tightening of the criteria in relation to people who, under the former provisions, 'escaped' jury service. The relevant provisions state that:

> ... every person shall be qualified to serve as a juror in the Crown Court, the High Court and county court and be liable accordingly to attend for jury service when summoned under this Act if -
> (a) he is ... registered as a parliamentary or local government elector and is not less than 18 nor more than 70 years of age;

---

[1] If somewhat mythically. See, also, the exposition of trial by peers in *Chapter 2*.

(b) he has been ordinarily resident in the UK, Channel Islands or the Isle of Man for ... at least five years since attaining the age of 13;

(c) he is not a mentally disordered person; and

(d) he is not disqualified for jury service [see below].

Related provisions abolish (except in the case of mentally disordered people) the categories of *ineligibility* for, and *excusal* from jury service as of right. The effect is that certain groups of people who formerly *could not*, or *need not*, do jury service are now required to perform jury service unless they can put forward a satisfactory reason as to why they should not do so. The provisions also amend the list of categories of people who are *disqualified* from jury service.

Ineligibility for and excusal from jury service

The new provisions remove the existing status of 'ineligibility' for jury service and of entitlement to be 'excused as of right' from a number of people who are now potential jurors. Under the former law, members of the judiciary,[2] other people concerned with the administration of justice and the clergy were ineligible. This is no longer the case. Other people, including those above 65 years of age, MPs, doctors, followers of certain religions and (in certain circumstances) members of the armed forces, were entitled to refuse to serve on a jury—but this entitlement has been removed. All such people now need to serve on a jury or to apply to be excused by putting forward their 'good reasons' (or where applicable for their jury service to be deferred). There are corresponding changes to the jury summoning offence provisions in the Juries Act 1974.

Disqualification from jury service

The 2003 Act also substitutes fresh categories of people who are disqualified altogether from jury service. These are people who are on bail or who have served, or are serving, custodial sentences or community orders of various types and the list has been updated to reflect changes in sentencing legislation, including those introduced by the 2003 Act itself. The new appears in a fresh Schedule 1 to the Juries Act 1974.[3] In summary, people are disqualified if they:

- are on bail (within the meaning of the Bail Act 1976);
- have at any time been sentenced in the UK, Channel Islands or Isle of Man to imprisonment for life, detention for life or custody for life, detention during Her Majesty's pleasure or that of the Secretary of State, imprisonment or detention for public protection, an extended sentence[4] or to a term of imprisonment or detention of five years or more;

---

[2] At least one Lord Justice of Appeal has served on a jury since the changes.

[3] As inserted by para. 15 of Schedule 33 to the CJA 2003.

[4] Under sections 227, 228 CJA 2003 or 210A Criminal Procedure (Scotland) Act 1995.

- have at any time in the last ten years in the UK, Channel Islands or Isle of Man served any part of a sentence of imprisonment or detention, or received a suspended sentence of imprisonment or suspended detention;
- have at any time in England and Wales had made in respect of them a generic community order, a community rehabilitation order, a community punishment order, a community punishment and rehabilitation order, a drug treatment and testing order or a drug abstinence order (including under court martial, or corresponding orders in other UK jurisdictions).[5]

Military, etc. personnel

With the abolition of 'excusal as of right', armed forces personnel who wish to avoid jury service will, like other people, need to apply showing 'good reason' why they should not serve. However, a commanding officer's certificate will be regarded as conclusive evidence of good reason for the purposes of these provisions, at least in so far as that, on its production, a jury service summons will be deferred. If there has already been a deferral, or the commanding officer certifies that absence would be prejudicial for a given period of time, then service personnel will be excused altogether from the obligation. This is without prejudice to their being summoned for jury service in future.

The Jury Central Summoning Bureau

Where someone has been summoned for jury service, he or she may be excused (on showing 'good reason') or his or her jury service deferred. This discretion currently rests with the Jury Central Summoning Bureau (sponsored by the Ministry of Justice), which administers jury summoning on behalf of the Crown Court (*Chapter 4*) as 'the appropriate officer' under the Juries Act 1974. The Lord Chancellor is required to issue guidance as to the manner in which the functions of the appropriate officer are exercised and for it to be laid before Parliament.

Jurors' allowances

Further changes allow jurors to be paid their statutory allowances (by the Court Service which administers this aspect) 'otherwise than by means of cash'. Some court facilities enable staff to obtain refreshments by non-cash means, such as a voucher system or 'swipe cards'. The new provisions will enable the Crown Court to extend such methods to jurors.

TRIAL WITHOUT A JURY: 'JUDGE-ALONE' TRIALS

Amongst the more controversial of the provisions in the CJA 2003 were those concerning 'judge-alone' or 'judge-only' trials. The provisions are narrower than

---

[5] Readers will note that some of these community orders no longer exist: see *Chapter 9*.

originally proposed. A proposal to allow defendants to apply for such trials was abandoned at the eleventh hour as part and parcel of a number of 'trade-offs' in the House of Lords so as to allow the CJA 2003 onto the Statute Book. The surviving provisions[6] allow trials without a jury, i.e. what have been dubbed 'judge-only' or 'judge-alone' trials, where:

- the prosecutor applies for this in relation to certain fraud charges; or
- the prosecutor applies for this where there is a danger of jury tampering; or
- a trial has collapsed because of jury tampering and the jury has had to be discharged, e.g. due to intimidation or bribery.

Application by the prosecutor in relation to certain fraud cases

Here, the prosecutor may apply to a judge of the Crown Court for the trial to be conducted without a jury. Provided that the judge is satisfied that:

> . . . the complexity of the trial or the length of the trial (or both) is likely to make the trial so burdensome to the members of a jury hearing the trial that the interests of justice require that serious consideration should be given to the question whether the trial should be conducted without a jury

he or she may make an order that the trial be conducted without a jury; and if not so satisfied must refuse the application.[7] It is important to note, in relation to this particular limb, that the judge can order trial without a jury. But he or she may not make such an order without the approval of the Lord Chief Justice or a judge nominated by him or her. In exercising the discretion, the trial judge must have regard to any steps that might reasonably be taken to reduce the complexity or length of the trial. A step is 'not to be regarded as reasonable if it would significantly disadvantage the prosecution'.

Application by the prosecutor in relation to jury tampering

The prosecutor may make similar application where jury tampering is anticipated. In this situation there are two conditions concerning which the judge must be satisfied, as follows:

> . . . the first condition is that there is evidence of a real and present danger that jury tampering would take place.

The relevant provisions give examples of cases where there may be evidence of such a 'real and present danger', i.e. a case where the trial is a retrial and the jury in the previous trial was discharged due to jury tampering; a case where

---

[6] Contained in Part 7 of the 2003 Act.

[7] See section 43 of the 2003 Act. For other items mentioned here see subsequent sections.

tampering has occurred in previous criminal proceedings involving the same defendant or defendants; or one where there has been intimidation, or attempts at intimidation, of a witness in the trial. The second condition is that:

> . . . notwithstanding any steps (including the provision of police protection) which might reasonably be taken to prevent jury tampering, the likelihood that it would take place would be so substantial as to make it necessary in the interests of justice for the trial to be conducted without a jury.

Discharge of a jury where there is jury tampering

This contemplates a quite different situation to those already outlined above: where there is a trial by jury but tampering actually happens during it. The position is then that where a judge is minded to discharge the jury 'and he or she is so minded because jury tampering has taken place', certain set procedures must be followed. The judge must inform the parties that he or she is so minded and of the grounds for this—and allow representations. Where, after considering any such representations, he or she discharges the jury, the judge may make an order that the trial is to continue without a jury 'if, but only if' he or she is satisfied that jury tampering has taken place and that to continue the trial without a jury would be fair to the defendant or defendants. All this is subject to the overriding consideration that if the judge considers it necessary in the interests of justice for the trial to be terminated, then he or she must terminate it.

When terminating a trial, the judge may make an order that any new trial be conducted without a jury if satisfied that both of the conditions noted above are fulfilled but nothing affects an application by the prosecutor being made in relation to any new trial that takes place following termination of a trial—or any other powers that the judge may have to terminate a trial.

Appeals and reasons for decisions: a note

As described in *Chapter 10*, the 2003 Act provides a right of appeal to the Court of Appeal to either the prosecution or defence against a determination to continue a trial in the absence of a jury, or to order a retrial without a jury because of jury tampering. Where a trial is conducted or continued without a jury, and a defendant is convicted, the judge is required to give his or her reasons for that conviction.[8] In the latter case, the court must be satisfied that the level and duration of the police protection that would be necessary for the relevant members of a jury hearing the trial would be excessively burdensome to a typical juror. Alternatively (or additionally), a court must be satisfied that the risk of jury tampering would remain sufficiently high despite any steps (including police protection) that could reasonably be taken to prevent it, so as to make it necessary in the interests of justice for the trial to be conducted without a jury.

---

[8] The jury does not give its reasons and its private deliberations are sacrosanct.

Jury challenges

Prosecuting counsel can challenge any juror without putting forward a reason by calling on him or her to 'stand by for the Crown', but this right of what is known as 'peremptory challenge' is rarely used in practice.[9] Both prosecution and defence can also challenge for cause, i.e. seek to reject a juror for good reason, e.g. that the juror is disqualified or ineligible, or because for reasons explained to the court—such as financial interest or strongly held views on a given topic—the juror in question might be biased or otherwise likely to prejudge the case.

Jury oath

Each member of the jury is required to swear on oath (or if he or she prefers to make an affirmation) as follows:

> I will faithfully try the several issues joined between our Sovereign lady the Queen and the prisoner at the Bar, and give a true verdict according to the evidence.

MAGISTRATES AND DISTRICT JUDGES

There are around 29,000 magistrates or 'justices of the peace' (JPs)[10] in England and Wales. They undergo special training but are essentially unqualified or 'lay'[11] magistrates and not paid other than their expenses and to reimburse any loss of earnings. They are members of the community drawn from a cross-section of society and are chosen for their character, integrity and judgement. They sit on the bench as a form of public service. Magistrates are advised at a senior level by justices' clerks and, on an everyday basis, by other qualified court legal advisers. In modern times, magistrates are addresses via the chair of the bench as 'Sir' or 'Madam' and, largely historically now, as 'Your Worships'.

Appointment of lay magistrates

Lay magistrates are appointed by the Lord Chancellor on behalf of the Sovereign following recommendations from local Advisory Committees on the Appointment of Magistrates. Most urban centres and counties have an Advisory Committee. A special arrangement exists in Greater Manchester, Merseyside and Lancashire, where appointments are made via the Chancellor of the Duchy of Lancaster. There has been a drive to broaden the bench, i.e. to make it more representative of the community it serves. This has led to more appointments from minority groups and disabled people, including since 1998 blind people (for whom training and other materials are translated into Braille). Advisory

---

[9] It has been argued that this ancient form of challenge should be dispensed with. It was at one time used to protect black defendants from having be tried by an all-white jury, but also sometimes in a purely cavalier fashion.

[10] For all practical purposes, 'magistrate' and 'justice of the peace' are synonymous.

[11] As noted in *Chapter 3*, the Ministry of Justice has discouraged the use of this term.

Committees thus look for applicants from a range of backgrounds and walks of life. They seek nominations by such methods as asking local organizations or businesses to encourage suitable people to come forward, and through notices, e.g. in the press and public libraries. There is nothing to prevent an individual putting himself or herself forward by contacting the secretary to the local Advisory Committee, completing an application form and adding the names of people prepared to recommend him or her. Political views are only relevant to prevent benches becoming weighted in any particular direction.

Duties and responsibilities

The main duty of a magistrate is to sit in court on a regular basis. The minimum requirement is 26 sittings a year. Most magistrates sit more than this and senior magistrates may find themselves sitting many more times. Apart from duties in their own PSA, magistrates may be called upon to sit elsewhere within the Commission of the Peace area on occasion, e.g. where someone closely connected with another bench is charged with an offence. Additionally, magistrates can volunteer to sit in the Crown Court alongside a judge to hear appeals (but no longer to sit on committals for sentence as they once did): *Chapter 10.*

Presiding justices

The magisterial hierarchy is noted in *Chapter 3.* For many years local benches have appointed 'court chairs', 'day chairs' or 'presiding justices'. Since 1996, only magistrates whose names appear on a list of approved court chairmen appointed by a local bench selection panel are eligible to act as such (except under supervision for training purposes). Similarly, no-one can preside unless they have undertaken an approved course of instruction (see, generally, under *Training for the Judiciary,* below).

District judges

There are also around 100 district judges (magistrates' courts).[12] These are full-time salaried magistrates, but otherwise of equivalent status to lay magistrates, although empowered to sit alone to hear cases and dispense justice and who, by virtue of their professional status and expertise, are likely to play a leading role in areas where they operate—principally London and larger urban centres, but also across many counties. Many district judges also sit as Crown Court recorders (see under the heading *Judges,* above). Despite the role of the district judge successive Lords Chancellor have reiterated that wholesale replacement of the lay magistracy by professionals is not an objective. Indeed, it is difficult to see how the public purse could afford to pay for the staffing of the thousands of magistrates' courts that are held daily in all parts of the country.

---

[12]   As opposed to district judge (county courts), a civil court appointment of similar standing.

Commission of the Peace

Magistrates are appointed to a Commission area and assigned to a Local Justice Area (*Chapter 3*). They must retire from the bench at 70 years of age when they are normally placed on the supplemental list (i.e. as opposed to the active list) after which they have a somewhat limited range of powers.

Magistrates' Association

The Magistrates' Association was established in 1920 and incorporated by Royal Charter in 1962. It enjoys the patronage of the Sovereign and publishes a regular journal, *The Magistrate* and an *Annual Report*. It responds to Government or government departments on proposals for reform and also to other criminal justice organizations, services, reform groups, etc. on matters affecting magistrates' courts. It also initiates projects and proposals of its own and publishes the *Magistrates' Courts Sentencing Guidelines,* which are now formulated in conjunction with the Sentencing Guidelines Council (SGC) (*Chapter 9*) and a range of other interested parties.

The vast majority of magistrates in England and Wales join the Magistrates' Association (by voluntary subscription) and take part in branch activities. There is a full-time secretary and staff. The association's headquarters are situated in Fitzrovia,[13] from where it operates through local branches based on a county or several counties. Each branch organizes its own events, meetings, training, social gatherings, etc. and, depending on its size, elects a given number of representatives to a national council of over 100 members which meets three times a year. The association has various standing committees, including, in the criminal justice sphere, a Sentencing of Offenders Committee.

TRAINING FOR THE JUDICIARY

The Judicial Studies Board (JSB) provides training and instruction for all full-time and part-time judges in England and Wales (including district judges) in the skills necessary for their role. The JSB is based at Millbank Tower, Westminster although many of its training functions take place at other locations. Noticeably, the JSB was one of the first organizations within the Criminal Justice System to take a stand on race (and other discrimination) issues, to the extent of setting up its own advisory board and providing extensive training and materials for judges and magistrates from the 1980s onwards. There are now highly developed schemes of training for judges at all levels.

---

[13] At 28 Fitzroy Square, London W1P 6DD. The premises were bequeathed to it by a former chair of the Magistrates' Association, Lord Merthyr of Borth-y-Guest.

Magistrates training

Before being appointed, candidates must give an undertaking to comply with the relevant requirements. If someone fails to complete an appropriate stage, he or she is expected to resign unless there is an acceptable explanation. There are schemes of Induction Training and Basic Training for new magistrates and comparable schemes for magistrates appointed to the specialist panels, i.e. youth court panel and family proceedings panel.[14] Various bodies are involved in providing training and materials: the Judicial Studies Board (JSB) (below); Magistrates' Association (below); and external bodies such as Cambridge University whose Board of Extra-Mural Studies runs courses at Madingley Hall.

JUSTICES' CLERKS

Formerly, justices' clerks were both the chief legal advisers to magistrates and managers of their courts. They are still the main legal advisers and courts must, in effect, operate under their auspices—but since the Police and Magistrates' Courts Act 1994 the administrator has been the justices' chief executive or equivalent status managing officer within the Court Service. The justices' clerk is free from direction in legal and judicial matters. However, he or she can direct his or her own court legal advisers—essentially people who deputise for him or her on a day-to-day basis in order that several courts can function simultaneously. Some justices' clerks are known as 'directors of legal services'. In the 1960s there were approaching 1,000 justices' clerks, but there are now around 100 people fulfilling that senior role[15] assisted by around 3,000 legal advisers.[16]

Duties and responsibilities

The justices' clerk will advise the magistrates on the law as it applies to the discharge of their responsibilities. In order to comply with the law and practice directions, he or she must advise 'on request', but can also act of his or her own initiative—and, in effect, must do so if the magistrates are about to go wrong in law. He or she may be invited into the magistrates' private retiring room but should never go there automatically and normally not do so unless specifically asked to do so. This invitation should only occur where there is a genuine need for legal advice or support. There is a duty to interrupt magistrates' private deliberations if by not doing so this would result in some legal error being made. The modern practice sanctioned in *Practice Directions* is for advice to be given or

---

[14] The magistrates' court has a wide-ranging family jurisdiction. It is possible in future that appointments may be made by the Lord Chancellor direct to either of these specialist panels (as already occurs in London)—as suggested by *Justice for All* in relation to the youth court panel.

[15] They must be barristers or solicitors of at least five years' standing.

[16] Notoriously, in 1922, the justices' clerk at Hay-on-Wye, Herbert Rowse Armstrong, was executed for the murder of his wife by poisoning, the only solicitor ever subjected to capital punishment.

repeated in open court. The parties can then comment if they so wish in the full knowledge of what advice is being tendered.[17]

Justices' Clerks Society (JCS)

The JCS (motto 'Putting Justice First') was founded in 1839 and incorporated in 1903. It is a professional body representing justices' clerks and assistant justices' clerks to magistrates and to district judges (magistrates' courts) in England and Wales and 'is committed to improving the quality of justice in magistrates' courts'. One of the main objects of the JCS is 'to keep under review the operation of the law, especially that administered by magistrates' courts, to point out its defects and to support and promote proposals for improvement'. Members of the JCS also play an active role in numerous bodies ranging from the National Criminal Justice Board (NCJB) to the Judicial Studies Board, in addition to developing their own initiatives and innovations within the Court Service.

LAW OFFICERS

The law officers of the Crown are the Attorney General and the Solicitor General. They are appointed from among the senior lawyer MPs of the party in power and are either a peer or a member of the House of Commons. Apart from his or her role in the courts, which may involve appearing as prosecuting counsel in high profile or nationally sensitive cases, the Attorney General has a political role which is to act as the government's principal legal adviser and in this capacity he or she answers members' questions in the House of Commons. Additionally, he or she is accountable to Parliament for the CPS and the SFO, the directors of which agencies report to him or her (*Chapter 7*). Along with the Lord Chancellor and Home Secretary the Attorney General is head of one of the three ministries with responsibilities for aspects of the CJS. The Attorney General is appointed by the Prime Minister, heads his or her own government department, the Office of the Attorney General, and is accountable to Parliament for the:

- Crown Prosecution Service;
- Serious Fraud Office;
- HM Treasury Solicitor's Department;
- Department of the Director of Public Prosecutions for Northern Ireland;
- CPS Inspectorate; and
- HM Revenue and Customs Prosecution Office.

The role of the Attorney General is some five centuries old. Certain prosecutions require his or her consent, or fiat, as it is called. There is also a broad public

---

[17] Which involves human rights considerations: *Chapter 2*.

interest duty, one example of which is that of appeal to the Court of Appeal where he or she considers that there has been an 'unduly lenient sentence' (*Chapter 10*). He or she is often described as being the guardian of the public interest and has a wide discretion to intervene as an external party in court proceedings or processes. The complexity of the role has attracted much public comment around several issues in modern times. These concerns have arisen following a number of events but are most strongly associated with the nature and legality of advice given to the Government concerning the legality of the Iraq War, interventions whereby a long-running criminal investigation into corruption at BAE Systems (now BAES) was ended by the SFO in the national interest,[18] and a degree of prevarication concerning who would or should take the final decision for or against prosecution in relation to the 2006-7 'cash for honours' investigation that cleared No 10 Downing Street of related criminality. Hence assurances by Government in the Green Paper, *The Governance of Britain*[19] that it is fully committed to enhancing public confidence and trust in the role. On taking up her appointment as Attorney General in 2007, Baroness Scotland,[20] announced that she would no longer be involved in a range of politically sensitive areas of decision-making, a stance that appears to have altered since that time and promised constitutional safeguards have not materialised.

CROWN PROSECUTORS

As explained in *Chapters 7* (which also outlines the nature of the prosecutor's role) the overall national head of the CPS is the Director of Public Prosecutions (DPP)[21]—who must issue a Code for Crown Prosecutors pursuant to section 10 Prosecution of Offences Act 1985—and the responsible Government law officer the Attorney-General (above). Crown prosecutors are usually solicitors, but may be barristers by training. Other senior personnel include a chief executive, directors of casework and policy, chief Crown prosecutors, assistant chief Crown prosecutors, area business managers and specialist higher court advocates. Crown prosecutors and senior Crown prosecutors operate at local level assisted by designated caseworkers (below).

Headquarters and the regions
The CPS has headquarters in London and York and operates under the now standard structure of 42 areas coinciding with police force and other agency boundaries across England and Wales. Each area matches police force boundaries

---

18 Subsequently, in 2008, found by the High Court to be a mere 'pretext' and unlawful.
19 (2007) Cm 7170: see also generally, *Chapter 15*.
20 The UK's first woman AG and also the first black AG.
21 The DPP originally had a limited responsibility for approving and supervising the prosecution of serious offences when prosecutions were generally conducted by the police or their solicitors.

apart from in London where one CPS area covers the City of London and the Metropolitan Police Service areas. This structure 'meets the Government's aim of a co-ordinated criminal justice system with national policies delivered locally'.

External representation and opinions

Largely speaking, the CPS functions through in-house lawyers and managers. However it does sometimes employ solicitors in private practice to act as its agents, and did so extensively in its early days. CPS agents have only limited authority concerning the conduct of a case. Also, it can happen that a case is unusually complex, involves specialist technicalities, or needs to be managed away from the distractions of day-to-day prosecution. It may then be more expeditious or cost-effective for the CPS to employ outside lawyers. Likewise it may be appropriate at the outset of a substantial case to take the opinion of counsel (i.e. a practising barrister) and to retain that person's services for all aspects of the future conduct of the case. Every such advocate prosecuting on behalf of the CPS is expected to be familiar with a booklet *CPS Instructions For Prosecuting Advocates* first published in 2000, which covers a range of day-to-day issues such as custody time limits, plea and directions hearings, disclosure of the prosecution case, racially aggravated offences and human rights issues.

Designated case workers

In 1998 the law was changed to allow CPS staff who are not fully qualified as lawyers to review cases and present them in magistrates' courts. The powers extend to a limited range of cases involving straightforward guilty pleas, including, e.g. minor thefts, simple possession of certain drugs and non-contentious motoring offences. Under the supervision of experienced Crown prosecutors, designated caseworkers divide their time between police stations (where they review cases) and local magistrates' courts. Before they can undertake this work they must pass an intensive training course validated by an external body and be formally designated as caseworkers by the DPP.

ADVOCATES

Lawyers are either barristers (also called 'counsel') or solicitors, according to their training. Both have rights of audience in the magistrates' court and barristers and authorised solicitors in the Crown Court. When appearing in court both are also known as 'advocates', i.e. they speak for their client on his or her 'instructions'—putting matters forward in the best light. This can be viewed as an essential feature of democratic society and a fair trial. No matter how unpopular the accused peron's alleged behaviour, he or she may always have someone who is professionally qualified to do so to speak on his or her behalf. Both professions have their own codes of conduct and ethics but, generally speaking, provided that they do not positively mislead the court there is no duty to actively disclose matters which are adverse to a client and which have not otherwise emerged in the proceedings (a consequence of the English adversarial system: *Chapter 2*).

The kind of advocate regularly seen in magistrates' courts is the local solicitor specialising in criminal (and often family) work. He or she will usually undertake state funded representation (below). Some solicitors find it cost-effective to employ recently qualified barristers for advocacy work. This is a common feature in London and other urban centres where there are barristers' chambers. Senior barristers are known as Queen's Counsel (or 'silks') and must normally appear in court accompanied by a junior barrister (although this allegedly restrictive practice is being questioned in the European Union).

CRIMINAL DEFENCE SERVICE (CDS)

Historically, local duty solicitor schemes provided legal assistance and advice to people when they were first detained by the police. There were no great formalities and such schemes did not guarantee any choice of solicitor, or for continued services by the same solicitor after the defendant was released from police custody or when he or she next appeared in court. Duty solicitor schemes in magistrates' courts provided a 'first aid' service to defendants in criminal cases who arrived at court without a lawyer. The same principle continues but a key aspect of reforms which took place in 2001 was the creation of a Criminal Defence Service (CDS) which now provides legal assistance to people suspected or accused of crimes through a mix of contracts with private and salaried defenders. The purpose of the CDS was set out in a circular from the then Lord Chancellor's Department[22] as being

> . . . to ensure access for individuals involved in criminal investigations to such advice, assistance and representation as the interests of justice require. The CDS will move to funding criminal defence services through a flexible system of contracts with private sector lawyers and salaried defenders, with the aim of achieving quality assured services and value for money. Suspects and defendants will have a choice of representatives.

The CDS operates under the auspices of the Legal Services Commission and only solicitors with a franchise from the LSC or who work full-time for the CDS can apply for a representation order for a defendant. The application, usually in the magistrates' court, can be made to a court or justices' clerk, the matter being referred to the court if he or she is not prepared to grant representation.

---

[22] Superseded by the Department of Constitutional Affairs and then the MOJ.

STATE FUNDED LEGAL REPRESENTATION

State funded legal representation is provided by what is generally called 'legal aid'[23] under a system which, historically speaking, took both the interests of justice and the financial circumstances of the applicant into account. The former Legal Aid Board was replaced by a Legal Services Commission (LSC) in 2001, that assumed responsibility for funding such advice and assistance in criminal proceedings. This reform—based on the Access to Justice Act 1999 and the Criminal Defence Service (Advice and Assistance Act) 2001—had various effects:

- legal aid as such was abolished and replaced by representation at public expense under the 1999 Act;
- legal aid orders were replaced by 'representation orders';
- a representation order is granted where this is in the interests of justice;[24] and
- all publicly funded representation in the magistrates' courts is now free of charge. There is no means test.[25]

Where a case is finalised in the Crown Court, the judge has a power to make an order at the end of the case requiring the defendant to pay some or all of the defence costs, known as a recovery of defence costs order (but not if a case starts and finishes in the magistrates' court).[26] Since then there have been a number of further reforms and cost-cutting measures in line with comparable initiatives.

Tensions and disincentives
Modern times have seen a significant number of solicitors moving out of this kind of work which they claim is no longer cost-effective following increased pressure to work within what they argue are diminishing budgets in real terms. Whether, ultimately, this is tantamount to a denial by all parties concerned of open access to justice is debatable. Indicative of the tensions, early in 2008, the LSC, Law Society and MOJ announced that they had finally 'reached agreement' on the best way forward following a Court of Appeal ruling on a Unified Contract for solicitors so as to 'ensure a period of certainty and stability for providers of legal aid'. The three organizations published a joint statement detailing the outcome of protracted negotiations saying among, other things, that it had been decided to delay until July 2009 the introduction of 'any best value

---

[23] A term which has continued in everyday parlance despite the newer 'state funded, etc' tag.
[24] The relevant considerations reflect what used to be known as 'the Widgery criteria' (named after Lord Widgery, Lord Chief Justice, who originally laid them down), e.g. whether: the accused is likely to lose his or her liberty; his or her reputation is at stake; the complexity of the proceedings; whether the accused will be able to understand the proceedings etc.
[25] Even a millionaire would qualify, it seems, if the interests of justice test is satisfied—assuming he or she does not wish to forego this and instruct and pay for a lawyer privately.
[26] There is thus and to this extent a disincentive to elect trial by jury.

tendering scheme for criminal defence services' that may be introduced and to make new arrangements in respect of 'historic un-recouped payments' made over a period of up to six years. The announcement concluded by saying:

> The legal aid reform programme continues, and the LSC and MOJ remain fully committed to its objectives of improving client access to quality services and providing value for money for the taxpayer.

THE McKENZIE FRIEND

As noted in earlier chapters, it is open to an accused person to represent himself or herself. He or she may also take along to court someone other than a lawyer to assist in this process, what is usually described as a 'McKenzie friend'[27] (even if that term may have been superseded in case law). With the permission of the court, that person may take notes, quietly make suggestions and give advice and support. As noted and it should be stressed, this needs to be authorised by the court—and the mechanism can only be used as a means of assisting the defendant and the court, not of hindering the proceedings, e.g. by filibustering, playing to the gallery, or otherwise interfering with the progress of the case. More generally, courts can hear from whoever they wish.[28] Conversely, the Courts and Legal Services Act 1990 acknowledged a general right for a court to refuse to hear someone who would normally have rights of audience for reasons which apply to him or her as an individual—but the court must give its reasons.

WITNESSES AND EXPERTS

A key contribution to the criminal process in court is made by witnesses attending to give evidence about events that they have seen, heard or otherwise experienced and who in many instances will also be victims of crime. The proper treatment of witnesses is high on the agenda within all the criminal justice agencies something which (together with Victim Support and witness schemes) is noted in *Chapter 13*. The role of the expert witness is noted in *Chapter 9*.

---

[27] One of those characters who spring up in the law from time to time and lend their identity to some legal concept, such as 'The Man on the Clapham Omnibus'—who became a by-word for reasonableness—and the unsuspecting Mr. Newton whose name is synonymous, in magistrates' courts, with the notion of plea of guilty where there are disputed facts, i.e. a 'Newton hearing'.

[28] A principle enshrined in the House of Lords ruling in *O'Toole v. Scott* [1965] AC 939.

INTERPRETERS

Increasingly, the need for interpreters[29] has been recognised in a wide range of criminal justice situations from the outset of an investigation to assistance in the prison setting, and indeed human rights considerations now often mean that such assistance is essential where the accused person's first language is not English (unless he or she clearly indicates that an interpreter is not required). In court, interpreters take a special oath (or affirm) to 'truly interpret' the evidence from one language to another, or by sign language to someone with impaired hearing. The task is a highly skilled one given the degree of precision required in legal proceedings, and the need to communicate information without adding to it, detracting from it or injecting any value judgment.

Courts, police and other practitioners now have, or have access to, lists of people who are qualified to interpret into and from English and other languages as well as interpreters skilled in dealing with sign language. People serving custodial sentences may or may not be fortunate enough to have ready or immediate access to an interpreter although this is an area where a number of initiatives have been developed by HM Prison Service, including remote interpreting over the telephone.

OTHER PEOPLE IN THE COURTROOM

Various other people are to be encountered in the courtroom including the usher who calls on cases, swears in witnesses and passes papers to and fro. There is also the police gaoler, prison officers or private sector security guards who take charge of prisoners and sometimes sit by them in the dock.[30] The media are usually present, for whom a press box is provided. In the Crown court there is frequently a stenographer who records the proceedings verbatim for the purposes of the official transcript on which any future appeal may be based. The role of the probation officer—who is regularly on the court scene attending to defendants and offenders or presenting a pre-sentence report (PSR)—is described in *Chapter 13*. Finally and importantly in the interests of visibility and transparency, there are any members of the general public who, as is their right, attend to observe the proceedings under the principle of open court which is outlined in *Chapter 2*.

---

[29]   See *Interpreters and the Legal Process* (1996), Colin J and Morris R, Waterside Press.

[30]   Many courtrooms do not have a dock as such and unless there is a security risk the accused person may appear in court without any sign of physical security. Escaping from lawful custody, physical or not, is a serious indictable offence.

CHAPTER 13

Community Provision

Community provision of various kinds exists alongside or in the hinterland of those CJS services provided by the statutory or public sector. It ranges across crime prevention or crime reduction initiatives and partnerships of the kind noted in earlier chapters to volunteering of all kinds. The role of one key community-based organization, Victim Support, is noted at the end of this chapter and also the closely allied Witness Service. 'Community justice' is a description that has been applied to emergent court-based schemes in some parts of England and Wales that are designed to engage the community as a whole in finding better solutions to the problems of law and order and anti-social behaviour (ASB)(below). This innovation is outlined in *Chapter 2*.

In terms of sentencing the key division between the generic community sentence and imprisonment (or other forms of incarceration) has already been noted in *Chapter 9* whilst the practical meaning of imprisonment and the work of HM Prison Service (HMPS) is expanded on *Chapter 14*. First, this chapter looks at the work of the Probation Service.

BACKGROUND

The National Probation Service (NPS) was created in 2001 as the modern-day incarnation of the former locally-based and welfare-oriented Probation Service. That service began as an advisory and befriending facility in the late-19th century, leading to formal recognition of its utility and the duties and responsibilities of the service and its officers being set out in the Probation of Offenders Act 1907. They had a duty to 'advise, assist and befriend' offenders that continued in one statutory form or another until the present arrangements superseded earlier provisions. The roots of the service can also be traced to philanthropic (often Quaker-based) initiatives and in particular to the work of the London Police Court Mission.[1]

From at least the beginning of the 1980s, the then locally-based service and HM Prison Service (HMPS) (*Chapter 14*) became increasingly committed to joint working to prevent offenders from re-offending in particular.[2] These efforts took place via various forms of supervision by probation officers (by offenders being 'on probation' as it was then styled), other community sentences that emerged

---

[1] For a fine historical account, see *Introduction to the Probation Service* (2001), edn. 2, revised reprint, Whitfield D, Waterside Press. Some commentators have noted that an original welfare-based ethos has taken second place as the Probation Service veers increasingly towards 'corrections'.

[2] See *Crime, State and Citizen: A Field Full of Folk* (2006), Faulkner D, Waterside Press, *Chapter 20*.

from the mid-1970s onwards, such as community service (later renamed 'community punishment' and now 'unpaid work') or within prison regimes. Many custodial sentences were and still are served partly in the community in any event (see, generally, *Chapter 9*). Indicative of the same kind of momentum, a Prisons and Probation Minister was appointed and, from 2002, a Correctional Policy Framework together with a joint Correctional Services Board and Correctional Services Accreditation Panel were created, the latter to validate programmes and courses. Overall, the aim was to maximise the numbers of offenders dealt with in the community, a theme that the present Lord Chancellor, Jack Straw MP, faced with a rising prisoner population, has returned to with some vigour in trying to persuade courts away from short sentences of imprisonment.[3] Similarly, the former Prison Ombudsman's office was enlarged to encompass the responsibilities of both services (see *Chapter 14*).

Ultimately, a National Probation Service (NPS) was created in 2001 and in 2004 the NPS and HMPS were then brought together—but still as separate and independently functioning bodies—under the umbrella of a National Offender Management Service (NOMS). This change followed a review of correctional services in England and Wales by Lord Patrick Carter, *Managing Offenders, Reducing Crime*, published in December 2003. The Government's response, *Reducing Crime: Changing Lives*, published in January 2004, announced the establishment of NOMS under a chief executive and a National Offender Manager. Ten Regional Offender Managers were appointed. It was announced that the 42 local Probation Boards would be replaced by independent Probation Trusts which would be under contract to NOMS to deliver probation services. The first six Probation Trusts came into operation in April 2008. A new structure for the MOJ was announced at the start of 2008, including the creation of an entirely fresh strategic post of Director General of Criminal Justice and Offender Management in addition to the chief executive of NOMS and with a level of integration at regional level to be introduced over a period leading up to 2010. The posts of chief executive of NOMS and Director General of the Prison Service were merged, so that the chief executive now manages public sector prisons and enters into service level agreements and contracts with Probation Boards and Trusts as well as private and voluntary sector providers of correctional services. The roles of Regional Offender Managers and Prison Service Area Managers will be merged, and each region will be managed by a Director of Offender Management. This new arrangement began in London and Wales in April 2008. Despite earlier, occasional suggestions that the two services should be merged into a single, unified 'corrections service', the separate roles and functions of probation officers, prison governors and prison officers still continue. With the creation of the MOJ, other fears came to the fore, not just about the proximity of the NPS and HMPS but also concerning their new, post-MOJ relationship to the

---

[3] Controversially in some instances. Exhortations of this kind inevitably invite questions when concerns about the nature and remit of the MOJ and judicial independence remain live issues.

courts with all three now looking to the MOJ for funding and other resources: see further the comments on the *Costs of Criminal Justice* in *Chapter 15*.

NOMS has developed an 'offender management' model in which a single offender manager takes overall responsibility for each offender sentenced to imprisonment or supervision throughout their time in custody and under supervision or licence in the community, to identify their needs and ensure that the right interventions are delivered to meet them. NOMS aims to apply the offender management model to all offenders subject to community orders and licences by the end of March 2009.

End-to-end sentencing

One outcome of joint-working between the Probation Service and HMPS was the development of 'end-to-end sentencing' or the 'seamless sentence'—put simply, effective mechanisms to ensure continuity and cohesion as between work with an offender inside prison and in the community following his or her release. This might, e.g. involve the setting-up of links between drug, alcohol or sex offending programmes in prison and in the community as well as communications between people who are at-risk of offending once released from prison, so that, e.g. this can be monitored during post-custody supervision and optimum use made of referrals to agencies such as those concerned with drug or alcohol misuse.[4]

THE PROBATION SERVICE

A National Probation Service (NPS) was established in April 2001 under the Criminal Justice and Court Services Act 2000. It took over the work of the 42 local Probation Services that existed across England and Wales and at the same time a new National Probation Directorate was established, based in London under a national Director of Probation. Initially a directorate of the Home Office, the Probation Service now comes under the MOJ and the Director of Probation is responsible to the chief executive of NOMS. The 2001 arrangements replaced those whereby area probation services operated under the auspices of local probation committees. At the same time, probation committees were replaced by Probation Boards (below) and there were significant changes in organization, structure, priorities, qualifying training arrangements for probation officers and day-to-day routines. The names of the main community sentences administered by the service were also changed under the 2000 Act and then again by the Criminal Justice Act 2003 when they became components of the generic community sentence.[5]

---

[4] A useful starting point is www.clinks.org Clinks was created in 1998 to strengthen and develop partnerships between voluntary and community-based organizations, HMPS and the NPS.

[5] One plan was to rename the Probation Service to give it a 'punishment' or 'corrections' edge. This was resisted by officers, the word 'probation' being retained in the agency's title but the names of community orders changed. Professor Mike Nellis, a seasoned commentator, noted at that time

Aims of the Probation Service

The aims of the Probation Service are now stated to be as follows:

- protecting the public;
- reducing re-offending;
- the proper punishment of offenders in the community;
- ensuring offenders' awareness of the effects of crime on the victims of crime and the public; and
- rehabilitation of offenders.[6]

The service also seeks 'to be a public service that protects the public, operates and enforces court orders and prison licences, and rehabilitates offenders to lead law abiding lives'. A 'collective aim' as expressed at its inauguration in 2001 is (paraphrased) to be a world leader in the design and implementation of offender assessment and supervision to reduce re-offending and improve public safety.

Organization and structure

The Probation Service now describes itself as a law enforcement agency and public authority. Under the Freedom of Information Act 2000, the National Probation Directorate (NPD) has undertaken to maintain a scheme for the publication of probation service information and methods of accessing that information.[7] Each year the Probation Service commences the supervision of some 175,000 offenders. Its caseload on any given day is in excess of 200,000. Approximately 90 per cent of those supervised are male and ten per cent are women. Just over a quarter of offenders serving community sentences are aged 16-20 and just less than three-quarters are aged 21 and over. Approximately 70 per cent of offenders supervised will be on generic community sentences and 30 per cent subject to a period of statutory licence supervision in the community as an integral part of a prison sentence.

Assessment and the management of risk

Virtually all Probation Service work with offenders combines continuous assessment and management of risk and dangerousness and the provision of professionally designed supervision programmes, with the aim of reducing re-offending. A main tool for this is the Offender Assessment System (Oasys).[8] Enforcement of the order or licence conditions is a priority. Each year the Probation Service assists magistrates and judges in their sentencing decisions through the provision of some 246,000 pre-sentence reports (PSRs) (see *Chapter 9* and also below) and 20,000 bail information reports (*Chapter 6*); and Probation Service staff supervise some eight million hours of unpaid work by offenders in

---

that it might have been better to have retained the well understood names of orders and to have changed the name of the service to, say, the 'Community Corrections Agency'.

[6] See www.probation.homeoffice.gov.uk (seemingly unchanged since the transfer to the MOJ).

[7] The scheme can be viewed at www.nps.org.uk

[8] Or eOasys as it applies in relation to assessments for electronic monitoring.

local communities, to ensure that they meet the requirements of their generic community sentence. The Probation Service also makes a critical contribution to decisions about the early release of prisoners through the production of reports (some 87,000 annually) which combine risk and dangerousness assessments with community supervision proposals in the form of a release plan. Where the victims of the most serious violent, including sexually violent, crimes are contactable and wish it, the impact of the offence and their concerns form a part of the pre-sentence reports or post-custody release risk assessments written by probation staff (around 50,000 cases per annum).[9] Many probation staff are seconded to work in youth offending teams, prisons and a wide range of other public protection and crime prevention or reduction partnership agencies, in particular for their risk-assessment skills.

Probation Boards and Trusts

Each Probation Board is composed of representatives of the local community appointed by the Lord Chancellor. The chief probation officer is a member of the board, which acts as the local employer as well as setting the local agenda against a background of national strategy. The chief probation officer for a local area is appointed by the Lord Chancellor who also has power to give directions to boards about how to fulfil their statutory responsibilities. There are 'default' powers whereby he or she can remove and replace boards if they fail to perform effectively. Probation Trusts will progressively replace Probation Boards, and will each appoint a chief executive. At national level there is a Probation Association (which has replaced the former Probation Boards Association from April 2008), the national employers organization which works with and on behalf of Probation Boards and Trusts.

Drug testing

The Criminal Justice and Court Services Act 2000 gave police power to drug test detainees in police custody (*Chapter 6*) and the courts powers to order drug testing of offenders under the supervision of the Probation Service and in relation to certain 'trigger' offences. Testing is restricted to specified Class A drugs, heroin and crack cocaine. The drug treatment requirement of the generic community sentence is mentioned separately in *Chapter 9*.

KEY ROLE OF THE PRE-SENTENCE REPORT

A central aspect of probation work is that of writing pre-sentence reports (PSRs) for consideration by courts before they decide upon sentence. PSRs are normally

---

[9] Under the Criminal Justice Act 1991 PSRs had, for the first time, to be 'in writing', whereas previously they were sometimes delivered by way of a short, impromptu speech in court by a probation officer following an short interview during a break in the proceedings. The practice was thus long since gone when the requirement for a PSR to be in writing disappeared under the Criminal Justice Act 2003, without explanation, discussion or rationale.

requested by courts in all the more serious cases, although they can be dispensed with where a court considers that a PSR is unnecessary.[10] In their modern form they were first introduced by the Criminal Justice Act 1991,[11] when the preparation and content of reports also became subject to *National Standards*. In more recent times, a form of PSR known as a 'specific sentence report' — or the SSR — has evolved. This is a more focused form of report which, at the request of the court, is directed towards the appropriateness of particular generic community sentence requirements and their suitability for the offender.

PSRs are confidential documents and the information in them is limited to what is relevant to the sentencing process. However, ever since the Pre-Sentence Report (Prescription of Prosecutors) Order 1998, Crown prosecutors are automatically entitled to receive a copy of the PSR, whilst the decision whether to disclose to other public prosecutors depends on an exercise of discretion by the court. *National Standards* envisage a copy being provided to the offender or its contents being brought to the attention of the offender by the report writer. This may mean reading it out in private to someone who has difficulty in reading, or asking an interpreter to read and explain it to an offender whose first language is not English. Since the Human Rights Act 1998 and in the normal course of events, a copy of the PSR is given to the offender and/or to his or her legal representative. By the same token it is important that offenders understood the contents of their PSR and are given a proper opportunity to consider and, where appropriate, comment on its contents to the report writer or the court.

Typically, a PSR begins by setting out basic information about the offence and offender (including his or her previous convictions, if any). It also contains a summary of the sources drawn upon to prepare the report and the steps taken to validate information. Information is then set out under various headings such as:

- an analysis of the offence or offences committed by the offender;
- an assessment of the offender himself or herself, including, e.g. information about his or her background, day-to-day activities, abilities, associates, attitudes, responsibilities and known problems, e.g. in relation to drugs, alcohol, mental impairment, employment (or lack of) and debt;
- assessment of the risk of harm to the public and the likelihood of re-offending (often described as a 'risk-assessment' as noted above); and
- a conclusion (including, where it seems to be appropriate, a sentence proposal that takes account of any general sentencing guidance or comments about what sentence the offender might expect to be made by the judge or magistrates when calling for the PSR).

---

[10] There are stricter criteria before a PSR can be dispensed with in relation to a juvenile: *Chapter 5*.

[11] Later consolidated in the Powers of Criminal Courts (Sentencing) Act 2000. Prior to 1991 courts relied on what were known as 'social enquiry reports' (or SERs) a term which serves to indicate how the ethos of probation work has changed.

As already noted earlier in this chapter, a specific sentence report (SSR) may differ in that the court will have requested given information around some key focus. Where appropriate, a PSR will be supplemented by specialist reports, e.g. from a doctor or psychiatrist and in particular where such reports have been ordered to be obtained by the court as part of the sentencing process. See, further, the note on *Medical and Psychiatric Services* later in the chapter.

PROBATION OFFICERS

Much of the day-to-day work of the Probation Service is carried out by what are often called qualified probation officers holding the degree-level Diploma in Probation Studies (DipPS), assisted by probation service officers (PSOs), for whom the entry requirements are less demanding. This work encompasses:

- *fieldwork:* attending court, writing PSRs (above), supervising offenders;
- *probation centre work:* running intensive courses for high risk offenders who attend a probation centre;
- *group work:* running offending behaviour groups, such as those based around the various levels of the sex offender treatment programme (SOTP), anger management, drug, alcohol or drink-driving education courses as well as everyday lifestyle matters such as personal finance;[12]
- *community punishment:* supervising non-probation officer staff, attending court, publicising schemes for offenders where appropriate;
- *probation hostels:* managing hostels, selecting and supervising residents;[13]
- *prison-related work:* working alongside prison officers in relation to bail information, sentence planning, throughcare and early release plans, forging links with outside supervisors, support organizations, rehabilitative and other pre-release and post-release work;
- *youth justice:* as a member of a youth offending team (YOT); and
- *bail information:* which is governed by *National Standards* and involves interviewing defendants, verifying information about their circumstances and supplying this to the Crown Prosecution Service (CPS).

Senior probation officer grades—implying management, co-ordination or specialist roles in relation to a geographical area or specialist sphere of operations—are senior probation officers, assistant chief probation officers and deputy chief probation officers. The Probation Service also employs a wide range of administrative and clerical staff as well as specialists in information, research, management systems and technology.

---

12   Comparable courses are run by or in conjunction with HM Prison Service: *Chapter 14.*
13   Some 100 approved hostels play a part in NPS 'public protection strategy', providing 'controlled environments for offenders on community sentences and post-custody licences'.

HM INSPECTORATE OF PROBATION

HM Inspectorate of Probation (HMIP) is a compact, autonomous unit responsible directly to the Lord Chancellor and charged with inspecting the work of the Probation Service. HMIP also provides ministers and officials with advice on probation matters and promotes the development of effective probation management and practice. Most probation inspectors are drawn from within the ranks of the Probation Service. Inspectors generally have considerable experience in the probation field, and may have worked through the grades to reach chief officer level. There is statutory provision allowing suitably qualified people from other disciplines to become probation inspectors. There are normally two kinds of inspection:

- *area* inspections, when two or three sections of a probation area's work (e.g. court reports, community sentences) are looked at in detail, with sampling exercises and face-to-face discussions between inspectors and probation staff taking place at all levels within the location being inspected. Such inspections are called 'Quality and Effectiveness Inspections' and make recommendations to the area concerned; and
- *thematic* inspections, when a particular type of work is examined, e.g. the preparation of PSRs or post-custody supervision (i.e. the supervision of prisoners following their release from prison: see below and *Chapter 14*). A thematic inspection will normally be carried out across several probation areas and the final report will contain recommendations to the Lord Chancellor about national issues as well as recommendations to local areas. Reports of thematic inspections can also contain recommendations concerning the performance of other agencies within the justice process and government departments with an interest in criminal justice.

As well as recommendations regarding action which needs to be taken to improve standards, reports by inspectors may also contain 'commendations' whereby government, Probation Boards and other people can become aware of good work. All such reports are open to public scrutiny.

MEMBERSHIP ORGANIZATIONS

As with other CJS services, probation staff have their own membership organizations. The Association of Chief Executives and Chief Officers of Probation (ACECOP) is a professional and representative organization for chief executives of Probation Trusts and chief officers of areas with Probation Boards. Napo—which represents probation officers and other staff working for the Probation Service—celebrated its centenary in 2007. It is a trade union, professional association and campaigning group which undertakes a range of activities, including in relation to training, representations to government and the publication of *Probation Journal* and *Napo News*.[14] There is also an Association of Black Probation Officers (ABPO).

SOCIAL SERVICES

Local authority social services departments work with many young or vulnerable people. This work is often carried out independently of the CJS proper under legal duties and responsibilities cast on local authorities and may be performed, e.g. by social workers or youth workers as an incidental part of their everyday employment. But it may also be an integral part of CJS work, e.g. where it is carried out by officers responsible for child protection or local authority members of youth offending teams (YOTs) (*Chapter 3*). Social services also have an integral role in relation to Multi-agency Protection Panel Arrangements (MAPPAs) (*Chapter 2*) and also possess emergency and longer-term statutory powers in relation to children and other vulnerable people, including mentally impaired, older or infirm people. The duties and responsibilities of local authorities in relation to Crime and Disorder Reduction Partnerships (CDRPs) are noted at various other points in this handbook.

EDUCATION SERVICES

Local education services are involved with the criminal justice process in a number of ways, including:

- preparing school reports on pupils appearing before the criminal courts, or alternatively providing relevant information to a YOT member who is preparing a PSR, for incorporation into that report;
- participating in a YOT;
- bringing prosecutions against parents for non-attendance at school by their children;
- providing or helping to provide education to prisoners and ex-prisoners as well as to those subject to community sentences as appropriate; and
- involvement in a range of multi-agency partnerships.

MEDICAL AND PSYCHIATRIC SERVICES

The National Health Service (NHS), local social services departments (above) and the voluntary sector provide a range of facilities for mentally impaired offenders

---

[14]   See www.napo.org.uk

who are diverted towards appropriate care at the pre-court stage (including as an alternative to prosecution); given community sentences with a requirement of psychiatric treatment; given hospital orders or remanded to hospital; made subject to guardianship orders or transferred from prison to hospital. In addition, medical services (including the Healthcare Service for Prisoners: *Chapter 14*) prepare reports on the medical and mental condition of defendants to assist courts in their sentencing decisions and HMPS and the Probation Service concerning post-custody and other community supervision. Some of the most serious and mentally impaired offenders are held in special hospitals in conditions of high security and under the auspices of doctors and psychiatrists (see, also, *Chapter 9*).

At many courts, 'duty psychiatrist' schemes and other court psychiatric assessment arrangements have been established: these enable courts to receive speedy professional advice which can also facilitate the (sometimes difficult to obtain) admission of offenders to hospital in appropriate cases.

THE PRIVATE SECTOR IN THE COMMUNITY

Private sector involvement with prisons is referred to in *Chapter 14*. Perhaps less well-known by the general public, is the extent to which the private sector is involved in the provision of CJS-related services in the community, including, in particular, in relation to the electronic monitoring (or tagging)[15] of offenders subject to curfew requirements (*Chapter 9*) or home detention curfew (*Chapter 14*) following release from prison on licence. The whole electronic monitoring service, from the supply and installation of equipment to the actual monitoring of those subject to surveillance, is the responsibility of private contractors. Neither should the role of the private sector in preventing crime in the community be underestimated given the vast nature of the security industry that provides everything from security alarms and CCTV systems to security guards, bodyguards, security vans and surveillance equipment. It is also the case that some programmes and services, including, e.g. those relating to biometric-testing and certain other scientific resources, are bought in from the private sector by the public sector. As already mentioned in *Chapter 11*, the Forensic Science Service (FSS) is a private sector organization known as a GovCo.

THE VOLUNTARY SECTOR

A wide range of organizations from the voluntary sector[16] are engaged in work with offenders. Many such organizations play a key part in work with offenders,

---

[15] For an overview of electronic monitoring, see, e.g. *The Magic Bracelet: Technology and Offender Supervision* (2001), Whitfield D, Winchester: Waterside Press.

[16] Other descriptions may be used, depending on exact status, e.g. 'non-statutory sector', 'charity'.

from national bodies such as the crime reduction charity Nacro—which works with 86,000 offenders and people at risk of offending each year—and Victim Support (below) to the Witness Service and small local charities that may, e.g. provide and manage a single hostel or local service (for example a drug rehabilitation scheme). Regular areas of work for the voluntary sector include:

- *accommodation:* providing hostels, shared housing and supported lodgings schemes for ex-offenders;
- *employment:* providing adult and youth training, work experience, and help and advice on finding employment;
- *education:* providing offenders with education in basic skills, and information, advice and help on participation in education courses;
- *bail:* providing accommodation and support for bailed defendants to help avoid unnecessary remands in custody;
- *mental health:* providing hostels, group homes, day care and advice services for people with a history of mental illness;
- *drug/alcohol misuse:* providing advice services, residential rehabilitation facilities and day care for people with drug and alcohol problems;
- *court-based services:* running help desks at courts providing on the spot advice and information to people attending court, as well as 'tea-bars' and refreshment facilities in some instances; and
- *prisoners' families:* providing support, help and advice to the families and friends of people serving prison sentences.

The voluntary sector also plays a substantial role in relation to HMPS: *Chapter 14*.[17] It is separate and distinct from personal 'volunteering' as such, which takes place across a wider range of activities and includes people, e.g. justices of the peace, special constables, who lend support to public sector organizations.

VICTIM SUPPORT

A striking example of the work of the voluntary sector is Victim Support (VS), which is a wholly independent national charity that helps people affected by crime. It provides free and confidential support to help people who are affected by CJS processes to deal with that experience, whether or not the crime is reported to the police or authorities. Victims of crime are contacted by local VS branches which can provide them or their family and friends with information and support. Members of the public can also phone a national helpline, Victim Supportline. Any citizen can volunteer to assist VS in its objectives, by practical support or by making a donation or shopping online.[18] VS also employs full-time

---

[17] See, also, *Prisons and the Voluntary Sector: A Bridge into the Community* (2002), Bryans S, Martin C and Walker, R, Waterside Press.

[18] See www.victimsupport.org.uk

paid staff. From 2008, various local member charities that were part of Victim Support across England and Wales began merging to form a single national charity, with full nationwide merger scheduled for the summer of 2008. Among its other services, VS has trained volunteers who offer:

- someone to talk to in confidence;
- information on police and court procedures;
- help in dealing with other organizations;
- information about compensation and insurance; and
- links to other sources of help.

This service is free and available to anyone, whether or not the crime has been reported and regardless of when or where it took place. As a result, VS is in contact with over one and a quarter million victims and witnesses each year. There is now provision for a Victims Commissioner and Advisory Panel.[19]

The Witness Service (WS)

VS (above) recognises that many witnesses 'feel worried about going to court, regardless of whether or not they were the victim of the crime'. Hence it also runs the Witness Service in every criminal court in England and Wales in order to provide witness care and give information and support to witnesses, victims, their families and friends when they go to court. In this context, it helps witnesses who are called to give evidence, whether prosecution or defence witnesses, and victims of crime, their families and friends who may be attending court for any reason, both children and adults. Witness Service staff and volunteers can provide, e.g. someone to talk to in confidence; a chance to see the court beforehand and learn about court procedures; a quiet place to wait; someone to accompany a witness into the court room when giving evidence; practical help (for example with expense forms); easier access to people who can answer specific questions about the case; and a chance to talk over the case when it has ended and to get more help or information. As with other aspects of VS, WS is free and independent of the police or courts. The police provide protection for witnesses as appropriate including under witness protection schemes and in extreme situations safe houses and armed guards.

---

[19] For further information, see www.cjsonline.gov.uk Note also the original *Victim's Charter* of 1990 that first publicly triggered a new approach to such matters.

CHAPTER 14

Custodial Provision

Lawful denial of liberty as a sanction against lawbreakers has existed since the Roman era (or even longer), but it is only in relatively modern times, within the last 200 years, that prisons and similar establishments have been places where people served terms of imprisonment ordered by a court as a punishment. Until the 18th century, prisons were used mainly for people who were awaiting trial, exile, execution, transportation or to enforce debts or other civil obligations.

In former times, prisons often operated under private ownership or as an adjunct to power, status or commerce (including as part of an inn).[1] The first public gaols were known as 'bridewells' and 'houses of correction' and were intended for petty offenders, miscreants, vagrants and people awaiting the visit of the judges 'on circuit'. They were largely administered by magistrates in their historic capacity as the local authority. Reliance on prisons as symbols of deterrence, shame and retribution or, gradually, more enlightened places where offenders might be educated, trained and rehabilitated, developed from a mix of law and order, politics and a tradition of penal reform.[2] In modern times, some prisons describe themselves as 'community prisons', which serves to emphasise the interests that the wider world has in what occurs behind prison walls and the contribution that local communities can make with regard to 'their' institutions.

HM PRISON SERVICE (HMPS)

Her Majesty's Prison Service (HMPS) operates under the Prisons Act 1952 and Prison Rules 1999 (and analogous provisions for young offenders). There is also a large accumulation of internal prison service orders (PSOs), instructions (PSIs) and HMPS manuals covering all aspects of prison life.[3] The former relative isolation of HMPS has been replaced by increased involvement with other agencies, including the Probation Service as already noted in *Chapter 13*, the police, Border Agency, Youth Justice Board (YJB) and voluntary, charitable and private sectors. Following the establishing of the National Offender Management

---

[1] It is not difficult to identify a vested interest in locking people up (or in many other forms of punishment), especially historically, but even without too great an imagination today.

[2] For an outline see *Introduction to Prisons and Imprisonment* (1998), Flynn N, Waterside Press; *Punishments of Former Days* (1992), Pettifer E, Waterside Press. For the debate on the purposes and utility of prison, see *Prison On Trial* (2006), Mathiesen T, 3rd edn., Waterside Press.

[3] From prisoners' telephone calls to race relations, work, pay, worship, discrimination and disability. HMPS also publishes *Prison Service News*, *Prison Service Journal* and *Prisons Video Magazine*.

Service (NOMS) in 2004, the director general of HMPS reported to the chief executive of NOMS. Since 2007 NOMS comes under the Ministry of Justice (MOJ) and in 2008 the post of director general of HMPS was merged with that of chief executive of NOMS. The latter now manages public sector prisons and contracts for the construction, development and management of private sector prisons.

Custody

HMPS seeks to combine security, control and safety in its 140 or so establishments for adults, young offenders and various auxiliary services—sometimes called 'the prison estate' or 'secure estate'. It provides a range of prisoner activities including various types of offending behaviour and treatment programmes, e.g. in relation to alcohol, drugs and sex offences. It also undertakes risk-assessments on prisoners so as to provide information to the courts or Parole Board (below).

HMPS is obliged to hold all adults (and some juveniles) remanded to custody by the courts pending their trial (*Chapter 8*) as well as those convicted and sentenced to a custodial term (or in custody after conviction awaiting sentence) (*Chapter 9*). The service must accommodate whoever arrives at the prison gate, regardless of capacity issues, convenience or problems, e.g. of language, religion, age or health. It has sometimes been necessary to hold several hundred 'overflow' prisoners in police cells, court cells or other temporary accommodation. An 'end-of-custody' scheme has allowed up to 1,500 short-term prisoners a month to be released around 18 days earlier than they would have been. The prison population has risen inexorably from around 42,000 in the late 1980s to a peak of around 82,000 in 2008.

Successive governments have tended to see prison building as 'the answer' whilst at the same time acknowledging the values of alternatives to custody (or even restorative approaches: *Chapter 15*). The prison building programme (that has a tendency to grow) is based on a projection of some 96,000 places needed by 2015, including, in a shorter timescale, three 'Titan prisons' to house around 2,500 prisoners each under the auspices of the private sector in (as yet) unspecified security conditions.[4] Typically, prisons in England and Wales each house from a few hundred prisoners up to 1,200 (as with HMP Wandsworth or HMP Wormwood Scrubs). There is a separate 'women's estate', the best-known establishment being Holloway Prison, north London. As there are only 17 prisons for women, female prisoners are often placed far away from their homes and find it difficult to maintain regular contact with their family and friends.

HMPS mission statement

The aims of HMPS are crystalised in its statement of purpose (or 'mission statement') which is prominently displayed in all HMPS establishments:

---

[4]   The Titan proposals have proved controversial. One of the authors (BG) is grateful to Lord Ramsbotham, former HM Inspector of Prisons, for explaining the negative ramifications.

Her Majesty's Prison Service serves the public by keeping in custody those committed by the courts. Our duty is to look after them with humanity and help them lead law abiding and useful lives in custody and after release.

MANAGEMENT AND STAFFING

HMPS became an executive agency in 1993. Since 2007, Ministers at the MOJ are responsible for general policy and the director general of HMPS for the day-to-day delivery of operational services.[5] In 2008, this post was combined with the post of chief executive of NOMS. A Prisons Board acts as the agency's senior management team which includes a number of non-executive directors from outside the service. Executive directors (in effect senior governor grades: below) take charge of designated areas of operation, such as healthcare, the high security estate, personnel, finance, life sentences and other regime activities.

Governors, prison officers and other staff

HMPS employs around 45,000 staff and spends over £1 billion a year on salaries, with overall running costs of some £2 billion. Some two-thirds of HMPS staff are uniformed prison officers[6]—and are called 'prison officers' whatever their rank, whilst over a thousand staff are what are termed 'governors' or 'governor grades'. There are also various operational support grades (OSGs). Each prison has a governing governor (sometimes called 'The Governor') with lesser-ranking governor grades in support and prison medical and education staff also falling within his or her oversight.[7] Prison officers with basic HMPS nursing training may be employed as hospital officers. The staff of healthcare units also includes state registered nurses. Qualified nurses are normally employed in women's prisons with their different regimes.[8] Other key staff and participants include:

- medical officers, prison doctors and psychologists who advise the governor on healthcare and mental health matters, provide reports and risk-assessments for courts or the Parole Board, and healthcare for prisoners;

---

[5] This distinction has not always proved straightforward as was notoriously demonstrated in 1998 when Home Secretary, Michael Howard MP dismissed his director general Derek Lewis following the escape of three high security prisoners from Parkhurst Prison on the Isle of Wight. Lewis, highly regarded, was the first and only DG recruited directly from the private sector, to which he returned.

[6] For an overview, see *The Prison Officer* (2001), Liebling A and Price, D, *Prison Service Journal*.

[7] See *The Prison Governor: Theory and Practice* (1998), Bryans S and Wilson D, Prison Service Journal.

[8] For the historical background to the modern-day arrangements, see *Invisible Women: What's Wrong with Women's Prisons* (1998), Devlin A, Waterside Press in which the fact that women's prisons were until modern times merely a variant of the male system is brought to the fore.

- education officers who run full-time or part-time education courses and evening classes (often provided under contract by colleges of further education or organizations running similar courses in the community);[9]
- librarians who staff prisoner libraries. These are of varying size, standard and accessibility, although the best provide a service equal to that in the community notwithstanding the constraints of prison life. Library catalogues include items from an official list of books and other documents which must be available in each prison for the use of prisoners;
- chaplains (from Anglican, Roman Catholic, Methodist, Muslim, Hindu, Pagan and other faiths depending on local arrangements) who provide opportunities for worship, spiritual counselling and pastoral care, supported by visiting ministers of other denominations and faiths;
- probation officers (*Chapter 13*) who work alongside prison officers on programmes and courses and undertake rehabilitative work, liaise with a prisoner's home probation officer, write reports for the discretionary release processes (see later in this chapter), and advise on issues of resettlement, sentence planning and links to the community;
- resettlement workers employed by voluntary agencies such as the crime reduction charity Nacro;
- staff from other agencies such as Jobcentre Plus who arrange Fresh Start interviews for prisoners seeking employment on release and the Citizens Advice Bureau which provides advice services in some prisons; and
- a wide range of administrative and clerical staff who handle contracts, accounts, calculate release dates, provide services to governors, internal boards, committees, etc. and keep related records.

Following NOMS being established, prisoners who will be on licence when released have a single 'offender manager', a probation officer based in the community. While he or she has overall responsibility for the offender, support is provided by an offender management team including 'offender supervisors' based in prison and in the community with day-to-day responsibility for ensuring that the offender's sentence plan is carried out.

Discipline
Until 2002, governors were responsible for disciplinary adjudications under a system whereby prisoners could have days added to their sentence for breaches of prison rules, but this practice fell foul of Article 6 of the European Convention On

---

[9] One complaint is the narrowness of much education provision that tends to focus on basic education or the acquisition of basic skills at the expense of broader educational topics. Nonetheless some prisoners still manage to study for higher qualifications or even degrees, often now with charitable funding. For a critique, see *Prison(er) Education: Stories of Change and Transformation* (2000), Wilson D and Reuss A, Waterside Press.

Human Rights (the right to a fair trial) (*Chapter 1*).[10] The adjudication function was then passed to visiting judges.

Prison establishments and regimes

Many prisons were built in Victorian or Edwardian times and may be listed buildings of architectural or historical interest. Others are less grand and many were constructed after the Second World War. Some 30 prisons have been built since 1980 or are at the planning stage, including those designed, constructed, managed and financed (DCMF) by private sector contractors and operated under a licence-type arrangement for a fixed number of years. The prison estate also includes converted castles, manor houses and military bases and one prison on land reclaimed from the sea by prisoners.[11] Prisons are styled 'HMP . . .' or in the case of young offender institutions 'HMYOI . . .'.

By 'regime' is meant how and when events occur within a prison on a day-to-day basis, ranging from the locking or unlocking of cells to activities such as work, education, meals, association with other prisoners, visits by outsiders (including legal visits by lawyers), offending behaviour courses, disciplinary adjudications and worship. Each regime will depend on the particular prison and the kind of prisoners held there as well as to some extent on the vision and initiative of a particular governing governor (the most senior governor in charge of a whole prison). The HMPS's mission statement apart (above), its stated aims include 'protecting the public', and providing 'positive regimes' and 'purposeful (or meaningful) activity' for prisoners. There are special regimes for life-sentence prisoners (below) and therapeutic communities at HMP Grendon (since 1960), HMP Dovegate (from 2001) and in smaller units at other prisons.[12] There are a number of open prisons without external walls and fences and two prisons which are styled 'resettlement prisons' where prisoners may be involved in 'working out' in the community as part of their progress towards eventual release.

Prison Governors' Association (PGA) and Prison Officers' Association (POA)

The PGA is the main membership body for governor grades and represents governors at all levels. It engages with the MOJ and other government departments on a range of prison-related, policy formation and day-to-day procedural issues and publishes a regular journal, *The Key*.[13]

The POA describes itself as 'the largest union in the UK representing uniformed prison grades and staff working within the field of Secure Forensic Psychiatric Care, with over 35,000 members in the public and private sectors'. It

---

[10]   *Okichukwiw Ezeh and Lawrence Connors* v. *United Kingdom* (judgement of 15 July 2002).

[11]   North Sea Camp Prison in Lincolnshire.

[12]   See, e.g. *Grendon Tales: Stories from a Therapeutic Community* (2001), Smartt U, Waterside Press.

[13]   Allusions to keys, locks and window bars are a central aspect of prison culture.

represents the interests of members across a broad range of professional issues, including, conditions of service, education, training, privatisation of prisons, health and safety, as well as structural or policy matters affecting, e.g. the MOJ and NOMS. It also provides various types of advice (including legal advice) and support to its members according to their employment-related needs.[14]

PRISONERS: RECEPTION AND REGIMES

At the time of writing the prison population has hovered towards an all-time high of over 82,000,[15] a rise of some 50 per cent over the past decade. Partly as a result of prison overcrowding concerns, in 2001 Lord Woolf, Lord Chief Justice, urged courts to consider whether, when sending someone to prison, a shorter sentence would suffice and later, in *R* v. *Kefford* (5 March 2002),[16] he indicated that prison overcrowding was a relevant consideration when deciding whether or not to send someone to custody, since it affected the ability of HMPS to tackle offending behaviour and reduce reoffending. Courts were reminded that they should heed the principle 'imprisonment only when necessary and for no longer than necessary'. In more recent times comparable sentiments have been expressed by Lord Phillips, Lord Chief Justice, whilst at the same time emphasising that sentencing is a matter for judges and magistrates, and that, in effect, judges should not pander to the administrative or other needs of the MOJ or its constituent parts. In 2002, the then Boards of Visitors (see later under *Independent Monitoring Board*) reported that overcrowding increased assaults, suicides and compromised security. From 1997, the 'tough on crime' agenda of the 1980s suffered a partial backlash in favour of a 'smart on crime' agenda. The Sentencing Guidelines Council is now the key body in issuing advice to courts (*Chapter 9*).

Reception into prison

From court, a prisoner will normally be taken to a local prison or remand centre, usually during the evening when the prison transport—i.e. prison vans now operated almost exclusively under private sector contracts—arrives to collect prisoners from a court centre at the end of the day's proceedings. A prisoner will arrive at reception and be required to shower or bathe, and receive a set of prison clothes. Women prisoners,[17] remand prisoners and, in some prisons depending on

---

[14] See further www.poauk.org.uk

[15] i.e. virtually at capacity, but well above the uncrowded capacity or 'certified normal accommodation' for which the prisons were intended. The Prison Reform Trust estimates that c. 20,000 prisoners are 'doubled-up' or 'trebled-up' in cells designed for smaller numbers. Taking a 'snapshot', there were exactly 82,283 prisoners in England and Wales on 14 March 2008.

[16] See also *R v Mills*, 14 January 2002, in the context of the women's estate.

[17] See *Invisible Women: What's Wrong with Women's Prisons?* (1998), Devlin A, Waterside Press.

the regime, men serving sentences are allowed to wear their own clothes. The prisoner will then be offered a meal, be given a number (which remains with the prisoner throughout his or her sentence) and often a brief medical interview before being taken onto one of the prison wings. During this or a later medical interview or examination the medical officer will assess the prisoner's fitness to work and whether he or she is a suicide risk. The suicide rate in prisons is roughly up to three times that of the general population despite extensive efforts and procedures to bring this down.[18] Young offenders, who are more likely to lack the inner resources to deal with imprisonment, are particularly vulnerable.

Prisoners may be fingerprinted and, within a day or two, photographed. On leaving reception, they are given a towel, sheets, wash-things, toothbrush and tooth powder, spare clothing, plastic cutlery, a plate, mug and pillowcase. He or she may be allowed to keep other personal items 'in possession' such as a radio, wristwatch, book, pen and paper. Some such items are allowed according to local practice (there is a standard list but of somewhat uncertain effect) and the discretion of the governor, who will be concerned to ensure the safety and security of prisoners generally. Other personal items will be stored in reception or at a central depot at Branston, Staffordshire.[19]

Local and other closed prisons are usually divided into a number of wings or halls, each often holding a different category of prisoner (below). Normally, prison wings have several levels or landings containing cells. Outside each cell is a small plate for a card containing the prisoner's number, surname, length of sentence, earliest date of release and religious affiliation. Some prisons have first night centres or other arrangements such as induction wings which avoid newly received prisoners having to go straight on to the main prison wings.

Categorisation and allocation
Sentenced adult men (i.e. aged 21 and over) are initially held in an observation, classification and allocation unit of a local prison or remand centre, after which they are placed in a security category, depending on their offence(s), the perceived risk of their escaping and the danger that they would present to the public should this happen. Sentenced adult male prisoners are categorised:

A Those whose escape would be highly dangerous to the public or the police or to the security of the State;

B For whom 'escape must be made very difficult';

C Cannot be trusted in open conditions but who do not have the will or resources to make a determined escape attempt; or

D Can reasonably be trusted in open conditions.

---

[18] Incidents are monitored by INQUEST (see www. inquest.gn.apc.org). See, also, e.g. *Deaths of Offenders: The Hidden Side of Justice* (1997), Liebling A (Ed.), Waterside Press.

[19] Hence references by prisoners to the fact that their belongings are 'in Branston'.

Unsentenced prisoners are automatically categorised B, unless provisionally placed in Category A. Women and young offenders are categorised simply for open or closed conditions, apart from a few women who are treated as if they were in Category A. Categorisation is reviewed at least every 12 months and prisoners tend to be moved to less secure conditions as they progress through their sentence and as part of a overall sentence plan or pre-release plan. The precise establishment to which an adult male sentenced prisoner is allocated will depend on his security category, sentence and the places or courses (such as the Sex Offender Treatment Programme (SOTP)) available. Many men serving 18 months or less serve their whole sentence in a local prison. Those serving longer sentences are often transferred to a training prison. Category A prisoners are allocated to a high security closed training prison (formerly a 'dispersal prison').[20]

There are also around 1,000 civil prisoners, mainly immigration detainees who are subject to a separate civil regime but within the same establishments as convicted or remand prisoners. Some prisoners are held in prison for non-payment of fines or other financial orders, usually for very short periods of time.

Rule 45

Vulnerable prisoners in need of protection (such as paedophiles, former police officers and supergrasses) and prisoners perceived as a threat to the maintenance of good order and discipline (GOAD) may be segregated from other prisoners under Rule 45 of the Prison Rules.[21] The former may request segregation, whereas GOAD prisoners are often segregated against their wishes. Some prisoners needing long-term protection are held in vulnerable prisoner units (VPUs). Some prisons hold only vulnerable prisoners (e.g. Whatton Prison) or have a large part of the prison used for this purpose (e.g. Stafford Prison and Wymott Prison). In modern times, considerable tensions have arisen between gangs in prison.

Sentence planning, drug and alcohol testing and sex offenders

Sentence plans are drawn up for prisoners serving 12 months or more and for all young offenders. These plans seek to ensure that the prisoner's time in custody is spent positively and that problems underlying offending behaviour are confronted. During their sentence many prisoners will join activities and work groups, offending behaviour courses and programmes which seek to address and remedy problems such as alcohol or drug abuse, gambling, aggression or sexual offending. All prisons have mandatory drug testing (MDT) and some also have additional voluntary drug testing (VDT). There are also a number of special schemes to

---

[20] The term 'dispersal' reflected a strategic decision taken after the Mountbatten Inquiry into prison security in the 1960s to disperse those prisoners who presented the greatest risk to a number of high security prisons rather than to concentrate them in a single establishment.

[21] Rule 47 in YOIs under comparable provisions (whilst such establishments exist).

rehabilitate people who misuse drugs and alcohol.[22] CARATS (Counselling, Assessment, Referral, Advice and Throughcare Services) teams provide the services described in their title.

Various establishments run sex offender treatment programmes (SOTPs) ('core', 'advanced' and 'booster') which aim among other things to counter denial and distorted beliefs; increase awareness of the effect on a victim; get prisoners to accept responsibility; and prevent relapse and high risk situations in future.

Education and training

As already intimated, education in many prisons currently focuses (somewhat contentiously) on the acquisition of basic skills rather than advanced qualifications, although there are opportunities to pursue a range of courses, including correspondence courses (some funded by outside organizations).[23] There is also a wide range of vocational training courses depending on the arrangements and facilities at a particular prison. However, the availability of fringe activities such as the arts which many people argue can lead to personal change has reduced considerably with increasing prison populations and the fact that such activities do not figure directly in HMPS key objectives.[24]

Temporary release

After serving a part of their sentence, prisoners can be considered for temporary release to take part in regime-related activities such as community service projects, employment, training or education, or for resettlement purposes, usually towards the end of a sentence (see, further, below).

LIFE SENTENCE REGIMES

The number of prisoners serving life sentences ('lifers') or other indeterminate sentences has increased from around 2,500 in the early 1990s to over 10,000 today. As noted in *Chapter 9*, lifers are subjected to a continuous process of review and risk assessment. Depending on their progress in prison, periodic downgrading of their security category will usually occur until they can enter open conditions and eventually begin the process of pre-release visits into the community, including in many instances on work-related schemes. Because of the time served under many life sentences (around 14 years on average and in some cases far more for

---

[22] Including the RAPt scheme: see *Drug Treatment in Prison: An Evaluation of the RAPt Treatment Programme* (2000), Martin C and Player E, Winchester: Waterside Press.

[23] See *Prison(er) Education*, etc. mentioned in an earlier footnote.

[24] See, e.g. *Inside Art: Crime, Punishment and Creative Energies* (2002), Brown M, Waterside Press. Drama is used in some prisons, see, e.g. *The Geese Theatre Handbook: Drama with Offenders and People at Risk* (2002), Baim C, Brookes S and Mountfield A, Waterside Press.

mandatory life sentences for murder) it is likely that a chain of HMPS and Probation Service personnel will be involved in carrying out the sentence plan and in resettlement, education, categorisation and assessment processes.

Lifers will typically complete an accumulation of offending behaviour courses and may undertake longer-term educational or other self-development projects. On release, they remain on licence for the rest of their natural lives and are subject to recall if their behaviour suggests that they might once again be a danger to the public. The requirement to report to a supervising probation officer can be removed after a period, but the licence remains in force. Some 40 'natural lifers' will never be released unless there is a change of policy or a European directive. In addition to life sentence prisoners, an increasing number of prisoners are now serving indeterminate sentences of imprisonment for public protection (see, generally, *Chapter 9*). This has caused serious problems for HM Prison Service, with many such prisoners unable to access offending behaviour programmes or other courses which could increase their prospects of release before the end of their minimum 'tariff' period.

THE PRISON DAY

A typical prison day begins between 7.30 and 8 a.m. in a closed prison, when cells are unlocked (known as 'unlock') and prison officers conduct a roll-call. Prisoners are also counted at regular intervals throughout the day. All cells now have sanitation, or access to sanitation, so that the practice of 'slopping out' plastic chamber pots into a communal sluice has virtually disappeared. Prisoners may collect hot water for washing and shaving, then their breakfast from heated trolleys to eat in their cells, while many collect a cold breakfast the evening before.

Regime activities begin around 8.45 a.m. Many prisoners will go to work, training or education classes, though some, mainly those in local prisons, may be inactive for much of the day. Prisoners are employed as cleaners, kitchen and laundry staff; in farming and gardening activities; in clothing, carpentry and engineering workshops; in assembling components for outside industry—and in sewing mailbags. Prisoners in some open and other training or resettlement prisons work outside prison with elderly people, physically disabled people and those with learning disabilities on community projects. In some prisons members of such groups enter the establishment to use sports or recreational facilities with the assistance of prisoners. Several prisons have won contracts in competition with the private sector to supply goods or services provided by prisoners.[25]

---

[25] One aim is to provide meaningful work, enhance self-esteem and bury the stereotypical image of prisoners 'sewing mailbags'. *The Bookseller* reported in 2002 that one contract bid was dropped: for drilling holes in overstocked books before pulping—perhaps a modern-day equivalent of the traditional moving of rocks across the prison yard so that other prisoners could move them back!

Prisoners employed within a prison can earn from £7 to £15 per week although more typically towards the lower end of this scale. Earnings, which can be higher in some privately managed prisons, can be spent in the prison shop[26] which prisoners usually visit (or order from) once a week to buy food, tobacco (but many prison wings are now no-smoking zones), toiletries, batteries, etc. Prisoners who do not have work or classes to go to are paid a flat rate allowance.

During the morning (and, in many establishments, the afternoon), prisoners in closed establishments exercise outdoors, weather permitting. In many places exercise involves walking with other prisoners in a ring in a yard. Prisoners in open prisons do not have exercise periods as such. Juveniles and young adults serving short sentences should have an hour of physical education each weekday. Physical education is popular with many prisoners. It raises self-esteem, provides a sense of achievement, serves as a means of letting out aggression, and prisoners are allowed to shower afterwards.

After lunch, activities are resumed. Some prisoners will receive visits from family and friends. Some prisons allow visits in the morning. Unconvicted prisoners can normally have visits by outsiders on at least three days a week, totalling a minimum of one and a half hours, and another visit at the weekend. Convicted prisoners are normally allowed a minimum of one visit every two weeks. Close relatives on income support or low incomes may get the cost of visits paid for by the MOJ.

The final meal of the day in local prisons, tea, is often eaten quite early, around eight or nine hours after breakfast, though many prisons have now introduced more flexible arrangements. Some prisons allow prisoners to prepare snacks on the wings and in certain places there are full-scale kitchen facilities.

Subject to there being adequate provision and staff cover, some prisoners will attend classes during the evening while others will be allowed to mix with other prsisoners ('association'), often by rota. Association may be withdrawn in the interests of security and control or if there are not enough staff to supervise it. Many prisoners not allowed association will be locked up—often with another prisoner[27] in a cell for one and typically measuring 12 feet by nine by eight. After lock up and lights out, the cell light is turned off from the outside.

REQUESTS AND COMPLAINTS BY PRISONERS

Formal interchanges between prisoners and HMPS are conducted via a mechanism known as 'requests and complaints'. The scheme provides a formal

---

[26] Traditionally known as 'the canteen' but this term seems to be disappearing. Many prison shops are now operated by private sector contractors and involve 'bagging systems', i.e. a kind of internal mail order with the goods arriving on the wing in bags for forwarding to individual prisoners.

[27] The practice of requiring three prisoners to share a cell largely ended in the 1990s.

mechanism for grievances, albeit that in practice prisoners are encouraged to discuss their concerns with prison officers to see whether these can be resolved informally (which the vast majority are). Under the revised scheme requests have been separated out from complaints and are dealt with by way of a simple applications procedure. Anything which proceeds beyond this stage is treated as a complaint. Complaint forms are freely available to prisoners on prison wings and completed forms are posted in locked boxes to which only a complaints clerk has access. Complaints are then considered and responded to in three potentially cumulative stages within the HMPS establishment:

- a response from the wing officer within three days (i.e. weekdays);
- a response from a governor grade within seven days; and
- a response from the governing governor within seven days.

A former HMPS headquarters appeal stage was abolished some years ago other than in the case of certain reserved subjects so that—once the above three stages are complete—a prisoner can now apply directly to the Prisons and Probation Ombudsman (below), ask to see a member of the Independent Monitoring Board (below), petition the Home Secretary or pursue the complaint outside the prison system through, e.g. the civil courts or his or her MP.

RELEASE FROM PRISON

Prisoners are normally released after breakfast.[28] Their property and clothes are returned from the prison store and fresh clothes supplied if necessary. Most sentenced prisoners are entitled to a discharge grant to cover immediate expenses (but only the equivalent of one week's income support payments except where a governor authorises a higher payment to someone who is leaving prison homeless) and a travel warrant back to their own area of the country. As already noted, 'end-of-custody' release has reduced the sentence of many short-term prisoners by some 18 days. These prisoners are not eligible for benefits and are given a lump-sum that they must survive on until technically no longer prisoners.

The Criminal Justice Act 1991 introduced fresh arrangements for the release of prisoners and for their supervision and liabilities after release. These arrangements were amended by the Criminal Justice Act 2003.[29] All sentences of imprisonment comprise a custodial part that is served in prison, and a part which

---

[28] The superstition being that a prisoner who fails to eat this breakfast will return to do so.

[29] The terms 'automatic unconditional release' (AUR), 'automatic conditional release' (ACR) and 'discretionary conditional release' (DCR) are normally used to signify the three main forms of release. The conditional release scheme applies to young people and juveniles in a modified form. Note that revised release arrangements affecting 'sentences below' 12 months were also introduced by the 2003 Act, but these remain to be implemented along with that scheme.

is served in the community (*Chapter 9*). Prisoners serving sentences of less than 12 months are released unconditionally after serving half their sentence; those serving longer sentences are released on licence with a requirement to comply with the conditions specified in the licence and are under the supervision of the Probation Service. If the sentence is a determinate term of 12 months or more, release on licence is at the half-way point of the sentence; if it is an indeterminate sentence, the Parole Board may order the release of the prisoner once he or she has served the minimum period (or 'tariff') specified by the sentencing court. With determinate sentences, the licence remains in force until the end of the sentence is reached. There are special provisions for the extended detention and supervision of certain serious offenders and lifers (below). The Lord Chancellor may release any prisoner on licence at any time if there are special compassionate reasons, but this power is rarely used.

A prisoner aged 21 or over serving a sentence of under four years may also be released early under what is known as home detention curfew (HDC), with a requirement for electronic monitoring.

Offenders who fail to comply with the conditions of their licence, or who commit further offences, can be returned to prison.

Aims of post-custody supervision

There are NPS *National Standards* for post-custody supervision. The aims are:

- the protection of the public;
- the prevention of re-offending; and
- the successful reintegration of the offender into the community.

As well as setting out frequency of contact and targets, a post-release supervision plan will identify resources which will:

- confront offending behaviour—challenging the offender to accept responsibility for his or her crime and its consequences;
- make offenders aware of the impact of the crimes they have committed on their victims, themselves and the community;
- motivate and assist the offender towards a greater sense of personal responsibility, to aid re-integration into the community; and
- remedy practical obstacles which impede rehabilitation, e.g. education, training, skills needed for employment, and action to counter drug or alcohol misuse, illiteracy or homelessness.

Conditionally discharged patients from mental hospitals

An offender who is adjudged to be seriously mentally ill and who poses a serious risk to the public can be made the subject of a restriction order for a specified period or indefinitely by the Crown Court under mental health legislation. In due course, the Lord Chancellor has the power to order that:

- the restriction order should cease to have effect; and
- the patient should be discharged absolutely; or
- the patient should be subject to conditions and to being recalled.

It is likely that supervision will be by a local psychiatrist and a 'social supervisor' who can be a probation officer or social worker. The discharged patient must live at an agreed address and is likely to be on supervision for at least two years. Concern about the patient can lead to the psychiatrist using civil powers to admit the patient to hospital compulsorily, or the Lord Chancellor can order a recall.

THE PAROLE BOARD

The Parole Board is an independent non-executive and non-departmental public body which makes risk assessments to inform decisions on the release and recall of prisoners. It operates in accordance with statutory directions, issued by the Lord Chancellor, which cover subjects such as the criteria to be used and the procedures to be followed. The board comprises a chair and some 80 members a small proportion of whom are full-time. Members include judges, psychiatrists, chief probation officers, criminologists and independent members. The board meets in panels of three or four to consider cases. Its role in relation to release of prisoners is noted under *Release* above. The Board publishes an annual report.

HM INSPECTORATE OF PRISONS

Each prison is inspected periodically by HM Inspector of Prisons or his or her team of full-time or specialist inspectors, the latter attached to the team for particular inspections or purposes. The inspectorate publishes an annual report and a report of each inspection, and carries out thematic inspections on particular aspects of the prison system. Essentially, the inspectorate looks at the treatment of prisoners, regime quality, the morale of prisoners and staff, the quality of healthcare, the way an establishment is managed and the physical condition of the premises. The chief inspector reports to the Home Secretary. HMPS is required to publish a considered reply. Reports have often been critical.[30] A number of chief inspectors have had a high public profile and have often been critical of conditions in custodial institutions and prison regimes and purposes generally.

---

[30] These can be viewed via www.justice.gov.uk (which still links to a Home Office-based web-site).

THE PRISONS AND PROBATION OMBUDSMAN

The Prisons and Probation Ombudsman acts, in effect, as a final appeal stage for grievances: he or she is totally independent of the agencies concerned but can make recommendations to HMPS, the Probation Service or Home Secretary. He or she is appointed by the Lord Chancellor. The ombudsman investigates complaints which have already been through all other stages in relevant procedures from:

- individual prisoners who have failed to obtain satisfaction from the requests and complaints system (above) (if eligible in other respects); and
- people who are, or have been, under the supervision of the Probation Service or housed in its accommodation or who have had pre-sentence reports (PSRs) prepared on them and failed to obtain satisfaction from the internal Probation Service complaints system (if eligible in other respects).

The ombudsman will reply to all people whose complaints have been investigated (the target is to do so within 12 weeks of determining eligibility), sending copies to the relevant service, and making any recommendations at the same time. He or she also informs complainants of the response to any recommendations made. The ombudsman publishes an annual report.

THE INDEPENDENT MONITORING BOARD (IMB)

Each establishment also has its own IMB,[31] a body of lay people who in effect are selected by the prison governor and appointed by the Lord Chancellor. It is intended to act as a 'watchdog' and oversee the activities of the prison and the treatment of prisoners. The IMB reports directly to the Lord Chancellor. IMBs have a long history, going back to the visiting committees under the Prison Act 1877. They were at one time the main disciplinary authority for the prison. Members of local boards, who like magistrates are unpaid volunteers, have open access to the prison to which they are appointed and may discuss matters with prisoners out of the hearing of prison governors or prison officers (subject to adequate security safeguards). Their role extends to approaching, consulting and advising the local prison governor on matters raised or observed, from a wholly objective, independent and fair-minded standpoint. The IMB has a full time secretariat based in Westminster and that provides information and training for members as well as co-ordinating applications to join the IMB and publishing annual reports. It has a regular journal, *The Independent Monitor*.

---

[31] Formerly known as Boards of Visitors and until 2007 a Home Office rather than MOJ responsibility. For further details of the modern-day board, see www.imb.gov.uk

CHAPTER 15

Royal Commission to a New Constitution

No short book on the CJS can hope to capture its full flavour or every aspect of its operation. Each chapter of this book could be extended many times over to deal with matters in greater detail or to highlight issues of the kind that commonly arise whenever any strand of the CJS is put under the microscope. The period since the early-1980s (at least) has been one of enormous change and as will now be clear to readers from earlier chapters this has tended to become accelerated of late. The as yet perhaps not fully worked-out move to a Ministry of Justice (MOJ) and its associated changes (*Chapter 1*) were 'one huge step for criminal justice and the UK Constitution' and any description of the CJS must now be given in this light whilst allowing for the fact that the situation remains fluid and dynamic.[1] Further change can be expected on many fronts and it is only by watching for developments with a close eye and scrutinising the detail that the full picture emerges. This contrasts markedly with a traditional, more gradual, measured and conservative[2] approach, not least in case the very fabric of the CJS begins to waiver. Again as noted in earlier chapters, it is important that underlying values and standards do not suffer. Hence, the note on constitutional reform at the end of this closing chapter, which contains a short selection of individual aspects of criminal justice and which is designed to convey something of the breadth and depth of the topic in a way that is less easy within the largely descriptive accounts in the handbook.

THE ROYAL COMMISSION

One of the most significant events for the CJS of the last 50 years was the Royal Commission on Criminal Justice announced in 1991[3] and chaired by Viscount Runciman of Droxford. Its terms of reference began by asking the Commission:

---

[1] The case for a MOJ had already been made by seasoned observers: see, e.g. *Crime State and Citizen: A Field Full of Folk* (2nd. edn. 2006), Faulkner D, Waterside Press.

[2] With a small 'c'. Some people might argue that the CJS is infused with a politically conservative agenda; others that human rights, insistence on due process or restorative justice are left-wing or even radical traits. Many proponents of the latter items might prefer to be described a liberal in their outlook—at the far end of the spectrum from (what are still called) 'hangers and floggers'.

[3] On the same day that the Court of Appeal quashed the convictions for murder in the iconic case of the 'Birmingham Six'—who served 16 years in prison for bomb attacks on public houses in 1974. It should be stressed that the Royal Commission was of the view that a wrongful acquittal was just as unjust as a wrongful conviction, whereas the until then prevailing wisdom (influenced

To examine the effectiveness of the CJS in England and Wales in securing the conviction of those guilty of criminal offences and the acquittal of those who are innocent, having regard to the efficient use of resources, and in particular to consider whether changes [were] needed . . .

The general tenor of the work of the Commission (and the preoccupation of the early-1990s) can be gleaned from the fact that it was required to look into the conduct of police investigations, the role of the prosecutor, the role of experts in criminal proceedings, the arrangements for the defence of accused people, the opportunities available for them to state their position and the extent to which the courts might draw proper inferences from primary facts, the conduct of the accused, and any failure on his or her part to answer questions. The Commission was also required to look into the powers of the courts in directing the course of proceedings, the possibility of their having an investigative role before and during a trial, pre-trial reviews (then very much the exception), and the court's duty when considering evidence, including uncorroborated confession evidence and the ease with which confessions can be 'manufactured', especially when people are made vulnerable.[4] Specifically, it was to look at the role of the Court of Appeal in considering new evidence on appeal and the then process by which alleged miscarriages of justice were investigated by the Home Office.

Proposals

In its 1993 report, the Royal Commission made 352 recommendations including for what is now the independent Criminal Cases Review Commission (*Chapter 10*), research and monitoring into areas of potential discrimination (see, further the general note in *Chapter 2*) and that judges should be able, in exceptional cases, to order the selection of a jury with up to three people from ethnic minority communities.[5] As to the police, they should be able to take samples from suspects for DNA-profiling, and it was recommended that a databank should be set up to contain samples from people convicted of serious offences (the origins of the database noted in *Chapter 11*). Also, there should be training in basic interviewing skills and the police themselves should be able to impose bail conditions (*Chapter 8*).

---

by the writings of the jurist, Sir William Blackstone (1723-1780)) was to the effect that 'a hundred acquittals are better than a single miscarriage of justice'. Also, in hindsight, the Commission seems to have marked the beginning of a move towards 'managerialism' in criminal justice, a greater balancing of systems, methods and process with purely justice-related outcomes, in contrast, e.g. to the more conventional stance of the Phillips Commission ten years earlier.

4   On which many defendants (including some of the Birmingham Six) had been convicted.

5   Never acted upon but revived in the Auld Report in 2001, though rejected by Government.

Famously, the Government rejected a recommendation that the *status quo* should be maintained in relation to the 'right of silence' and in the Criminal Justice and Public Order Act 1994 it created inroads into that right (*Chapter 2*). Recommendations that committal proceedings in magistrates' courts should be abolished and that defendants should lose the right to insist on trial by jury for certain offences, whilst not enacted, later resurfaced in a new guise in the 2002 White Paper, *Justice for All*[6] and now at least find some expression in the new allocation and sending provisions that have existed since 2003 (*Chapter 8*).

As can also be seen from earlier chapters, various of the Commission's recommendations concerning disclosure of the prosecution case were acted upon, whilst those concerning pre-trial procedures to assist in clarifying and defining the issues in the case before trial became, over the years, a part of day-to-day practice and an underlying theme within the Code for Crown Prosecutors, aspects of the Criminal Justice Act 2003 and modern day practice. A more open system of sentence discounts is now both statutory and a practice that operates under the tutored eyes of the Sentencing Guidelines Council (SGC). Similarly, the idea that judges might give an indication of sentence so that the defendant can take this into account when deciding whether to plead guilty is now a mainstream approach. Many less prominent recommendations have also been woven into the fabric of the everyday work of the CJS, such as those for the tape-recording of police interviews.

A distinct change of approach

What is especially interesting is the way in which, in 1993, such deliberation was given to any matters that might involve significant change. As was customary even beyond the confines of such a major exercise, there was wide-ranging consultation and a notable respect for experts or practitioners who were experienced in CJS matters. This contrasts markedly with the situation by 2007 when an entirely new ministry, central to the work of the CJS was formed without prior warning or meaningful consultation; events which, however sound aspects of those changes might be, followed on from a period when criminal justice legislation was being enacted virtually wholesale (and with corresponding structural and administrative changes to many of the services involved).[7] Neither, in more modern times, has there been a great deal, if any,

---

6 (2002) Cm 5563.

7 It can, of course, be argued that this is not comparing like with like, that the Commission was about major and very significant reform, the MOJ largely about 're-arranging the furniture'. But it would be difficult to think of a more seismic event in the history of the English legal system or Constitution that occurred with so little public scrutiny. The CJS as described in this handbook has changed markedly in the past ten years often in a situation of low visibility, and hence certain comments concerning *The Governance of Britain* at the end of this chapter.

regard for history. It might be thought that this type of 'progress' is reminiscent of the Blair era as a whole, that the idea that 'history has little to offer and can get in the way'.[8] There have been suggestions that the time is ripe for a new Royal Commission that would look at the CJS as a whole and the developments that have taken place from a more fundamental and less immediate perspective.

PARTNERSHIP AND WORKING TOGETHER

Partnership, 'working together', or 'multi-agency working' have been a regular feature of public affairs since at least the 1980s. They have become part of the stock-in-trade of the police, local authorities, probation officers, prison officers and even, in their own modified way, the courts. With the restructuring, renaming and readjusting of government departments in 2007, various new contexts arose in which liaison and communication between the MOJ, Home Office and other central government departments became essential. Not least in this originally were developments in relation to youth justice, where the key department in terms of youth justice is the Department for Children, Schools and Families.[9] Many other and more localised or 'grass roots' partnerships arrived at over the years underpin the modern-day work of the CJS and its day-to-day operation. Quite apart from inter-agency liaison within the mainstream CJS, there are, e.g. many voluntary sector organizations that provide services to the courts, prisons and probation officers, to witnesses, and to victims of crime as 'partners' (see, especially, *Chapter 13*). Some are of a charitable nature, others offshoots of the private sector or campaign groups. They range from alcohol, drug treatment and gambling projects to refuges for women suffering as a result of domestic violence and support groups for prisoners or secondary victims of crime (i.e. the families of those most directly affected by it). These groups are sometimes described as part of 'the wider justice family' (*Chapter 2*) and even if not involved in the day-to-day provision of services, are frequently consulted about their relevant interests. The modern-day situation is a long way from that which prevailed in the early days of working together when there was often suspicion, mistrust or even inter agency-obstruction around, e.g. 'territorial' or 'jurisdictional' issues.

---

[8] In *Great Hatred, Little Room: Making Peace in Northern Ireland* (2008), Jonathan Powell, chief of staff to Tony Blair, Prime Minister, devotes a whole chapter to 'The Burden of History', which is instructive re the actions of New Labour on all fronts since coming into power in 1997. Success in Northern Ireland with the peace process shows once and for all how history can hinder matters!

[9] If not sometimes strictly the lead: the MOJ retains many related responsibilities. In 2008, it emerged that tensions had initially existed between the relevant Ministers but suggestions that they had 'come to blows' in Cabinet were dismissed as mere tittle-tattle.

At a strategic level

All CJS service now share similar objectives in relation to crime prevention, crime reduction, bringing offenders to justice or dispensing justice. Post-creation of the MOJ, it and not, as previously, the Home Office, has lead responsibility for criminal law (as described in *Chapter 2*). But arrangements exist within Government whereby the Home Office, in liaison with the MOJ, can seek to bring in legislation where, e.g. there is a need to do so in order to confront terrorism or other immediate threats to public safety. Similarly, the Home Office is to the fore in relation to police procedures, such as those concerning powers of arrest, to search people or property, and of arrest and detention.[10] Where issues concern police procedures and the criminal law—such as the admissibility of evidence obtained during an investigation—there is a partnership in terms of the oversight of Parliamentary legislation that rests on longstanding mechanisms for collective agreement and the opportunities now provided, since 2007, by the high-powered and increasingly influential Cabinet Committee on Crime and Criminal Justice System (CCCCJS).[11] Bodies such as the National Criminal Justice Board (NCJB), Office for Criminal Justice Reform (OCJR) and Sentencing Guidelines Council (SGC) all play their part in terms of partnership at the highest level (albeit the latter with the standard reservations concerning judicial independence: *Chapters 1 and 12*). Thus, a former Lord Chancellor, Lord Falconer noted that:

> Prior to the [MOJ] ... government arrangements meant that the vast bulk of expenditure on justice issues was [by] the Home Office, with courts and prosecutors in two very much smaller outposts. Now the MOJ has responsibility for much of the policy which affects what goes on in the courts, and the work of many of the delivery agencies. The MOJ must work closely with the other agencies and departments ... most notably the new slimmed down Home Office itself and the police, the Attorney General and prosecutors, and social service departments who connect closely with the Family Justice System ... We do want to see better outcomes.

Sentencing policy[12] falls to the MOJ in discussions with the SGC and others, but the MOJ also leads a modern, collective process to determine whether legislation, offences and changes to the existing sentencing framework accord with the Government's broader criminal justice, sentencing and penal policies,

---

[10] As contained, e.g. in statutes such as the Police and Criminal Evidence Act 1984 (PACE), Criminal Justice Act 2003 and Serious and Organized Crime and Police Act 2005.

[11] For a fuller explanation of these highly significant developments at a strategic and policy-making level, see *The New Ministry of Justice: An Introduction* (2007), Gibson, B, Waterside Press.

[12] In the broader, more general, of the two senses of 'sentencing policy' noted in *Chapter 7*.

including via the CCCCJS (above). It remains to be seen how far this will involve realistic levels of consultation and how the SGC and judiciary will respond.

VICTIMS AND RESTORATIVE JUSTICE

The proper treatment of victims of crime has already been noted in *Chapter 9* in relation to sentencing and *Chapter 12* when looking at *Other people in the courtroom*. Compensation to victims is a central feature of the CJS and there have been a number of initiatives to improve their situation, in particular via Victim Support, the victim surcharge as now regularly added by courts to sentences, when reporting crime and when appearing as witnesses to give evidence. A court can also make a restitution order to ensure that, where possible, e.g. stolen property is returned to the victim, whilst the Criminal Injuries Compensation Authority (CICA) handles claims in respect of violent crime (*Chapter 9*). There also what are known as 'victim-less' crimes (such as failure to comply with regulations or those laws designed to protect the community as a whole rather than individuals, such as tax evasion, benefit fraud or many regulatory offences). It was victims that the early criminal law set out to protect in former times when the local community and only later the Crown and state took over responsibility to avoid direct action, including the ancient blood feud. As the CJS became more sophisticated, this thinking became more and more lost within an adversarial system of justice that encourages conflict rather than repairing the harm that offences cause to people or communities as well as to priorities such as punishment and retribution. This is now being partly recouped within the kind of measures noted in this section.

Issues concerning victims of crime and adversarial methods are inextricably interlinked with competing claims as to the benefits of restorative justice (RJ).[13] RJ has no fixed definition but connotes repairing the harm done and restoring harmony between victim and offenders; what Martin Wright as long ago as 1982 described in a seminal work on the subject as 'making good'[14] and, in more modern times, David J Cornwell as 'doing justice better'.[15] RJ has entered

---

[13] Often with upper case letters, i.e. Restorative Justice.

[14] *Making Good: Prisons, Punishment and Beyond*, 2nd edn (2008), Waterside Press. For a wideranging survey of RJ, its history, philosophy and present uses, see, also, *Restoring Respect for Justice: A Symposium* (2nd edn. 2008), Wright M, Waterside Press. Comparable sentiments by the Relationships Foundation, Cambridge, are contained in *Relational Justice: Repairing the Breach* (1994), Burnside J and Baker N (Eds), Waterside Press.

[15] *Doing Justice Better: The Politics of Restorative Justice* (2007), Cornwell D J, Waterside Press, which includes extensive references to other authoritative works and commentators worldwide. RJ also has connections to conflict resolution generally, e.g. in the Truth and Reconciliation Movements of South Africa and, latterly, Northern Ireland.

mainstream thinking on crime and punishment and has been the theme of various official pronouncements, initially largely in relation to juveniles, including through referral panels and referral orders (*Chapter 5*), and gradually more generally across the CJS.[16] It has featured regularly in Government consultation papers and Ministerial pronouncements of commitment to its principles but, whatever such support, has yet to break through in practical terms in the everyday work of most practitioners. But its methods have been introduced into some prisons consistently with that variety of punishment and including in relation to relatively serious offences.[17] Ultimately, the idea behind RJ is to considerably reduce (if not largely eliminate) the use of more punitive measures in favour of those which involve problem-solving and a reduction in tensions and conflict.[18]

Restorative justice can be traced to more socially-cohesive and less blame-oriented times and ways of life (as far back as the 12th century at least). It is often linked to 'sentencing circles' as were known to exist in various parts of the world (especially New Zealand, Australia and the Middle East), whose aims have included, e.g. acknowledgement of wrong or harm by the offender (sometimes involving what is called 'shaming' within his or her own community), demonstration of remorse, e.g. via an apology, or physical or financial reparation, and reintegration and rehabilitation. Whereas conventional forms of sentence can be viewed as *exclusionary* in nature (particularly custody), restorative approaches are viewed as *inclusionary*.[19]

True restorative justice remains something of an ideal, but aspects of social inclusion are, it is argued by adherents of RJ, invaluable if offenders are not to become marginalised or labelled as outcasts (particularly at an early stage in their lives), thus further fuelling any existing preconception that they may have, e.g. of worthlessness, lack of self-esteem or having a stake in society. Such matters can be intertwined with other forms of disadvantage that all need to be tackled simultaneously and in a way free from more patronising forms of help and support. So it is this kind of thinking that certain modern-day pronouncements by policy-makers are designed to encourage, even though the CJS and its sentencing framework remains largely geared to the punishment approach typified by the criteria of the sentencing framework described in *Chapter 9*. But RJ has become 'a force to be recognised', whose adherents exist world wide and in relation to which many local initiatives (often styled

---

[16] But nowhere near as emphatically as it might: see, especially, *Doing Justice Better*, above.

[17] *Restorative Justice in Prisons: Making it Happen* (2006), Edgar K and Newell T, Waterside Press.

[18] Hence restorative methods also feature, e.g. in schools and industry. The international computer conglomerate Hewlett Packard, e.g. purports to be 'a non-conflict company'.

[19] There are thus connections to be made between RJ and initiatives to avoid social exclusion.

'partnerships')[20] have been developed with voluntary, charitable or sometimes public sector support. Neither should the links between RJ and community justice (*Chapters* 2 and 13) be discounted, nor the occasional (if sometimes strangely equivocal) exhortations of ministers-of-state to judges and magistrates to avoid the use of imprisonment. There is a national Restorative Justice Consortium (RJC) of RJ-based organizations,[21] which describes RJ as follows:

> RJ processes give victims the chance to tell offenders the real impact of their crime, to get answers to their questions and to receive an apology. It gives the offenders the chance to understand the real impact of what they've done and to do something to repair the harm. RJ holds offenders to account for what they have done, personally and directly, and helps victims to get on with their lives ... RJ can take place when the offender has already been sentenced, in prison or in the community. It can take place when an offender has pleaded guilty in court, but before the judge passes sentence. It can be used as an alternative to prosecution for less serious crimes ... Restorative processes are also being used successfully outside the CJS, for example, in schools, workplaces, care homes, health services and communities.[22]

Certain offenders, particularly if young or immature, often fail to appreciate the real impact that offending has on other people. Among other things, RJ is a way of making that connection and at the same time encouraging offenders to put right the harm they have caused, in some cases by repairing damage, achieving something for themselves and the community, and in carefully managed situations writing to or meeting with and apologising to a victim as an integral part of RJ and in line with its reparative thinking. Research has shown high levels of satisfaction by victims who have participated in an RJ process.

COSTS AND CRIMINAL JUSTICE

It is sometimes said the 'justice is not for sale', words which concisely embrace a multitude of related issues. England and Wales has come a long distance from the days of 'basket justice' as it was called, when the local magistrates, quite literally, sat in court with a basket or bowl before them to receive bribes. It was only from the 18th century onwards that such practices fully disappeared. Later, when the rules of natural justice were articulated, it became clear that bias, especially a financial interest but also vested interest due to relationships between a judge or magistrate and, e.g. an accused person or witness was (and

---

[20] Hence, e.g. the influential UK Thames Valley Partnership: www.thamesvalleypartnership.org

[21] In 2008, Jack Straw MP, Lord Chancellor, gave the keynote speech at the AGM of the RJC, combining assurances of ministerial commitment to RJ with encouragement to its supporters.

[22] See www.restorativejustice.org.uk

remains) a reason why someone should not adjudicate.[23] Even within the past 30 years there have been major corruption inquiries into activities within certain police forces or prisons and individual officers despite, in some cases, obstructive tactics that appear to have been based around the idea that certain illicit gains were a perk of the job. Even commissioners of the Metropolitan Police Service (MPS) who sought to tackle such matters were at the time vilified for their efforts. At a different level, there have been concerns about the profits from speed cameras being used to fund extra resources within police forces. Over and above other protections, practices, standards and monitoring that may now exist within these or similar institutions, such considerations are now, as appropriate, subsumed within the fair trial provisions of the European Convention On Human Rights and Fundamental Freedoms (*Chapter 2*).

In more modern-times a different kind of cost consideration has arisen but one that reverberates, if more subtly, in a similar way. First, there is what has been described as a 'criminal justice industry': the implication being that some people gain from its processes because, in this regard, 'crime pays', whether in terms of careers, the supply of resources or other benefits. The role of the private sector has been noted in earlier chapters. It is, e.g. the profit motive that causes people to invest in prison building, security or the provision of items such as CCTV cameras, Taser-guns or even private DNA-testing facilities. There is a vested interest in punishment, in other words, which should cause some claims or policies to be viewed with circumspection. Second, there is the CJS itself and the tensions that may be caused by budgets, which may, in a post-MOJ world fall to be shared by those with competing interests, such as prisons and community-based organizations. Hence the need, also, for judges and magistrates, if they are to remain independent to be ring-fenced in terms of their own costs and resources. This, again, is perhaps more understated than might first appear, since the ways in which pressure can be brought to bear are many and various. Only a Lord Chancellor committed to his or her duty to protect the independence of the judiciary will be able to deal with such matters.

Financial Implications of Decision-Making

In the day-to-day world of criminal justice politics and management, Ministers, Parliament and managers of CJS services have to face the problem that spending money on more 'bobbies on the beat' or more places in prisons is always popular (except among a comparatively small number of human rights activists and penal reformers), and yet it is always difficult show that such

---

[23] Or, in lesser instances, at the very least declare the interest and stand down unless there is a clear waiver by an affected party. The common law rule is that 'financial interest cannot be waived', no matter how small. One ruling of the House of Lords was voided because a Law Lord owned shares linked to a litigant. The rule is at its strongest in criminal proceedings.

expenditure is cost-effective and gives value for money in the way that modern management and financial accountability demand. Both may give the public a vague sense of re-assurance, but neither has been shown to have any measurable effect on crime. Penal reformers in particular have for many years claimed that some of the money spent on prisons could be used to better effect on provision for sentences served in the community, or on preventive work outside the CJS altogether. A further consideration is that, especially for young offenders and YOTs (*Chapter 3*), the cost of preventive work (including work with offenders themselves) is usually a charge on local services and local funds, while the cost of custody and probation supervision is borne by central government. Local services thus have a built-in incentive to move 'difficult' people towards custody and the CJS if they are able to do so.

The financial implications of decision-making are most problematic in relation to sentencing. It is a necessary and so far uncontested condition of justice and judicial independence that judges and magistrates should in any particular case be able to impose whatever sentence justice requires, without being constrained by its cost. But it is not so obvious that sentencing practice more generally should not have some regard to cost and what the country can afford, and it can be argued that the judges of that should not be the judiciary but democratically elected Members of Parliament and Ministers. In any case, notional cost is one thing and actual physical capacity is quite another. Prisons have never yet closed their doors on the courts because they were full, and it seems unthinkable that they should ever do so. But the situation has sometimes come close to that, and the courts have for some time accepted, reluctantly, that they should not include conditions (say for drug treatment) in community orders if the National Probation Service or other providers of such resources do not have the capacity to give effect to them.

The sensitivity of the relationship between sentencing and prison capacity has ebbed and flowed throughout the last 30 years and has become more acute. Governments have tried various ways of alleviating it, using both persuasion and legislation, of which the suggestion for a Sentencing Commission (see *Chapter 9*) is the most recent.

CONSTITUTIONAL AFFAIRS

There is no direct outward correlation between everyday matters of crime and punishment and the UK Constitution. The two are separate and relatively 'compartmentalised' topics of study in most educational institutions and on the face of things only overlap when some high principle such as trial by peers (*Chapter 2*) is in issue. Increasingly, however, it seems plain that constitutional forces or influences do touch on ordinary decision-making across the CJS. In relation to the courts there was a need for legislation to bring the UK into line with its European obligations. The Constitutional Reform Act 2005 now ensures that the Lord Chancellor no longer directly influences appointments to the judiciary, or is involved in the disciplining or removal of judges.[24] Initially in the 2008 Green Paper, *The Governance of Britain*[25] and then the 2008 White Paper, *Constitutional Renewal*,[26] the Government announced proposals to give Parliament more power to hold the Government to account and to strengthen its relationship with citizens, if need be through a (still long off it would seem) Bill of Rights, and sets out further proposals to accompany a draft Constitutional Renewal Bill that, if enacted, would further distance him or her and the Executive from judicial matters.[27] The SGC is one of several examples of the way in which the Lord Chief Justice, now head of the judiciary in place of the Lord Chancellor, takes the lead in matters of justice and criminal justice rather than a Minister, as was the position before the 2005 Act. These are matters of high import whose ultimate workings affect the whole context in which criminal justice and the court at the hub of the CJS (*Chapter 1*) operate. Unless judges feel comfortable with their arrangements in this regard, then those services where there is a need for independent decision-making but which are not affected by principles of the 'high judicial' kind—and which are perhaps vulnerable to greater ease of direction or manipulation—ought perhaps to be very concerned.

Democracy and justice

Central to these constitutional developments are longer term aims for the 'democratisation' of Britain that have also become intermingled with notions of Britishness, whereby citizens, including children, might be expected to outwardly demonstrate their allegiance to the Crown or state (as incoming migrants are already after passing an appropriate Citizenship Test). While such moves are controversial, it is surely uncontroversial that such people might also be expected to be pro-active in matters of law and order, whether by refraining from criminal offending or in terms of crime prevention or, e.g. reporting wrong-doers to the authorities. There is thus, potentially, a new and largely constitutionally driven context for the CJS in which greater transparency ought to occur in relation to such often stated ideals as a broader-based judiciary, initiatives to counter social exclusion and improved mechanisms for consultation before CJS services are reorganized or new legislation happens, especially that concerning what most people would see as basic rights, e.g. to

---

[24]   In so far as they can or could be removed administratively rather than by Parliament.

[25]   (2007), Cm 7170.

[26]   *The Governance of Britain: Constitutional Renewal* (2008), Cm 7432, Vols. 1-3.

[27]   See www.governance.justice.gov.uk (a sub-domain of www.justice.gov.uk) where full and up-to-date details about potential short-term and longer-term constitutional changes can be found.

protest, go about their business without undue intervention by the other authorities, including in terms of the accumulation of data or surveillance, the fear of a disproportionate dawn raid on their homes, or being criminalised by legislative overkill, much of which will be beyond their comprehension.[28]

Also at the centre of concerns of this kind has been the role of the Attorney General (*Chapter 12*) and those mechanisms that have allowed people who are in power to act in ways which do not withstand scrutiny when placed against expectations of behaviour by citizens, whether they are being criminalised through anti-social behaviour orders, a plethora of offences, or enforcement processes that are potentially alienating due to their type, intensity or extent.

A time to re-examine the CJS

The UK does not have a written Constitution, something of which UK citizens sometimes profess themselves to be quite proud. In the past there may have been no shortage of assurances that the country was better off without one. Yet the UK has already been obliged to accept that some of its most venerated institutions, including the role of the Lord Chancellor, were in fact faulty and below international standards—whilst even the best of constitutional lawyers will admit to some vagueness about what the UK Constitution means, contains or entitles its citizens to. As with constitutional matters, so with crime and punishment: neither is just about rights, but also responsibilities. If there is to be serious constitutional reform, then this represents an opportunity to re-examine various contexts in which the CJS on the one hand and an unwritten constitution on the other may fall short of the ideal. The underlying question may be whether something in the nature of a social contract—or at the very least an improved level of openness and, correspondingly, public support—is needed if crime prevention measures are to work better and outcomes and responses to offending are to have a generally less punitive edge. There may be more constructive forms of investment, financial or otherwise, than are achieved via an escalating prisoner population, but these are unlikely to be acceptable unless the context in which the CJS operates becomes less about political posturing, more open and visible as the proposals for democratic change suggest that all matters of a public nature should be, and, ultimately, more about resolving law and order problems in a rational way.

---

[28] As a great deal of modern-day CJS-related legislation is of lawyers or even courts and judges. The principle that everyone is presumed to know the law—encapsulated in the maxim 'ignorance of law is no excuse'—resonates of a different era: see, in particular, the comments concerning the volume of criminal justice legislation under *Criminal Law* in *Chapter 2*.

Glossary of Words, Phrases, Acronyms and Abbreviations

absconding Fleeing: **(1)** bail; or **(2)** from prison by overstaying temporary leave or walking out of an open prison (as contrasted with an escape from conditions of physical security).

acceptable behaviour Usually 'low level' behaviour (that may, or may not, fall short of a criminal offence or anti-social behaviour (ASB)) but that is to be discouraged. The term is used mainly in the context of acceptable behaviour contracts with supervisors, youth justice teams (YOTs), or in relation to diversion or intervention schemes. See the explanation of 'contract' in the *Glossary*.

accused Someone who has been charged with an offence but who has not yet stood trial.

ACECOP Association of Chief Executives and Chief Officers of Probation.

ACPO Association of Chief Police Officers.

AEO Attachment of earnings order.

AG Attorney General.

agency/service Words commonly used to refer to bodies within, or connected to, the CJS.

AJF Area Judicial Forum: *Chapter 3*.

allocation Procedure for determining: **(1)** the appropriate venue as between a magistrates' court and the Crown Court: see *Chapter 2*; **(2)** the particular prison that a prisoner will be sent to at any given time: *Chapter 14*.

alternative A word used since at least the 1980s to describe a different/parallel means of approaching a given situation, as in 'alternative to prosecution' (*Chapter 7*); 'alternative to custody' (*Chapter 9*).

ancillary order One which is additional to a main sentence: *Chapter 9*.

APA Association of Police Authorities.

arraignment A procedure in the Crown Court: see *Chapter 4*.

ASB/ASBO Anti-social behaviour/order.

BCU Basic Command Unit (of the police).

bench Common way of referring to the judge or magistrates, deriving from the raised bench on which they normally sit when in court.

Best Practice Term used to signify the generally accepted way of discharging a particular (usually meaning an administrative) task with a view to achieving a high standard.

Border Agency That securing UK borders, mainly at ports and airports: *Chapter 11*.

British Crime Survey An important source of information about levels of crime and public attitudes to crime. BCS results play a part in informing criminal policy. The annual survey measures crime in England and Wales (originally Scotland also, but it and Northern Ireland now have their own such surveys) by asking members of the general public about crimes they have experienced in the previous year. The BCS includes crimes which are not reported to the police, and is a key alternative to police records. It collates information about: the victims of crime; the circumstances in which incidents occur; and aspects of offending behaviour—so as to inform crime reduction measures and to gauge their effectiveness. It is also an important source concerning perceptions of crime, anti-social behaviour and public attitudes towards the CJS, including the police and the courts. In particular, it looks at common and other attitudes to crime, e.g. at fear of crime and views about the measures needed to avoid it.

BTP British Transport Police.

CA (or C of A) Court of Appeal.

CARATS Counselling, Assessment, Referral, Advice and Throughcare Services.

Case conference A multi-agency discussion/meeting that focuses on aspects of a specific case in order, e.g. to consider reports, progress, problems or developments.

CCCCJS Cabinet Committee on Crime and the Criminal Justice System.

CCRC Criminal Cases Review Commission.

CCTV Closed circuit TV used for surveillance.

CDH Criminal directions hearing (*Chapter 8*).

CDRP Crime and Disorder Reduction Partnership.

CDS Criminal Defence Service.

CENTREX Former name for the main nationwide police training agency, since part of the NPIA.

CEOP Child Exploitation and Online Protection Centre.

chambers (1) 'In chambers' (or 'in the judge's chambers') rather than in a courtroom, e.g. for a directions hearing, or sometimes where aspects of a case are heard in camera. **(2)** Barristers' chambers, i.e. the normal description for barristers' 'offices', which are grouped together in 'a set of chambers'.

charge A word that can bear various subtleties of meaning as explained in *Chapter 8*.

CICC Criminal Injuries Compensation Commission.

CICS Criminal Injuries Compensation Scheme.

CID Criminal Investigations Department.

civil behaviour order Generic term that has emerged to encompass a range of orders based (initially) on civil powers (but backed by potential criminal sanctions), especially anti-social behaviour orders, including those that can be made by the civil courts.

CJA Criminal Justice Act (various years).

CJS Criminal Justice System.

CJU Criminal Justice Unit.

CLS Community Legal Service.

code Usually meaning an official or statutory set of instructions or guidance, such as policing-related PACE Codes or the Code for Crown Prosecutors.

contract Term used to signify a consensual (but sometimes more one-sided) arrangement, as with: **(1)** a 'contract' between a probation officer or youth justice worker and an offender whereby the requirements of a generic community sentence are implemented; **(2)** similarly a 'going straight contract' to assist someone in avoiding offending behaviour, especially juveniles; or **(3)** a 'contractual fine' within the burgeoning industry whereby private sector interests issue their own penalty charges, e.g. for unlawful parking, wheel clamp release, overstaying in a car park, or minor 'contractual infringements' within privately owned town centres, etc. The term is also regularly used in relation to the private sector generally.

CPRC Criminal Procedure Rule Committee.

CPS Crown Prosecution Service.

'cracked trial' A trial that falls through at a late stage, e.g. due to a change of plea or a witness disappearing—events that disrupt court schedules/listing arrangements and are hence a target of initiatives to avoid such outcomes.

CRB Criminal Records Bureau.

CRP Crime Reduction Programme.

CSO Community support officer (but often PCSO).

DAT Drug action team.

DCR Discretionary conditional release from prison, i.e. subject to conditions.

deportation of an alien, e.g. at the end of his or her sentence, or if not entitled to remain in the UK, or whose leave to do so has expired.

designated case worker CPS employee who is qualified to deal with some matters in court.

discipline Usually a reference to prison discipline as enforced under the *Prison Rules*.

disclosure The exchange of information concerning aspects of the prosecution or defence case as described in *Chapters 7* to *9*.

discontinue Stop a prosecution, i.e. by a Crown prosecutor after a charge has been made.

discretion A word that encapsulates the idea that the person making a decision has a choice and that, in making it, he or she should take relevant matters into account and discount irrelevant ones—act fairly, even-handedly, proportionately, reasonably. Hence, e.g. judicial discretion; prosecution discretion; police discretion. In a CJS context, the word also connotes the idea that discretion must be actively exercised, not evaded or ignored.

DNA Deoxyribo Nucleic Acid. The genetic material of a cell which may be a unique form of evidence of identification.

domestic court A court of a State as opposed, e.g. to the European Court or an international tribunal, sometimes called a 'national court'. Note also, however, that the description may be used in a different sense to describe certain family proceedings arrangements, especially in the magistrates' court.

double jeopardy At risk of conviction the second time around: See *Chapter 2*.

DPP Director of Public Prosecutions (head of the CPS).

DTTO Drug treatment and testing order (former): but see the further explanation in *Chapter 9*.

due process According to proper entitlements, procedures, rights, rules, etc.: see *Chapter 2*.

ECHR Either: **(1)** European Convention On Human Rights and Fundamental Freedoms; or **(2)** European Court of Human Rights.

either way offence One that can be tried in a magistrates' court or Crown Court: *Chapter 2*.

enforcement The carrying out of a sentence, if need be by bringing further proceedings against the offender for default, breach or prohibited misbehaviour (as, in the latter case, with the requirements of a generic community sentence, restraining orders or internal prison discipline).

equivocal plea Neither 'guilty' nor 'not guilty'.

establishment General description of any HMPS-related premises/institution.

evidential test First part of a twin test applied by the CPS to see if a prosecution should occur: *Chapter 7*.

expert witness One deemed as such by the court and hence, thereafter, able to give opinion evidence in a given case: *Chapter 9*.

FPN Fixed penalty notice.

generic community sentence Since 2003, the only form of community sentence available for adults, but with various requirements: *Chapter 9*.

GOAD Good order and discipline (in prison).

grave crime One where a juvenile can be sent to the Crown Court for trial: see *Chapter 3*.

grounds and reasons Usually meaning those under the Bail Act 1976, which must exist before a court can refuse bail to someone.

FSS Forensic Science Service.

'hanger and flogger' An opinionated individual whose views reflect a highly disciplinary, retaliatory and harsh approach to crime and punishment.

HDC Home Detention Curfew.

heavy end offence/offender A term sometimes used for offences/offenders at the more serious end of the offending scale from whom the public must be protected, especially violent/sex offenders.

HM Her Majesty's, e.g. HM Prison Service.

HMCS HM Court Service.

HMI HM Inspectorate, e.g. HMIC = HM Inspectorate of Constabulary; HMCIC = HM Chief Inspector of Constabulary.

HMPS HM Prison Service.

HO Home Office.

House of Lords In a legal context, the final UK appellate court pending the opening of the Supreme Court: *Chapters 5* and *10*.

Howard League A leading penal reform organization named after the 18th century penal reformer John Howard, see www.howardleague.org

Human rights Fundamental and inviolable legal or other rights, especially those protected by the European Convention On Human Rights and associated provisions: *Chapter 2*.

IMB Independent Monitoring Board (i.e. in relation to a prison: *Chapter 14*).

indictable only offence One that can only be dealt with in the Crown Court.[1]

indictment A process in the Crown Court: *Chapter 4*.

inherent powers Those which exist by virtue of the very nature of a person's appointment, office, role, etc., but that must be exercised fairly, reasonably or (in the case of judges and magistrates) judicially.

interdependence Term used to describe the relationship between CJS services: *Chapter 1*.

intervention plan Usually meaning a plan to confront offending or otherwise unacceptable behaviour as devised by a YOP or YOT for a juvenile: *Chapter 5*.

IPCC Independent Police Complaints Commission: *Chapter 11*.

IPS Identity and Passport Service: *Chapter 11*.

ISPP Indeterminate sentence for public protection: *Chapter 9*.

J Judge or, more commonly, Mr/Mrs/Ms Justice, the latter signifying a judge of the High Court.

JAC Judicial Appointments Commission.

JCO Judicial Communications Office.

JCS Justices' Clerks' Society.

JCSB Jury Central Summoning Bureau.

JIG Judicial Interests Group: *Chapter 3*.

JO Judicial Office (i.e. that of the LCJ).

JP Justice of the peace.

JSB Judicial Studies Board: *Chapter 12*.

JTAC Joint Terrorism Analysis Centre.

judge-alone (or judge-only) trial One without a jury under the provisions of the Criminal Justice Act 2003, in certain limited circumstances described in *Chapter 12*.

label/labelling Terms used to signify (many and various) criminological theories which argue that particular words can cause those to whom they are applied to be adversely categorised or stereotyped, causing them, e.g. to have the same self-image/'act up to type'.

L Ch Lord Chancellor For most purposes the terms Secretary of State for Justice and Justice Secretary, i.e. the head of the MOJ, and Lord Chancellor, a historic title, are now interchangeable: for a fuller explanation, see *The New Ministry of Justice*.

LCJ Lord Chief Justice.

LCJB Local Criminal Justice Board.

lifer A life sentence prisoner: *Chapter 9*.

LJ Lord Justice of Appeal.

LSC Legal Services Commission.

MA Magistrates' Association.

mandatory sentence/order One that a judge/magistrate must pass/make by law.

MAPPAs Multi-agency Protection Panel Arrangements: *Chapters 2 and 11*.

MCA Magistrates' Courts Act (various years).

McKenzie friend Someone other than a legal representative who a court allows to help a defendant and who is normally, but not necessarily, a lay person.

MDT Mandatory drug-testing.

mercy A quality recognised in sayings such as 'justice must be tempered with mercy', 'throwing oneself on the mercy of the court' (by pleading guilty without more ado); and the Royal prerogative of mercy.

MOD(P) Ministry of Defence (Police).

MOJ Ministry of Justice.

MPS Metropolitan Police Service.

MPSO Money payment supervision order.

Nacro National crime reduction charity working with offenders and people at-risk of offending, see www.nacro.org.uk

Napo Representative organization for probation staff.

National court See domestic court (above).

National Policing Plan See *Chapter 11*.

National Standards Standards applicable nationwide re an agency, e.g. those of the NPS.

NAYJ National Association for Youth Justice.

NCJB National Criminal Justice Board.

NDPB Non-departmental public body, e.g. SOCA.

NIS National Identification Service.

NNWA National Neighbourhood Watch Association.

no case to answer Procedure whereby a case will not proceed beyond the prosecution evidence: *Chapter 9*.

NOMS National Offender Management Service.

non-conviction Term sometimes applied to a fixed penalty (i.e. as opposed to conviction).

non-police matter Something that is either: **(1)** outside the purview or interests of policing altogether, e.g. because it is not a crime or deserving of other law and order interventions; or **(2)** a criminal matter that is dealt with by a law enforcement agency other than the police, e.g. an HM Revenue and Customs matter. Hence, also, expressions such as 'non-police court'; and note how, historically, 'domestic' incidents (i.e. within families or other closed groups) were often wrongly so treated.

non-statutory Not related to or deriving from an Act of Parliament, e.g. an agreed *Code* or *Protocol*, or a voluntary or charitable organization rather than one established under CJS-related or other legislation.

NPIA National Policing Improvement Agency.

NPP National Policing Plan: *Chapter 11*.

NPS National Probation Service: see *Chapter 13*.

NSPCC National Society for the Prevention of Cruelty to Children.

Oasys Offender Assessment System: *Chapter 13*.

OCJR Office for Criminal Justice Reform.

offender Someone who has been convicted of an offence, whether or not yet sentenced.

offending behaviour Neutral term that is commonly used to describe the conduct that was involved in the offences that have been committed by someone,

---

[1] Legal definitions sometimes include either way offences within a broader definition of this term: *Chapter 2*.

i.e. rather than 'crime' or 'crimes' and that is intended to avoid labelling and confrontation.

OJC Office for Judicial Complaints.

PACE Police and Criminal Evidence Act 1984.

paperwork Any process that is conducted 'on the papers', but especially a written plea of guilty or a paper committal/sending for trial.

PB Parole Board.

PCSO Police community support officer.

PGA Prison Governors Association.

PNC Police National Computer.

POA Prison Officers Association.

Police authority A local board for policing matters that forms part of a three-cornered arrangement with its chief constable and the Home Secretary: *Chapter 11*.

POTF Persistent Offender Task Force.

pre-cons Previous convictions.

presumption of innocence The longstanding rule that an accused person is always presumed innocent throughout criminal proceedings unless and until found guilty in a court or he or she voluntarily pleads guilty.

Prison Rules Those for the internal operation of prison discipline, that derive from statute.

private sector A function which originates in the commercial world, as in relation to privately managed prisons, the security industry, electronic monitoring.

protocol Usually meaning a flexible variety of inter-agency agreement or understanding.

PRT Prison Reform Trust, see www.prisonreformtrust.org.uk

PSI HM Prison Service Instruction.

PSO HM Prison Service Order.

PSR Pre-sentence report (usually meaning by a probation officer or YOT member).

public interest test Part of the twin test applied by the CPS to see whether there should be a prosecution: *Chapter 7*.

QBD Queen's Bench Division (of the High Court of Justice): *Chapter 5*.

Queen's evidence An accused person or suspect is said to 'turn Queen's evidence' where he or she gives evidence for the prosecution against a co-accused (usually), in the expectation that he or she might be treated more leniently than might have been the case or, in the extreme, might not be arrested or charged.

RAPt Rehabilitation for Addicted Prisoners Trust: see www.rapt.org.uk

recognizance A legally enforceable promise at the behest of the court, as e.g.: in relation to bail by a surety; or a bind over.

rectification The putting right of an error after it has been made without the need for an appeal or litigation, especially where it is discovered soon or immediately.

regime Usually a reference to: (1) the structure of the daily arrangements within a prison (*Chapter 14*); or

(2) the overall official requirements that an agency must operate within at any given time.

requirement An obligation imposed, e.g. (1) by law on a court or officer, especially as part of due process; (2) by the order of a court on an offender, especially one which forms part of a generic community sentence; (3) similarly re post-custody supervision.

requests and complaints (R&C) The nationwide system in prisons for processing applications by prisoners and that has various stages and targets for responses, etc.

review Word used in various contexts when matters are re-considered, e.g. a review of: PACE detention; a court decision by the High Court ('judicial review'); a file by the Crown prosecutor; a conviction by the CCRC.

right of audience The right to appear in a given court as an advocate/legal representative.

risk assessment An informed assessment of the risk posed in a given situation by, e.g.: (1) an offender; or (2) a situation, e.g. terrorists, hostage-taking, a demonstration, gathering.

RJ Restorative justice: *Chapter 15*.

RJC Restorative Justice Consortium.

RSPB Royal Society for the Protection of Birds.

RSPCA Royal Society for the Prevention of Cruelty to Animals.

RTA Road Traffic Act (various years).

RTO Road traffic offence.

Rule 43 A rule whereby vulnerable prisoners can be kept apart from others (now in fact Rule 45 but the old number persists!).

SAP Sentencing Advisory Panel.

SAR Suspicious activity report—as must be made to the relevant authorities by banks, lawyers, accountants, etc.: *Chapter 11*.

SARA Scanning, Analysis, Response, Assessment. A modern, problem-solving approach to policing: see *Chapter 11*.

sending Term used where a magistrates' court transfers a case to the Crown Court following its allocation decsion: *Chapter 8*.

separation of powers Constitutional doctrine that compartmentalises the different roles of the Executive, Legislature and Judiciary so that they operate independently: *Chapter 2*.

SFO Serious Fraud Office.

SGC Sentencing Guidelines Council.

SI Statutory Instrument.

SCI Street Crime Initiative.

security Money or valuables deposited with a court by the accused or a third party as a guarantee that the accused will attend in answer to bail—and that will normally be forfeited if the latter does not do so.

sit/sitting Words regularly used to signify the holding of a court hearing, i.e. when judges or magistrates will sit on the bench and hear cases in a courtroom. Contrast also, 'sitting in chambers'.

SOCA Serious Organized Crime Agency.

SOCO Scene of crime officer.

SOTP Sex Offender Treatment Programme.

Statute Book Metaphor for the totality of legislation enacted by Parliament, as in the term 'on the Statute Book'. All Acts of Parliament (aka 'statutes') appear in writing soon after being passed and are contained in 'volumes', one or more per year, e.g. Vol. 1 of 2010 (or sometimes by reference to the year of the reign of the Sovereign, especially in older texts, records, etc.)

Strand ('The Strand') The Royal Courts of Justice in The Strand, central London.

summary justice That: (1) dispensed by magistrates; (2) other speedy or instant forms of resolving conflict or issuing fine notices.

surety An amount promised to a court as a guarantee that someone else, or the person making that promise, will surrender to bail.

sus 'On suspicion', as with the 'sus laws' that underpin police stop and search powers.

suspect Someone who investigators consider may be guilty of an offence but who has not been charged. Hence, also, e.g. prime suspect.

suspended sentence A sentence of imprisonment that does not take effect within a given time period unless later ordered by the court, because the offender has committed another offence: *Chapter 9*.

tagging Electronic monitoring, i.e. the fitting of an electronic tag—as part of (or alongside) a generic community sentence, or as an integral part of a home detention curfew.

target The focus of, e.g. an investigation, project, operation, budget, time limit, etc.

tariff (1) The period set by a judge as the minimum that must be served in prison before someone can be considered for release from an indeterminate sentence or life sentence. **(2)** Description used for a guideline punishment, i.e. 'the going rate'.

taxation The official, quasi-judicial process for assessing a bill of costs and authorising the correct level of payment, including from the public purse.

testimony Evidence given on oath by a witness in the courtroom (or possibly in other evidence-taking situations allowed by law).

threshold A legal or practice-based hurdle that must be overcome before a power can be used, e.g. re a generic community sentence; imprisonment; bringing a prosecution.

TIC An offence for which an offender is not prosecuted (but which he/she admits) which is taken into consideration when he/she is sentenced for other matters: *Chapter 9*.

time limit One for a given stage of court or other proceedings, as with PACE detention, 'custody time limits' or an appeal.

timetable That set by a judge, magistrate or justices' clerk with a view to progressing criminal proceedings, especially in relation to a criminal directions hearing.

TVL TV Licensing (i.e. the licensing and prosecuting authority re TV licence offences).

'two strikes' English variant of the USA's 'three strikes and you're out' law under which offenders receive a life sentence for a third offence (USA), or second offence (UK): and see the further notes in *Chapter 9*.

UKAEC UK Atomic Energy Constabulary.

Unlock National Association of Ex-offenders, see www.unlock.org.uk

Up-tariffing Phenomenon whereby, given a range of powers of punishment, courts tend to gravitate upwards in the scale when using them, leaving little room for manoeuvre on any later occasion that the offender is before a court for a subsequent offence.

user group Meeting of interested parties, in relation to court administration, in particular.

VDT Voluntary drug-testing.

verdict (1) The initial outcome of a criminal case in the sense of the decision as to whether the accused is guilty or not guilty. **(2)** More loosely, any decision arrived at after considering competing versions of events, priorities, arguments or claims.

voluntary sector A part of the CJS comprising volunteers and non-statutory organizations, e.g. Victim Support, Witness Service: *Chapter 13*.

VPS Victim Personal Statement, i.e. one made by the victim of an offence for the attention of the judge or magistrates at the sentencing stage in his or her case and that sets out, e.g. information about the effect of the offence on the victim or his or her family; and also the extent of any physical, mental, emotional or possibly financial damage. As matters stand, this information exercise does not affect the actual sentence that will be imposed; but is one of a number of developments to enhance the standing of the victim within the CJS: see *Chapters 9, 12* and *13*.

VPU Vulnerable Prisoner Unit (i.e. in prison).

VS Victim Support, see www.victimsupport.org.uk

warrant card A special form of identity card issued to police officers and that should be shown whenever authority is exercised unless the police officer is clearly in uniform.

what works Expression symbolising the notion that the CJS should try to use those outcomes that have been proved by evidence-based research and/or experience to work in terms of crime prevention and crime reduction.

Woolf Report Usually meaning that in 1991 by Lord Woolf into prison disturbances.

written plea A written plea of guilty in the magistrates' court under the paperwork procedures for minor offences: *Chapter 9*.

WS Witness Service, see the WS web-site.

YJB Youth Justice Board: *Chapter 3*.

YOI Young offender institution.

YOP Youth offending panel: *Chapter 3*.

YOT Youth offending team: *Chapter 3*.

Index

The New Ministry of Justice
An Introduction ~ Bryan Gibson

'Will set a standard of solidity and credibility... enthusiasm is kept within bounds and visionary schemes dealt with in measured terms': *Justice of the Peace*

'The author is to be applauded for having produced the first word on these new departments': **Jamie Bennett, HMPS,** *Prison Service Journal*

160 pages | September 2007 | ISBN 978-1-904380-35-1

The New Home Office
An Introduction ~ Bryan Gibson

'A sound and practical book that is useful for both the newcomer and the seasoned practitioner. For a small book, it is incredibly comprehensive and yet easy to read': *The Justices' Clerk*

'This is a book that should be read by everybody involved in the Criminal Justice System' *Internet Law Book Reviews*

'These two guides will prove invaluable for anyone trying to get their head around the 21st century new world of criminal justice': *Thames View*

172 pages | September 2007 | ISBN 978-1-904380-36-8

Both with a Foreword by **David Faulkner**

These are the first books to describe the **post-2007 arrangements.** They combine a full description of the developments with historical background and contextual analysis. A must for anyone wishing to understand strategic developments, policy-dynamics and modern-day shifts in relation to the administration of justice and law and order in England and Wales.

Available individually, or as a **three book set** with *The Criminal Justice System*

Full details and ordering **www.WatersidePress.co.uk**

≈ WATERSIDE PRESS